Group Dynamics
for Teams

Group Dynamics for Teams

Daniel Levi

Sage Publications
International Educational and Professional Publisher
Thousand Oaks ▪ London ▪ New Delhi

For information:

Sage Publications, Inc.
2455 Teller Road
Thousand Oaks, California 91320
E-mail: order@sagepub.com

Sage Publications Ltd.
6 Bonhill Street
London EC2A 4PU
United Kingdom

Sage Publications India Pvt. Ltd.
M-32 Market
Greater Kailash I
New Delhi 110 048 India

Printed in the United States of America

Library of Congress Cataloging-in-Publication Data

Levi, Daniel, Ph.D.
    Group dynamics for teams / By Daniel Levi.
      p. cm.
    Includes bibliographical references and index.
    ISBN 0-7619-2254-7 (pbk.: paper)
    1. Teams in the workplace. I. Title.
    HD66 .L468 2001
    658.4'036—dc21   00-011857

02   03   04   9 8 7 6 5 4 3 2

Acquiring Editor:	Jim Brace-Thompson
Editorial Assistant:	Shannon Helm
Production Editor:	Diana E. Axelsen
Editorial Assistant:	Cindy Bear
Typesetter/Designer:	Marion Warren
Indexer:	Jeanne Busemeyer
Cover Designer:	Jane M. Quaney

CONTENTS

ACKNOWLEDGMENTS

Many people helped to shape the development of this book. My understanding of work teams, including both manufacturing and professional teams, was fostered by the many opportunities I had to study and consult with actual teams in industry. Andrew Young and Margaret Lawn (formerly of Nortel Networks) and Don Devito (formerly of TRW) created a number of opportunities for me to work with teams in the United States and abroad. Most of my research and consulting on work teams were performed with Charles Slem, my partner at Cal Poly, San Luis Obispo. In addition, I had the opportunity to work with engineering teams at Cal Poly as part of a NASA-supported program to improve engineering education. This project was supported by Russell Cummings, Joanne Freeman, and Unny Menon of the College of Engineering at Cal Poly as well as the engineering graduate students who worked with me, especially Lawrence Rinzel and Maria Cacapit. As a teacher of group dynamics, I learned a lot by co-teaching with Fred Stultz and Robert Christenson.

The support of people at Sage Publications has been invaluable, especially from my editor, Jim Brace-Thompson. Both Kathy Johnson and Sara Kocher labored diligently to improve my language and make the text more readable. My wife, Sara, also deserves special credit for her thoughtful reviews and supportive presence throughout this process.

INTRODUCTION

There are two sources of information about teamwork. On the one hand, there is a large body of research in psychology and the social sciences called *group dynamics* that examines how people work in small groups. This research has been collected over the past century and has developed into a broad base of knowledge about the operation of groups. On the other hand, the use of teams in the workplace has expanded rapidly during the past two decades. Management researchers and applied social scientists have studied this development so as to provide advice to organizations about how to make teams operate more effectively. However, these two areas of research and knowledge often operate along separate paths.

The purpose of this book is to unite these two important perspectives on how people work together. It organizes research and theories of group dynamics so that this information can be applied to the ways in which teams operate in organizations. The concepts of group dynamics are presented so that they are useful for people who work in teams and enlarge their understandings of how teams operate. It is hoped that this integration will help people to better understand the internal dynamics of teams so that they can become more effective team leaders and members.

The larger goal of this book is to make teams more successful. Teams and groups are important in our society, and learning teamwork skills is important for individual career success. The book presents many concepts related to how groups and teams operate, but many chapters also contain applications sections with techniques and activities that are designed to develop teamwork skills. Teamwork is not just something one reads about and then understands; teamwork develops through guided experience and feedback.

This book provides a framework for teaching about teams and improving the ways in which teams function.

OVERVIEW

The 17 chapters in this book cover a wide range of topics related to group dynamics and teamwork. These chapters are organized into the following four parts: characteristics of teams, processes of teamwork, issues teams face, and teams at work.

| PART I: CHARACTERISTICS OF TEAMS

Chapters 1 and 2 provide an introduction to group dynamics and teamwork. Chapter 1 explains the differences between groups and teams. The purpose of using teams in organizations and why they are increasing in use are examined. The chapter concludes with a brief history of both the use of teams and the study of group dynamics.

Chapter 2 explores the characteristics of successful teams. It explains the basic components that are necessary to create effective teams and examines the characteristics of successful work teams. In many ways, this chapter establishes a goal for team members, whereas the rest of the book explains how to reach that goal.

| PART II: PROCESSES OF TEAMWORK

Chapters 3 through 6 present the underlying processes of teamwork. Chapter 3 examines the processes that relate to the forming of teams. Team members must be socialized or incorporated into teams. Teams must establish goals and norms (operating rules) so as to begin work. These are the first steps in the stages of team development.

Chapter 4 presents some of the main concepts from group dynamics that explain how teams operate. Working together as groups affects the motivation of participants both positively and negatively. Team members form social relationships with each other that help to define their identities as teams. Teams divide their tasks into different roles so as to coordinate their work. The actions of team members can be viewed as either task oriented or social, both of which are necessary for teams to function smoothly.

One of the underlying concepts that defines teamwork is cooperation. Teams are a collection of people who work cooperatively together to accomplish goals. However, teams often are disrupted by competition. Chapter 5 explains how cooperation and competition affect the dynamics of teams.

Team members interact by communicating with each other. Chapter 6 examines the communication that occurs within teams. It describes the communication process and how teams develop communication patterns and climates. The chapter also presents practical advice on how to facilitate team meetings and develop skills that help to improve team communication.

| PART III: ISSUES TEAMS FACE

The third part of the book contains seven chapters that focus on a variety of issues that teams face in learning to operate effectively. Chapter 7 examines conflict in teams. Although conflict often is viewed as a negative event, certain types of conflict are both healthy and necessary for teams to succeed. The chapter explains the dynamics of conflict within teams and discusses various approaches to managing conflict in teams.

Chapter 8 describes how power and social influence operate in teams. Teams and their members have different types of power and influence tactics available to them, and the use of power has wide-ranging effects on teams. In one important sense, the essence of teams at work is a shift in power. Teams exist because their organizations are willing to shift power and control to teams.

For many types of teams, their central purpose is to make decisions. Chapter 9 examines group decision-making processes. It shows under what conditions teams are better at making decisions than are individuals and the problems that groups encounter in trying to make effective decisions. The chapter ends with a presentation of decision-making techniques that are useful for teams.

Chapter 10 presents the leadership options for teams, from authoritarian control to self-management. The various approaches to understanding leadership are reviewed, with an emphasis on leadership models that are useful for understanding team leadership. Self-managing teams are examined in detail to illustrate this important alternative to traditional leadership approaches.

The different approaches that teams use to solve problems are examined in Chapter 11. The chapter compares the ways in which teams actually solve problems to the ways in which teams should solve problems. A variety of problem-solving techniques are presented that can be used to help improve the ways in which teams analyze and solve problems.

Creativity, which is one aspect of groups that often is criticized, is discussed in Chapter 12. Groups can inhibit individual creativity, but some problems require groups to develop creative solutions. The chapter examines the factors that discourage creativity in groups and presents some techniques that foster group creativity.

Chapter 13 examines the ways in which diversity affects teams. In one sense, if everyone were alike, then there would be no need for teamwork. Teams benefit from the multiple perspectives that come from diversity. However, group processes need to be managed effectively for these benefits to be realized.

| PART IV: TEAMS AT WORK

The final section of the book presents a set of issues that relate to the use of teams in organizations. Chapter 14 examines the relationship between teams and the cultures of their organizations. Organizational culture defines the underlying values and practices of an organization. Teams are more likely to be successful if their organizations' cultures support them. This relationship is reciprocal because using teams can cause organizational cultures to change.

Although teams often are thought of as people interacting directly with each other, Chapter 15 examines the impacts of teams that interact through electronic communication. Computer-based communication technologies allow for the creation of teams whose members are dispersed around the world. The use of these technologies changes some of the dynamics of how teams operate and how organizations use teams.

The different types of applications of teams in the workplace are presented in Chapter 16. Teams can be created among factory and service workers, professionals, or managers. These different types of teams create different opportunities and risks for organizations. Regardless of the types of teams, there are issues that organizations need to manage to support the use of teamwork.

The final chapter examines team building, that is, the various approaches for improving the ways in which teams operate. There are a variety of approaches that organizations can take to help develop more effective teams. One of the keys to the development of effective teams is creating a mechanism to provide good feedback to teams so that they can improve their own performance.

LEARNING APPROACHES

Learning how to work in teams is not a matter of simply reading about group dynamics. Teamwork is a set of skills that need to be developed through practice and feedback. Besides presenting information about the ways in which teams operate, this book contains two other types of material that are helpful for developing teamwork skills: application sections and activities.

Many chapters in the book end with application sections. The purpose of these sections is to provide practical advice about how to apply the concepts in the chapters. These sections focus on presenting techniques rather than theories and concepts. They can be applied to the teams one belongs to or can be used on a group in a class to practice the skills.

All chapters in the book end with activities. Each activity is designed to examine a topic in the chapter and includes a set of discussion questions that apply what has been learned to actual teams. Some of the activities are structured discussions or small group exercises. However, most of the activities are structured observations of the ways in which teams operate. One of the most important ways in which to improve both one's teamwork skills and the operation of teams is to learn how to be a good observer of group processes. These observation activities are designed to develop these skills.

For the observation activities, there are several options that can be used. If the observers belong to functioning teams, then they can observe the teams to which they belong. For example, a teamwork class might have students working on project teams. The observation activities can be used as a way in which to study and provide feedback to the project teams. Groups also can be created in class settings and given assignments on which to work. There are many books on small group activities that can be used to create assignments for the groups. A class could use several groups with an observer assigned to each group, or a single group could perform while being surrounded by many group process observers. Finally, students could be asked to find a team that they can observe as part of an ongoing class project.

Each of the activities includes objective, activity, analysis, and discussion sections. The structure of the activities makes them suitable for homework assignments or for entries in group dynamics journals. The basic structure of the written assignments would include answering the following questions: What did you observe? How did you analyze this information? How would you apply this knowledge?

By working through the information and activities presented here, team members will gain practical skills and knowledge that can be directly applied to improve the operations of teams and the success of teamwork.

PART I

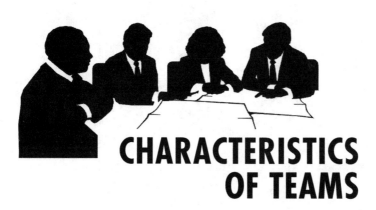

CHARACTERISTICS
OF TEAMS

Chapter 1

UNDERSTANDING TEAMS

A team is a special type of group in which people work interdependently to accomplish a goal. There are many different types of teams that are used by organizations for a variety of purposes. The use of teams to perform work has a long history, but during the past few decades their use by organizations has expanded rapidly due to changes in the characteristics of workers, the nature of jobs, and the structure of organizations. The scientific study of group dynamics has evolved to a point where it provides many useful insights about how teams operate and how they can be improved.

》 LEARNING OBJECTIVES

1. What are the characteristics of a group?
2. How is a team different from a group?
3. How are teams used by organizations?
4. How are traditional work groups different from teams and self-managing teams?
5. Why is the use of teams by organizations increasing?
6. What are the main historical trends in the use of teams?
7. How has the study of group dynamics changed over time?

DEFINING GROUPS AND TEAMS

A group is more than just a collection of people; it has several distinguishing characteristics (Table 1.1). A group exists for some reason or purpose, so it has a goal that is, to some extent, shared by the group members. The people in a group are connected to each other. They typically recognize that they have this connection, and it binds them together so that they collectively share the impact of things that happen to fellow group members. Group members interact with each other; communication often is viewed as the central mechanism of a group. The people in a group recognize and acknowledge their membership. Formal and informal rules and roles of the group control the interactions of group members. The people in a group influence each other, and the desire to remain in the group increases the potential for mutual influence. Finally, a group satisfies members' physical and psychological needs, so individuals are motivated to continue participation.

From a psychological perspective, there are two processes that define a group: social identification and social representation (Hayes, 1997). *Social identification* refers to the recognition that a group exists separate from others. It is the creation of a belief in "us versus them." Identification is both a cognitive process (classifying the world into categories) and an emotional process (viewing one's group as better than other groups). *Social representation* is the shared beliefs, ideas, and values that people have about the world. Belonging to a group, over time, changes the ways in which its members view the world. The group develops a shared worldview through its members' interactions with each other.

Most definitions of teamwork classify a team as a special type of group. To some theorists, the distinction between groups and teams is fuzzy; teams are simply groups in work settings (Parks & Sanna, 1999). Other theorists focus on how the behavior of teams differs from that of typical groups. Teams have been defined as structured groups of people working on defined common goals that require coordinated interactions to accomplish certain tasks (Forsyth, 1999). This definition emphasizes one of the key features of a team—that members work together on a common project for which they all are accountable. However, there are other qualifiers that can be used to distinguish between groups and teams.

One common distinction relates to application. Teams typically are engaged in sports or work activities. They have applied functions, and team members' roles are related to their functions. For example, in sports teams, members have specific roles assigned to them such as pitcher and shortstop. Teams usually are part of larger organizations, and their members have specialized knowledge, skills, and abilities related to their tasks. This is why we typically do not talk about a family as a team; in a family, roles are inherited and not directly related to tasks. This distinction also appears in research on groups and teams. Research on groups typically is done in laboratory settings, whereas research on teams typically is done in field studies that focus on the actual use of teams in the workplace.

TABLE 1.1
Characteristics of Groups

Goal orientation	People joining together for some purpose or to achieve some goal
Interdependence	People who have some type of relationship, see connections among themselves, or believe that they share a common fate
Interpersonal interaction	People who communicate and interact with each other
Perception of membership	Recognition that there is a unity or collectiveness to which people belong
Structured relations	Roles, rules, and norms that control people's interactions
Mutual influence	People having an impact on each other due to their connections
Individual motivation	People's personal needs being satisfied by their membership in the group

SOURCE: Johnson, D. W., & Johnson, F. P., *Joining Together,* 6th ed. Copyright © 1997 by Allyn & Bacon. Reprinted/adapted by permission.

Group is a more inclusive term than *team.* Groups range in size from two to thousands, whereas teams have a narrower range of sizes. A dating couple may be considered a group but not a team. Political parties and social organizations are groups but not teams. A team typically is composed of 4 to 20 people who interact with each other directly (although this interaction may occur through computers and other communication devices). A team is not simply people who belong to the same group or who are co-acting in the same place.

Katzenbach and Smith (1993) focus on performance in their definition of teamwork. In addition to team members having a common purpose, there are performance goals connected to this purpose for which everyone in the team is held mutually accountable. Katzenbach and Smith also believe that the concept of a team should be limited to a fairly small number of people with complementary skills who interact directly. This helps to distinguish teams from work groups whose members jointly do the same tasks but do not require integration and coordination to perform the tasks.

Hayes (1997) focuses on power in her definition of teams. A team must actively cooperate to achieve its goals. For this to occur, a team needs to have independence, responsibility, and the power to operate. A team is not a group of people who perform a task under the rigid control of an authority figure. For a group to become a team, it must be empowered and have some authority to act on its own. In addition, team members are more likely to work together cooperatively and provide assistance to each other than are members of other types of work groups.

Because there is not a firm dividing line between a group and a team, the use of these terms in this book is somewhat arbitrary. When referring to research on group dynamics, especially laboratory research, the term *group* is used. When talking about applications in work environments where people are interdependent, the term *team* is used. In the in-between cases, *group* and *team* are used interchangeably.

TYPES AND PURPOSES OF TEAMS

Organizations can use teams in a variety of ways. Because of this variety, there are many ways of classifying teams. These classifications help to explain the psychological and organizational differences among different types of teams. One important distinction is the relationship of teams to organizations. Teams vary depending on how much power and authority they are given by organizations.

| HOW TEAMS ARE USED BY ORGANIZATIONS

Teams are used to serve a variety of functions for organizations. The day-to-day operations of organizations can be shifted to teamwork (e.g., factory production teams, airline crews). Teams can be formed to provide advice and deal with special problems such as teams created to suggest improvements in work processes. Teams help to manage coordination problems by linking different parts of organizations such as budget or planning committees composed of members from several departments. Finally, teams can be used to change organizations by planning the future or managing the transition.

Obviously, teams can come in mixed packages. Concurrent engineering teams are teams composed of members throughout an organization whose task is to oversee the design, manufacturing, and marketing of new products. For the people who work in the research and development area of an organization, being in a concurrent engineering team is part of their day-to-day activities. However, the other members of the team are there on a part-time temporary basis to deal with coordination, special problems, and implementation of change. The research and development staff may define the characteristics of a new product, whereas representatives from other departments may comment on the technical aspects related to production.

Sundstrom (1999a) identifies six types of work teams based on the functions they perform. *Production* teams, such as factory teams, repeatedly manufacture or assemble products. *Service* teams, such as maintenance crews and food services, conduct repeated transactions with customers. *Management* teams are composed of managers or executives who work together to plan, develop policy, or coordinate the activities of an organization. *Project* teams, such as research and engineering teams, bring experts together to perform a specific task within a defined period of time. *Action* or *performing* teams, such as sports teams, entertainment groups, surgery teams, and airline crews, typically engage in brief performances that are repeated under new conditions and that require specialized skills and extensive training or preparation. Finally, *parallel* teams are temporary teams that operate outside of normal work such as employee involvement groups and advisory committees that provide suggestions or recommendations for changing an organization.

| CLASSIFYING TEAMS

Teams can be classified in a number of ways besides by the types of activities they perform, but there is no agreed-on classification system for work teams (Devine, Clayton, Philips, Dunford, & Melner, 1999). Researchers have suggested classifying teams by how long they exist (permanent vs. temporary), how much internal specialization and interdependence they require, and how much integration and coordination with other parts of the organization is needed (Mohrman, 1993; Sundstrom, DeMeuse, & Futrell, 1990). One of the most important distinctions among types of teams relates to their amounts of organizational power (Hayes, 1997). When an organization uses teams, rather than individual workers, to perform tasks, it is giving the teams some power and authority to control the operations of its members. This shifting of power affects leadership, decision making, and how team members' work activities are linked.

There are three options for organizing people into work groups: a traditional work group, a traditional team, or a self-managing team. The differences among these types are presented in Table 1.2. *Traditional work groups* are part of the organization's hierarchical system. They are led by supervisors or managers who control the decision-making process. Group members typically work on independent tasks that are linked by the managers or work system.

Traditional teams are given some power and authority, so they are somewhat independent of the organization's hierarchy. Their leaders are selected by management and given some managerial power. Leaders can use a variety of techniques for making decisions in the teams such as using the teams to provide advice about decisions (consultative) and having the teams vote to make decisions. Team members' work activities are interdependent and are coordinated by the leaders.

Self-managing teams are given significantly more power and authority, so they are more independent of the organization's hierarchy. Team members typically select their leaders, so the leaders have limited power and must facilitate, rather than control, their teams' operations. The leaders must rely on democratic or consensus decision making because they do not have the authority to make the teams accept decisions. Team members' work is highly interdependent, and all team members work together to coordinate activities.

WHY ORGANIZATIONS ARE USING TEAMS

The traditional approach to organizing people to perform a task is called *scientific management* (Taylor, 1923). In this approach, managers or technical experts analyze the task and divide it into small activity units that are performed by individuals. The system is designed so that each activity is linked, and individuals work separately to complete the entire task. It is the role of management to design the system and control the operations of the people in it. It is the role of the workers to perform the specific task. In other words, managers think and control, whereas workers act.

This traditional approach works very well under certain conditions. It requires that the task remain the same for some time because it is hard to change the system. It requires that the process be not too complex or easily disrupted because the people doing routine activities are not aware of what happens in other parts of the system. It focuses on productivity and often ignores concerns about quality and customer service because these factors require more commitment to the job. It assumes that there are workers who are

TABLE 1.2
Organization of Teams

	Traditional Work Group	Traditional Team	Self-Managing Team
Power	Part of organization's hierarchy; management controlled	Linked to organization's hierarchy; some shift of power to team	Linked to organization's hierarchy; increased power and independence
Leadership	Manager or supervisor controls	Leader has limited managerial power; selected by organization	Leader is the team's facilitator; selected by the team
Decision making	Authoritarian or consultative	Consultative, democratic, or consensus	Democratic or consensus
Activities or tasks	Independent	Interdependent; coordinated by leader	Interdependent; coordinated by team members

willing to perform routine activities under controlled situations because that is the nature of work.

Scientific management is the best approach given these assumptions. The time and expense of developing teams is not needed under these conditions. Teams are important when the goal is to improve the way in which a product is made or a service is provided, when the job is complex, when customer service and quality are important for success, or when rapid change is necessary. Because team members have increased autonomy and are developing new skills, teams can support the retention of people who want more from work than just money. It is these conditions that create the need for teams. Modern organizations are shifting to teamwork because of changes in the characteristics of people, jobs, and organizations.

| CHARACTERISTICS OF PEOPLE

Scientific management operates under a negative set of assumptions about workers called *Theory X* (McGregor, 1960). Theory X managers assume that people are basically lazy, do not like to work, want to avoid responsibility, and need to be coerced so as to be motivated. Given these assumptions, a command-and-control organizational system makes sense. However, these assumptions might not be valid, especially for the most desirable workers.

An alternative set of managerial assumptions, called *Theory Y,* is based on the belief that work is a natural activity for people, people want responsibility, and there are a variety of ways in which to motivate people. Rather than requiring control to operate, Theory Y focuses on gaining commitment to the task and getting people to accept responsibility for their work. The goal in this perspective is to design a job that people will want to perform rather than trying to force people to perform a job they dislike.

The shift to a commitment-based organization, based on employee responsibility, autonomy, and empowerment, is one of the core notions of teamwork. This transition helps to improve the quality of people's jobs, increase internal motivation, and improve job satisfaction (Orpen, 1979). For many people, the amount of autonomy and responsibility in a job is one of the most important factors in evaluating a job (Finegan, 1993). Often, the best way in which to change an organization so as to make people's jobs more satisfying is to shift to teamwork.

| JOB CHARACTERISTICS

The changing nature of people's jobs is encouraging the use of teamwork. Many jobs are changing from routine work to nonroutine work (Mohrman, Cohen, & Mohrman, 1995). These nonroutine jobs involve more complexity, interdependence, uncertainty, variety, and change than do routine jobs. These new jobs are difficult to manage in traditional work systems but are well suited for teamwork.

Nonroutine jobs are found in a number of contemporary work settings. In factories, as jobs become more complex due to technology or other factors, teams become a good way in which to handle this increasing complexity (Manufacturing Studies Board, 1986). In modern computer-oriented factories, the typical worker operating a single machine all day is being replaced by a team of workers who monitor, troubleshoot, maintain, and manage a complex and integrated work system. The technology is integrated, so the employees need to be integrated as well.

These changes also affect professional work. Imagine designing a new product for the marketplace. The design, manufacturing, marketing, and sales of the product require expertise from a variety of disciplines and support from many parts of an organization. Few individuals possess all of the necessary knowledge and expertise, so a diversity of knowledge is gained by using a team approach. In addition, using teams that contain members from several parts of the organization enhances support within the organization for the new product. The team members help to coordinate the project throughout the organization.

Complexity creates several issues that relate to teamwork. Problems or tasks that are complex often require multiple forms of expertise to complete. No one person may have all of the skills or knowledge to complete a task or solve a problem, but a team may have sufficient expertise to deal with the task. Complexity also implies problems that are confusing or difficult to understand and solve. Here, the value of teamwork is not in multiple forms of expertise but rather in multiple perspectives. People learn from the group interactions in teams, and this helps them to gain new perspectives in analyzing problems and developing solutions.

As jobs become more interdependent, it becomes increasingly difficult for managers to control the flow of information. Everyone needs to be aware of the changes occurring that affect their jobs and to coordinate with others about how to deal with these changes. Teams become a necessity to promote coordination in a rapidly changing organizational environment.

Work is becoming more varied. Increasingly, complex technical systems do not require routine operation but do require monitoring and troubleshooting. Changes in technology and markets require flexibility to meet new demands. Teams provide a mechanism for creating jobs that are more responsive to the changing work environment.

| ORGANIZATIONAL ISSUES

The rate of change in technology and other aspects of business seems to be continually increasing. Markets are expanding so that competition is global. Communications technology allows for the creation of new ways in which to integrate the operations of organizations. It is difficult to keep up with these changes using traditional approaches to the design of organizations. The changing business environment is forcing organizations to change the ways in which they operate. Business organizations need to reduce costs, improve quality, reduce the time for creating new products, improve customer service, and increase their ability to change so as to adapt to an increasingly competitive environment.

Organizations are changing to meet these new demands, and the new characteristics of organizations increase the importance of teamwork (Mohrman et al., 1995). One important area of change has been a shift to simpler organizational hierarchies. This transition is being driven by a desire to save costs and to increase flexibility in organizations by reducing layers of management. The new organizational forms have fewer managers, and to a certain extent, they substitute teams for managers.

In the new organizational forms, teams replace many of the traditional management functions. Teams provide a way in which to integrate and coordinate the various parts of an organization. They are able to do this in a more timely and cost-effective manner than are traditional organizational hierarchies. Teams execute tasks better, learn faster, and change more easily than is the case with traditional work structures. These characteristics are needed by modern organizations.

Although the use of teamwork has expanded dramatically in all areas of organizations, it has not been universally successful. Teamwork has become a management fad, and this has created its own set of problems. Organizations sometimes introduce teams in situations where they might not be appropriate. Managers sometimes implement teams without changing the organizational contexts or supplying sufficient resources or training. Organizations sometimes call groups of employees *teams* without really changing the nature of work or the organizational reward systems.

HISTORY OF TEAMS AND GROUP DYNAMICS

The use of teams in organizations has changed significantly over the past century. During this period, the scientific study of group dynamics has developed into an interdisciplinary research field.

| FOUNDATIONS OF TEAMWORK

Historically, there have been two major ways of organizing people for work. One approach uses a structured hierarchy and is based on the model established by the military. Command and control is the dominant theme. Everyone has a single job and a single boss, and everyone's primary activity is to do what he or she is told. The alternative is a small group or family approach, which is the model for traditional farming and the guild system for manufacturing. Here, the organization is fairly small, commitment often is for life, people work their way up through the system as they learn new skills, and work is a collective activity.

The industrial revolution of the early 1900s shifted most work organizations into the hierarchical approach and used scientific management to design organizations and jobs (Taylor, 1923). Jobs were simplified, so the advantages of the skilled workers created by the guild system were minimized. Professionals—from accountants to engineers—were brought into the hierarchy to make sure that the production system operated efficiently. It was a system that worked well but created problems. It alienated the participants (who then became increasingly difficult to motivate), it became more difficult to set up as the technical systems became more complex, it was more difficult to change because the structure was inflexible, and it had difficulty in successfully incorporating new goals beyond efficiency such as quality.

The scientific management model of organizations began to be questioned during the 1920s and 1930s. The rise of unions and other types of worker organizations demonstrated that there were problems with people's relationship to work. This led to an increased interest in the social aspects of work.

The Hawthorne studies inadvertently raised questions about whether one could ignore the social relations aspects of work (Mayo, 1933). These studies were a series of research projects designed to examine how environmental factors, such as lighting and work breaks, affected work performance. They revealed that social factors had an important impact on performance. Group norms controlled how people performed. In some cases, because people were being studied, they tried to perform better (what social scientists now call the *Hawthorne effect*). In other cases, group norms limited or controlled performance. Workers all did the same amount of work at the same pace to protect each other, so making changes in physical conditions had little effect on performance. This research led to the *human relations movement,* which focused on the social aspects of work.

Following World War II, researchers in the United States and Europe developed additional concerns related to the standard approach to work. They recognized that although the military looked like a hierarchical system, the troops actually operated using teamwork. Research showed that organizing people into teams was one way in which to improve the operations of organizations and improve productivity.

During the 1960s and 1970s, organizational psychologists and industrial engineers refined the use of teams at work. The development of *sociotechnical systems theory* (STS) captures this knowledge (Appelbaum & Batt, 1994). STS provides a way in which to analyze what people do at work and then to decide what is the best way of organizing them. According to this theory, teams should be used when jobs have technical uncertainty rather than routinization, when jobs are interdependent and require coordination to perform, and when the environment is turbulent so that flexibility is required. Many jobs today meet these criteria.

The most famous applied examples of STS were in the Volvo car facilities in Sweden. The assembly-line approach to work was redesigned to be performed by *semi-autonomous groups*. This approach, during the 1970s, became part of the *quality of worklife movement* in the United States. Although there were several successful demonstrations of the value of using teams at work in Sweden and the United States, this teamwork approach did not become popular.

The contemporary emphasis on teamwork has its origins in another change that occurred during the 1970s. The rise of Japanese manufacturing power resulted in high-quality inexpensive products being distributed throughout the global marketplace. This caused companies throughout the industrial world to change the ways in which they operated so as to reduce costs and increase quality at the same time. When business experts visited Japan to see how Japanese manufacturers achieved these goals, they found that teamwork in the form of *quality circles* seemed to be the answer. Quality circles are parallel teams of production workers and supervisors who meet to analyze problems and develop solutions to quality problems in the manufacturing process.

Throughout the 1980s, companies in the United States and Europe began experimenting with teamwork in the form of quality circles (and later *total quality management*) as a new way in which to organize workers. The jobs that people performed still were primarily individual. However, workers were organized into teams as a way in which to improve quality and other aspects of production. The early examples were primarily attempts to copy the Japanese approach. This met with mixed success, partly because of cultural differences. By the late 1980s, teamwork was spreading in organizations as new approaches were developed.

The *quality movement* launched the current emphasis on teams, but other factors have been sustaining it. The increased use of information technology, the downsizing of layers of management, business process reengineering, and globalization all have contributed to the use of teams. Teamwork in U.S. companies expanded rapidly during the 1990s, and the use of teams has expanded to include more professional and managerial teams. Current studies suggest that 85% of companies with 100 or more employees use some type of work teams (Cohen & Bailey, 1997). In addition, some organizations are restructuring and using teams as a central way in which to integrate various parts of their organizations (Mohrman et al., 1995).

| FOUNDATIONS OF GROUP DYNAMICS

There is an unfortunate gap between our understanding of work teams and the study of group dynamics. The scientific study of groups began at the turn of the 20th century with the work of Norman Triplett (Triplett, 1898). His research showed the effects of working alone versus in a group. For example, he observed that bicycle racers who pedaled around a racetrack either alone or in groups were faster in groups. This effect has been called *social facilitation* because the presence of other people facilitated (or increased) performance. (Later research showed that performance was increased for well-learned skills but was decreased for less well-developed skills.)

The early studies in psychology all had a similar perspective in that they were designed to show how groups affected individual performance or attitudes. Although this was group research, the focus was on individuals. Psychologists did not treat groups as an entity appropriate for scientific study.

This perspective changed during the 1940s due to the work of Kurt Lewin and his followers (Lewin, 1951). Lewin created the term *group dynamics* to show that he was interested in the group as a unit of study. For the first time, psychologists took the study of groups seriously rather than just looking at the effects of groups on individuals. The initial work on how groups operate created a new research paradigm in psychology and the social sciences. Lewin's innovations in research methods, applications, and focus still define much of the study of group dynamics.

Lewin developed a new approach to research in psychology. He began with a belief of the importance of theory: "There is nothing so practical as a good theory" (Lewin, 1951, p. 169). His innovation was in refining how theories in psychology should be used. He developed an approach called *action research*. In action research, scientists develop theories about how groups operate and then use these theories in practical applications to improve the operations of groups. The process of applying the theory and evaluating its effects should both help to refine the theory and improve the operations of groups.

One of Lewin's primary concerns was social change. He believed that it is easier to change a group than to change an individual. If one changes the behavior of an individual, then once the individual returns to his or her everyday life, the influence of the people around the individual tends to reverse the behavior change. If one changes the behavior of a group of people, then the group will continue to reinforce or stabilize the behavioral change. Lewin developed models of organizational change and group dynamics techniques that still are used today.

During the 1950s and 1960s, the study of group dynamics expanded rapidly. It grew beyond the field of psychology to become more interdisciplinary. Researchers from sociology, anthropology, political science, speech and communication, business, and education now study different aspects of groups. Although psychological research is dominated by laboratory research on how groups operate, many of the other fields of study emphasize applied research.

Today, the study of group dynamics is an accepted academic discipline in a number of fields. As a theoretical area of study, it is fairly stable rather than growing. However, it is growing as an applied field as more organizations become interested in using groups and teams.

SUMMARY

Groups are more than just collections of people. Groups have goals, interdependent relationships, interactions, structured relations, and mutual influence. Individuals are aware of their membership in groups and participate to satisfy their personal needs. Although the distinction between groups and teams is not completely clear, the term *teamwork* typically is used to describe groups that are parts of organizations. Team members work interdependently to accomplish a goal and have the power to control at least part of their operations.

Organizations are shifting away from individual work performed in hierarchical work structures and toward team-based operations. Changing goals in organizations, which must deal with the evolving work environment, are driving this change. People are demanding meaningful work, jobs are becoming increasingly complex and interdependent, and organizations are finding that they need to be more flexible. All of these changes are encouraging the use of teamwork.

Organizations use teams in a number of ways. Teams provide advice, make things or provide services, create projects, and/or perform specialized activities. Teams also vary according to the amounts of power they have, their types of leadership and decision making, and the tasks they perform. These factors define the differences among work groups, teams, and self-managing teams.

Working in small groups was common before the industrial revolution, but scientific management simplified jobs and created hierarchical work systems. The Hawthorne studies of the 1930s demonstrated the importance of understanding the aspects of work related to social relations. Following World War II, researchers began to experiment with the use of work teams. STS during the 1960s presented a way in which to analyze work and identify when teams should be used. However, it was the rise of Japanese manufacturing teams during the 1980s that led to the increased use of teamwork in the United States. Paralleling this growth in the use of teams, the social sciences developed the field of group dynamics, which focuses on understanding how groups operate. Today, group dynamics is a scientific field that provides information that can be used to help improve the operations of teams.

ACTIVITY: GROUPS VERSUS TEAMS

Objective. There is no clear distinction between groups and teams. The purpose of this activity is to examine the implicit definitions that people have of these terms.

Activity. Create a list of groups and teams. Using Activity Worksheet 1.1, classify these examples as groups, teams, or somewhere in-between groups and teams. Compare your classifications to those of other members in your group. Try to reach agreement on the classifications by discussing how you decided.

ACTIVITY WORKSHEET 1.1
Groups Versus Teams

Groups	In-Between Groups and Teams	Teams

Analysis. When your group has reached agreement, analyze the lists and develop rules to define when a group becomes a team:

1. _____

2. _____

3. _____

4. _____

Discussion. Imagine that you are working in an office and your manager decides to organize the employees into a team. Using the rules you have developed to define a team, what advice would you give to the manager about how to create a team?

Chapter 2

DEFINING TEAM SUCCESS

A successful team completes its task, maintains good social relations, and promotes its members' personal and professional development. All three of these factors are important for defining success. To perform effectively, a team requires the right types of people, a task that is suitable for teamwork, good internal group processes, and a supportive organizational context. Group members need both an appropriate set of task skills and the interpersonal skills to work as a team. Although teams can perform a wide variety of tasks, appropriate team tasks require members' work to be integrated into the final products. The internal group process should maintain good social relations while organizing members to perform the task. Finally, the organizational context needs to support the team by promoting cooperation, providing resources, and rewarding success.

Researchers have conducted a number of studies on work teams to determine what characteristics predict success. Successful teams have clear goals, good leadership, organizational support, appropriate task characteristics, and mutual accountability with rewards. However, the characteristics that predict team success vary depending on the type of team being studied.

➤➤ LEARNING OBJECTIVES

1. What are the three criteria used to define team success?
2. Why is team success more than just completing the task?
3. What factors determine whether a group has the right set of people?
4. In what types of tasks are groups better than individuals? Why?
5. What are the important parts of the group process?

6. How does an organization provide a supportive context for teams?
7. What are the characteristics of successful teams?

NATURE OF TEAM SUCCESS

One of the prerequisites to studying and understanding teamwork is to define the nature of team success. The research on groups and teams has used a variety of measures to study the functioning of groups. Often, research examines these internal measures of group functioning and tries to relate them to external measures of team success.

Measuring the success of teamwork can be difficult. The characteristics that team members and leaders believe are important for success might not be the same characteristics that managers believe are important (Levi & Slem, 1996). Team members focus on the internal operations of the team; they look at the contributions that each member brings to the team and how well members work together. Managers focus on the team's impact on the organization; they are concerned with results, not with how the team operates. There is a danger in using too simplistic a view of success because it can cause one to focus on the wrong factors when trying to improve a team.

According to Hackman (1987), there are three primary definitions of team success that relate to the task, social relations, and the individual. A successful team completes its task or reaches its goals. While completing the task, team members develop social relations that help them to work together and maintain the group. Participation in the team is personally rewarding because of the social support, the learning of new skills, and/or the rewards given by the organization for participation.

| COMPLETING THE TASK

From a management perspective, the obvious definition of team success is performance on a task. A successful team performs the task better than individuals and better than other ways of organizing people to perform the task. Although this definition might seem simple, measuring the performance of teams can be difficult. For complex tasks, there might not be alternatives to teamwork, so it is not possible to compare group and individual outcomes. For many professional tasks that require creativity or value judgments, there might not be clear ways in which to determine which solutions are best (Orsburn, Moran, Musselwhite, Zenger, & Perrin, 1990). One approach to these measurement problems is to determine whether the products or outputs of the team are acceptable to the owners, customers, and team members. However, these three perspectives might not agree with each other (Spreitzer, Cohen, & Ledford, 1999).

Completing a task successfully as a team is a measure of success, but project success is not a demonstration of team success. Could the task have been completed without using a team? What was the benefit of using a team for performing the task? Often, for a particular task, there is not much advantage to using a team. In fact, there are disadvantages because time is "wasted" in developing the team instead of focusing on the task. The advantages of using a team to perform a task occur when unforeseen problems arise and when the team will work together on future tasks.

If a project runs smoothly, then people working individually under supervision often can perform the necessary task. However, if a project encounters difficulties, then the value of a team is demonstrated by the ability of the team members to use multiple perspectives to solve problems and to encourage and motivate each other during the difficult period. Although a team consumes time in its development, as people learn to work together, they are better able to handle future projects. Many of the benefits of creating a team occur over the long run rather than in the first project the team performs.

| MAINTAINING SOCIAL RELATIONS

Measuring the results of a team's task performance does not completely capture the definition of team success. A successful team performs its task and then is better able to perform the next task assigned to it. This is the social relations, group maintenance, or viability aspect of teamwork (Sundstrom, DeMeuse, & Futrell, 1990). An important value of teamwork is building the skills and capabilities of the team and organization. For this to happen, the team must have good internal social relations, and performing in the team should encourage participants to want to work in the team in the future.

A team needs to develop the social relations among its members. The social interactions that are necessary for teamwork require group cohesion and good communication. Cohesion comes from the emotional ties that team members have with each other. Good communication depends on understanding and trust. When team members do not develop good social relations, they do not communicate well, have interpersonal problems that interfere with task performance, and are not able to reward and motivate each other. This limits the ability of the team to continue to operate.

A good example of the problem of too much focus on task performance and ignoring social relations can be seen in the computer development team described by Kidder (1981). The team successfully developed a new computer system. However, in the stress of competition and time pressure, the team members burned themselves out. At the end of the project, everyone was happy about his or her success, but the team members no longer wanted to work together. Was the team a success? Yes, it completed its task, but no, it failed to develop social relations that encouraged successful teamwork in the future. The capabilities of the team were lost at the end of the project because of the exclusive focus on the task. So, the organization benefited by getting a new computer, but it did not improve its ability to use teams to successfully design new computers in the future.

INDIVIDUAL BENEFIT

The third aspect of team success concerns the individual. Participating in a team should be good for the individual. Teamwork should help to improve an individual's social or interpersonal skills (Katzenbach & Smith, 1993). In the workplace, being in a team with professionals with different expertise, or with workers having other skills, should help to broaden an employee's skills and knowledge and make him or her better aware of the perspectives of other disciplines. In addition to personal development issues, participating in a team should help an employee's career in the organization. Successful contributions to a work team should be reflected in the employee's performance evaluations (O'Dell, 1989).

There are a variety of personal benefits that can come from teamwork that help to satisfy people's social and growth needs. People should enjoy working in teams because it increases the amount of social and emotional support they receive. Teams also can be great learning experiences. Team members share their knowledge and expertise, and as they learn how to be good team members, they also develop communication, organizational, and management skills.

Obviously, these personal benefits are more important to some people than to others. People vary in their social needs, so people low in social needs will be less rewarded by teamwork. Some people already have good teamwork skills, whereas others do not care whether they learn these skills, so the latter will receive fewer rewards from teamwork. Also, the social and learning benefits from teamwork primarily come from successful teams. Working on dysfunctional teams may teach members to avoid working on teams in the future.

In addition to the personal benefits, participating in a team should help one's career in the organization. Unfortunately, this often is not the case. Most organizations focus on managing individuals rather than on managing teams. Even when most of one's time is spent working in a team, the typical performance evaluation system focuses on what an individual produces rather than on the success of the team. Being a good team player might go unrecognized, while people who differentiate themselves and stand out get rewarded. This conflict between individual and team success is one of the major unresolved problems with teamwork in many organizations.

CONDITIONS FOR TEAM SUCCESS

The success of a team depends on four conditions (Figure 2.1). First, the team must have the right group of people to perform the task. Second, the task must be suitable for teamwork. Third, the team needs to combine its resources effectively to complete the task. Fourth, the organization must provide a supportive context for the team. A team can be an effective way for an organization to improve the way in which it operates (Guzzo & Dickson, 1996). However, teamwork is not a universal solution to an organization's problems. A team requires each of these four conditions to be successful. If the organization does not meet these conditions, then the value of teamwork might be limited.

| GROUP COMPOSITION

A group's performance depends on the qualities of the individuals who are performing the task. These qualities can be viewed in three different ways. First, the group must contain people with the knowledge, skills, and abilities that match the requirements of the task. Second, the group must have members with the authority to represent the relevant parts of the organization and the power to implement the group's decisions. Third, the group's members must have the necessary group process skills to operate effectively.

Some groups fail because their members do not have the needed knowledge, skills, and abilities to perform their tasks. The level of skills of the individuals in a team correlates with the success of the team. Good teams have

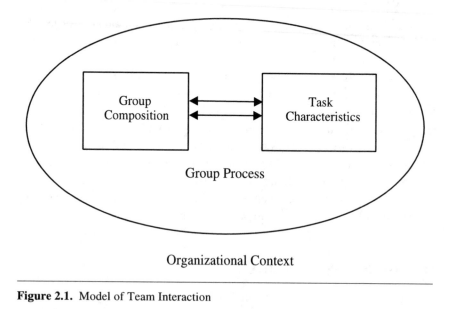

Figure 2.1. Model of Team Interaction

good team members. In their study of highly successful groups, Bennis and Biederman (1997) determine that much of the success of these groups was due to the leaders' ability to recruit highly competent team members. High-performing leaders are not afraid to hire people better than themselves.

Part of creating an effective group is making sure that there is the necessary diversity of knowledge and skills. Research teams that are interdisciplinary are more productive than teams composed of individuals with similar backgrounds. Groups whose members have differences of opinion are more creative than like-minded groups. Management teams with members of different backgrounds are more innovative than homogeneous teams (Guzzo & Dickson, 1996). However, diversity alone is not always a benefit to groups. The advantages of diversity occur when people are highly skilled and when their skills are different. Diversity of knowledge and perspective is a benefit when group members are committed to their groups' goals.

For some types of groups, composition is not about skills but rather about representation. Task forces, as well as other types of teams that help to integrate parts of a larger organization, require team members to simultaneously be committed to their teams and represent outside interests in their teams (Gersick & Davis-Sacks, 1990). The value of these teams is breadth of perspective and commitment to implementation of decisions. For example, concurrent engineering teams are an approach to research and development that includes members of manufacturing and other departments in the design of new products. The manufacturing representatives help to ensure that the new design is sensitive to the needs of manufacturing, and their participation encourages support of the new product in manufacturing.

Concurrent engineering teams were developed to deal with the problems created by bureaucratic divisions within an organization. Before the use of this approach to design and manufacturing, the work of research and development was separate from that of manufacturing. Research and development often used the most advanced technology available because designers like to be innovative. It was not designers' job to be concerned with production issues. The result sometimes were designs with overly expensive parts that were impossible to manufacture with the organizations' existing manufacturing technologies. Concurrent engineering teams deal with these issues early in the design process.

Groups also require that team members have the skills to work together as a group. These skills can be used as a selection criterion for group members, can be taught to the members, or can be brought into teams through the use of facilitators. These skills can be grouped into interpersonal skills, problem-solving skills, and teamwork skills (Carnevale, Gainer, & Meltzer, 1990). Interpersonal skills include cross-cultural tolerance, interviewing skills, active listening, effective nonverbal communication, ability to provide feedback, and negotiation skills. Problem-solving skills help to improve the effectiveness of teams by providing approaches to analyzing problems and making decisions. Teamwork skills promote an understanding of group processes and dynamics and also provide skills to manage group processes effectively.

| CHARACTERISTICS OF THE TASK

A team's ability to perform one type of task well does not necessarily generalize to other types of tasks. The mix of abilities in the group might make it better at certain types of tasks. Teams can be used to perform a variety of types of tasks, and tasks also vary in how well suited they are for group work. McGrath (1984) has a system that explains the different types of tasks that teams perform, whereas Steiner (1972) has a system that explains the different ways in which team members' efforts can be combined.

TABLE 2.1
McGrath's Model of Team Tasks

Goal	Tasks	Cognitive-Behavioral Dimension	Cooperation-Conflict Dimension
Generate	Planning, creative	Cognitive and behavioral	Cooperation
Choose	Intellective, decision making	Cognitive	Cooperation and conflict
Negotiate	Cognitive conflict, mixed motive	Cognitive and behavioral	Conflict
Execute	Competitive, performance	Behavioral	Cooperation and conflict

SOURCE: Adapted from McGrath (1984).

McGrath (1984) developed a classification system to describe the types of tasks that groups perform. The system is based on the four group goals—generate, choose, negotiate, and execute—with each goal having two related tasks (Table 2.1). These eight tasks vary along two dimensions: cognitive-behavioral and cooperation-conflict. Group tasks range from purely cognitive activities (e.g., decision making) to behavioral activities (e.g., making something). Tasks also range from cooperative activities in which members work together (e.g., generating creative ideas) to conflict-oriented activities in which members may disagree or compete with each other (e.g., negotiating differences).

Generation includes tasks that focus on the creative generation of new ideas and tasks to generate plans for behavioral action. Choosing deals with intellective tasks such as problem-solving activities when there are correct answers and decision-making tasks when there are no correct answers. Negotiation includes tasks aimed at resolving conflicting viewpoints and mixed-motive tasks aimed at resolving conflicts of interest. Execution refers to competitive tasks that deal with resolving conflicts of power and performance tasks designed to make things or provide services.

The suitability of a task for a group depends on the demands of the task (Steiner, 1972). Task demands vary along three dimensions (Table 2.2). Some tasks are divisible and can be broken down into subtasks for individual group members, whereas other tasks are unitary. Some tasks require a

TABLE 2.2
Steiner's Demands of Group Tasks

Issue	*Options*	*Task Types*
Can the task be divided?	Subtasks exist	Divisible
	No subtasks exist	Unitary
Is quantity more important than quality?	Quantity	Maximizing
	Quality	Optimizing
How are the individual's inputs related to the group's product?	Added together	Additive
	All group members must contribute	Conjunctive
	Average of the individuals	Compensatory
	Select from individual judgments	Disjunctive
	Group decides how to organize	Discretionary

SOURCE: *Group Dynamics*, 3rd ed., by D. R. Forsyth. Copyright © 1999. Reprinted with permission of Wadsworth, a division of Thomson Learning.

high rate of production (maximization), whereas other tasks require high-quality solutions (optimization). Finally, tasks combine the efforts of the group members in different ways. The group's work can be added together, limited by the last member, averaged, selected, or combined in any way the group desires.

Additive and conjunctive tasks usually are divisible and maximizing; the subtasks can be identified, and the quantity of output is emphasized. Additive tasks combine the group members' contributions together such as when a group paints a house or sells a product. The productivity of a group will exceed that of an individual group member. However, it often is less than the sum of individuals working alone because this type of task tends to reduce the motivation of the individual performers. Conjunctive tasks are not completed until all of the group members have completed their parts. An example of this would be working on an assembly line. Although the group's performance is limited by the worst-performing member, the group can compensate for this in several ways. It can encourage the poor performer to work harder, it can provide advice and support to the poor performer, or it can assign the poor performer to the easiest part of the task.

A compensatory or disjunctive task typically is unitary and optimizing; the task is not easily dividable into subtasks, and the quality of the output is emphasized. A compensatory task averages the input of the group members to create a single solution. An example of this type of task would be when the group leader asks for all group members' opinions and then forms a single recommendation from the responses. The average score is better than the opinions of most of the individual members. In a disjunctive task, the group must generate a single solution that represents the group's product. Typically, the group discusses the issue until its members agree on a solution. The decisions of juries and the problem-solving actions of technical teams are examples of disjunctive tasks. A group usually performs better than individuals in this type of task, but usually not better than the best individual in the group. The problem in formulating a correct group decision is how to evaluate the opinions of the group members. To be successful, someone has to generate the right answer, and the group must decide to adopt it.

When the group is able to decide how it wants to perform a task, it is called a *discretionary task*. Discretionary tasks can be divisible or unitary as well as maximizing or optimizing. Self-managing teams would be an example of groups working on discretionary tasks because they are allowed to decide how to best perform their tasks. The performance of a group on a discretionary task is variable because it depends on whether the group selected an appropriate method to perform the task.

Both McGrath's (1984) and Steiner's (1972) systems for classifying team tasks are useful for understanding what a team does. McGrath's (1984) system explains the different types of tasks that a team actually performs. A team might perform only one or two types of tasks such as a factory team that primarily performs a physical task and might do some problem solving. Other types of teams might perform many different types of tasks such as a project team that both designs and produces a product. Understanding the range of tasks that a team performs is important for the selection and training of team members.

Steiner's (1972) system acknowledges that a team performs a variety of tasks that can be combined in different ways. The team's work may be organized as an additive task (where each person's job is relatively independent) or as a conjunctive task (where team members shift roles to keep the process going smoothly). Steiner's work has been useful in explaining the benefits of and problems with different ways of combining tasks. For some types of tasks, organizing work into teams can create synergies that make performance better than people working independently. However, using teams also might create performance losses due to coordination and motivation problems. (These performance losses are discussed in more detail later in Chapters 4 and 9.)

| GROUP PROCESS

Having the right people and the right type of task does not guarantee success. Team members must be able to combine their efforts successfully. Teams sometimes do not reach their potential because their internal processes interfere with success. Effective teams must organize themselves to perform their tasks, develop social relations to support their operations, and have leaders who provide direction and facilitate the teams' operations.

Groups primarily engage in two types of activities: making decisions and performing tasks. For both of these activities, internal group processes can limit success. Groups can encounter problems with decision making. Groups are imperfect decision makers that do not always fully use the collection of knowledge and skills available to them. Group decisions can be disrupted by personal biases, distorted by the desire to maintain good relationships, and/or impaired by the desire to make decisions quickly. Rather than taking a structured approach to problem solving, groups often become prematurely committed to the first acceptable solution. Creative alternatives to solving problems might not be voiced in groups due to the fear of being criticized by other members.

Even when groups are organized with the sole purpose of performing certain tasks, group process issues can have both positive and negative impacts on performance. Highly effective groups have task-oriented goals and norms. These groups will outperform collections of individuals. However, things can go wrong. A group might have unclear goals or norms that do not encourage performing its task. Rather than encouraging performance, working in a group might lead to reduced effort by individual members. (This problem, called *social loafing,* is discussed later in Chapter 4.)

Internal social relations should provide support for a group to perform its task. Group members need to communicate well, work cooperatively together, and provide emotional support for each other. Groups with high levels of group cohesion and good social relations are more effective. However, a group can be riddled with conflict and divided into cliques or act competitively rather than cooperatively, and communication within the group can break down.

It is the responsibility of the leader to provide a direction for the group and to facilitate its internal processes. There is no set of rules that a good leader can mechanically follow. Groups need different types of leadership depending on their tasks and their maturity. The use of teams often changes the nature of leadership because team leaders do not have the same amount of power and authority as do traditional managers in organizations.

| ORGANIZATIONAL CONTEXT

The organizational context has a significant effect on whether teams operate successfully (Guzzo & Dickson, 1996). Teams can be used as a way in which to improve the operations of organizations, but teams are sensitive to their organizational environments. Teams need the right organizational conditions to be successful. The organizational contexts relate to the cultures of organizations, the amounts of support that organizations provide for teams, and organizations' feedback and reward systems.

Teams are more likely to be successful in organizations that have supportive organizational cultures. Supportive cultures encourage open communication and collaborative efforts. Power and responsibility are given to teams so that they can control their own actions. Although the use of teams can help to change organizations' cultures, it can be difficult to get this change process started due to the limits imposed by existing cultures.

There are a number of organizational supports that should be provided to teams so as to help make them function more effectively (Hackman, 1990b). Teams perform better when they have clear goals and well-defined tasks. They must be provided with adequate resources including financial, staffing, and training support. Reliable information from organizations is required for teams to make decisions, to coordinate their efforts with other parts of the organizations, and to plan for future changes. Finally, teams should have available to them technical and group process assistance. They need technical help to solve their problems, and they need facilitation or coaching to deal with interpersonal difficulties.

Building effective teams requires the efforts of both team members and their organizations. To improve on how team members operate, a team needs feedback on its performance and an incentive to change. To a certain extent, the team can evaluate itself, and team members can provide support for each other. However, an effective team requires feedback and rewards from the organization for good performance. Without this, team members will not focus on the goals that the organization has established for the team.

CHARACTERISTICS OF SUCCESSFUL TEAMS

What makes for successful teams? A number of researchers have tried to answer this question. Their typical approach is to find examples of successful teams and then use interviews and surveys to try to determine what makes these teams successful. Although the research approaches are similar, the types of teams that researchers investigate often are different. In addition, the types of questions that are used to examine the teams differ depending on the backgrounds of the researchers. Several approaches to defining the characteristics of successful teams are presented in what follows to illustrate the characteristics that successful teams have in common.

Hackman (1987) is an organizational psychologist whose specialty area is job design. His research has examined a wide variety of types of teams, both at work and in the laboratory. He lists the following five factors as necessary for the successful development and use of teams:

1. *Clear direction and goals:* Teams need goals to focus their efforts and evaluate their performance.
2. *Good leadership:* Leaders are needed to help manage the internal and external relations of teams and to orient teams toward their goals.
3. *Tasks that are suited for teamwork:* Tasks should be complex, important, and challenging so that they require the integrated efforts of team members and are not capable of being performed by individuals.
4. *Necessary resources to perform the jobs:* The resources that teams need include both material resources and training and personnel resources.
5. *Supportive organizational environment:* Organizations must give sufficient power and authority to allow team members to make and implement their decisions.

Levi and Slem (1995) are psychologists who examined teamwork in high-tech companies. They studied factory production teams and engineering research and development teams to determine a set of factors related to team success. They found the following five factors:

1. *Evaluation and rewards:* Teams need fair and objective criteria for evaluation, team members' performance evaluations should relate to

their contributions to their teams, and members should be rewarded when their teams are successful.

2. *Social relations:* Teams need training in social skills so that they can resolve internal conflicts and function smoothly.
3. *Organizational support:* Management, the organizational system, and the organizational culture must support the use of teams.
4. *Task characteristics:* Teams need clear direction and goals, tasks that are appropriate for teamwork, and work that is challenging and important.
5. *Leadership:* Leaders need to facilitate teams' interactions and provide assistance to teams when problems occur.

Larson and LaFasto (1989) are experts in group communication. They studied a variety of teams from business, sports, and government. Like the previous studies, they found that clear goals with standards of excellence, principled leadership, and external support and recognition are important success factors. In addition, their research indicates that a results-oriented structure, competent team members, a unified commitment, and a collaborative climate are important.

Katzenbach and Smith (1993) are management experts who studied upper level management teams primarily in large organizations. They found that clear performance goals, common approaches and methods for completing tasks, and a sense of mutual accountability are factors related to success. In addition, they believe that a team performs best when there is a small number of team members, members have adequate levels of complementary skills, and there is commitment to a common purpose.

Table 2.3 presents the characteristics of successful teams that are listed by most of the preceding researchers. Teams require clear, well-defined goals to provide direction and motivation and to allow performance to be evaluated. Leaders help to keep teams focused on the goals and facilitate (but do not control) teams' activities. Organizations' cultures and systems must be compatible with teamwork, and organizations must supply teams with the necessary power and resources (e.g., personnel, financial, training) to perform the tasks. Tasks must be suitable for teamwork. They should require the coordinated efforts of people and be both challenging and motivating. Finally, team members should have a sense of common fate or mutual accountability, and their efforts must be evaluated and rewarded in a fair manner.

Although it is useful to try to determine the factors that characterize successful teams, this approach is limited. The differences found by the researchers reflect both different research approaches and different types of

TABLE 2.3
Characteristics of Successful Teams

	Hackman (1987)	Levi and Slem (1995)	Larson and LaFasto (1989)	Katzenbach and Smith (1993)
Clear goals	X		X	X
Appropriate leadership	X	X	X	
Organizational support	X	X	X	
Suitable tasks	X	X		X
Accountability and rewards		X	X	X

teams studied. Cohen and Bailey (1997) conducted a meta-analysis of work teams during the 1990s. Their review of 54 studies of work teams shows that the factors important for success are different for production, professional, and managerial teams. For example, for self-managing production teams, the amount of organizational support is very important, but the quality of leadership is relatively unimportant. On the other hand, professional project teams often are dependent on high-quality leadership because of the nonroutine nature of their tasks.

SUMMARY

The definition of team success relates to teams' tasks, social relations, and impacts on their members. Successful teams complete their tasks and do so in a collective way that is better than using only individuals to perform the tasks. Teams need to develop good social relations to support their task activities and to help the teams maintain their existence. Participating in teams should be a benefit to their members, both in terms of learning new skills and in terms of advancing their careers.

The success of a team depends on the composition of the group, the task, the group process, and the organizational context. There are three important aspects to group composition. A group needs to have members with the right set of knowledge, skills, and abilities to complete its task. For some types of groups, the members need to represent the relevant parts of an organization so that there is a sense of participation in the decision and support for its implementation. Finally, group members need to have the interpersonal skills to work together as a team.

Teams perform a variety of types of tasks that require different sets of skills. The tasks that groups perform can be analyzed by examining whether they can be divided, whether they focus on quantity or quality, and how members' inputs relate to the products. For a task where the group's work is simply added together, the group does not perform any better than the same number of individuals working alone. When the poorest performing member limits completion of the task, the group performs better because it can compensate for individual problems. For a task that requires the group to make a quality decision, the group often performs better than individuals working alone. When the group is allowed to decide on how to perform a task, success depends on how well the group structures the task.

The group process connects the members of the group to its task. Successful group processes organize the group to complete the task, develop supportive social relations, and have leaders to provide direction and facilitation. For each of these steps, the group must overcome obstacles that interfere with its interpersonal dynamics.

The organization provides a context for a team. The organization's culture needs to support the team by creating an environment that encourages collaboration and allows the team to control its internal operations. The organization's systems can support the team by providing direction, resources, information, and assistance. One of the most important aspects of the organizational context is the willingness of the organization to provide feedback to the team on its performance and to reward successful performance.

Researchers from a variety of perspectives have identified several common features of successful teams. Teams have clear goals that provide direction and motivation. Their leaders structure the tasks and facilitate group processes. Their organizations provide supportive contexts for the teams to grow. The tasks that teams perform are well suited for teamwork. Finally, team members are held mutually accountable for the success of their teams, and they are rewarded for their efforts. Although these are characteristics of successful teams, the importance of these various characteristics changes depending on the type of teams.

ACTIVITY: UNDERSTANDING TEAM SUCCESS

Objective. Why are some teams successful, whereas others are unsuccess-ful? This activity tries to use your experience with teams to answer this question.

Activity. Think about a time when you were on a successful team. Using Ac-tivity Worksheet 2.1, write a description of the team at that point in time. (What was it like being on the team? What was the team like?) Think about a time when you were on an unsuccessful team. Write a description of the team at that point in time.

ACTIVITY WORKSHEET 2.1
Successful and Unsuccessful Teams

Successful team:

Unsuccessful team:

Analysis. Compare the two descriptions of successful and unsuccessful teams. What characteristics can explain the differences between these two teams? Compare your answers to those of other group members. Are the characteristics similar? Develop a group answer to the following question: What are the characteristics of successful teams?

1. _____

2. _____

3. _____

4. _____

Discussion. Using your list of the characteristics of successful teams, what advice would you give a team leader about how to establish and run a team?

PART II

PROCESSES OF
TEAMWORK

Chapter 3

TEAM BEGINNINGS

Teams develop through a series of stages that reflect changes in their internal group processes and the demands of their tasks. One of the most important insights of the stage perspective is that teams often are not productive at the beginnings of projects.

There are several issues that a team should address when it is first formed so as to become more effective. The team needs to orient or socialize new members into the group. This socialization process assimilates the new members while accommodating their individual needs. The purpose or objective of a team needs to be defined by the creation of team goals. Developing team goals is an important process that helps to avoid problems, provides directions, and increases motivation. The team needs to develop rules, or group norms, by which to operate. These norms define what is appropriate behavior for group members.

There are techniques to help teams form social relations, develop team norms, and clarify the definitions of their tasks. By focusing on these issues at the beginning, teams can be productive more quickly.

▶ LEARNING OBJECTIVES
1. Understand the main stages of group development.
2. How do the demands of a project change the way in which a team operates?
3. What are the implications of team development stages?
4. How do evaluation, commitment, and role transitions affect group socialization?
5. What are the main characteristics of team goals?
6. What are hidden agendas? How do they affect a group?
7. What are the main functions of group norms?

8. What are the positive and negative effects of group norms?
9. What can a team do to help improve the beginning stages of a team project?

STAGES OF TEAMWORK

Research on project teams shows that the start-up activities take longer than anticipated. For many professional design projects, most of the design work occurs during the last half of the allotted time (Gersick, 1988). The main reason for this slow start is that it takes time to decide on the definition and goals of a project and to develop the social relations and procedures for effective teamwork. Defining the project often is the most difficult part of a team's task. The team needs time to develop social cohesion and functioning group norms before it can focus on performing the task.

An understanding of the dynamics of team projects and group development can help to speed up this process and reduce frustration caused by what members might perceive as a slow start to a team's project. Teamwork is not a smooth process; the team goes through stages and has its good and bad periods. It is important is to develop the capabilities of the team while working on the team's task.

A variety of approaches have been used to explain the changes that groups go through during their existence. Stage theories of group development focus on how the internal group processes change. Project theories attempt to describe how groups change based on the tasks that they perform. Finally, there are alternative theories that explain group process changes as cycles rather than as stages.

| GROUP DEVELOPMENT PERSPECTIVE

There are a variety of stage theories of group development. However, most of the theories have similar elements. The theories try to explain why it takes time for a group to develop before it becomes productive. In addition, they try to explain why the group goes through periods of conflict during its development. Table 3.1 presents the best-known group development stage theory, developed by Tuckman and Jensen (1977). This theory focuses on the development of the internal relations among the team members. (A similar theory developed by Wheelan [1994] focuses on how group members develop independence from the leader.)

TABLE 3.1
Stages of Group Development

Stage	Activity
Forming	Orientation: Members getting to know each other
Storming	Conflict: Disagreement about roles and procedures
Norming	Structure: Establishment of rules and social relationships
Performing	Work: Focus on completing the task
Adjourning	Dissolution: Completion of task and end of the group

SOURCE: Adapted from Tuckman and Jensen (1977).

A group starts with the *forming* stage, where few measurable accomplishments occur. During this stage, group members get to know each other and learn how to operate as a group. Members tend to be polite and tentative with each other as well as compliant toward the leader. They often feel uncomfortable and constrained because they are not familiar with the rest of the members. Group members are confused and uncertain about how to act, and they need to spend time defining their goals and planning how to do their tasks. This stage ends when a level of familiarity has been reached so that group members are comfortable interacting with each other.

The *storming* stage that follows often is characterized by conflicts among group members and confusion about group roles and project requirements. Disagreements over procedures may lead to expressions of dissatisfaction and hostility. Group members may begin to realize that the project is more difficult than was anticipated and may become anxious, defensive, and blameful. The members can become polarized into subgroups as conflict about their roles and about their views of the task expands. Although this conflict might be unpleasant, it is important because it promotes the sharing of different perspectives and leads to a deeper understanding of the members' positions. Not only does this conflict clarify the group's goals, but its resolution also leads to increased group cohesion.

The group begins to organize itself to work on the task during the *norming* stage. Here, the group becomes more cohesive, conflict is reduced, and team confidence improves. The group has established some ground rules (or norms) to help members work together, and social relations have developed enough to create a group identity. Increased levels of trust and support characterize group interactions. Although differences still arise, they are handled through constructive discussion and negotiation.

Next is the *performing* stage. The group has matured and knows how to operate, so it now can successfully focus on the task. If the group has developed norms and successfully built social relations, then it can easily handle the stress of approaching deadlines. The group focuses on performance through collective decision making and cooperation. Studies of many types of groups show that most performance occurs during this stage near the end of the group's project (Hare, 1982). However, not all groups get to this stage; they can get bogged down in the earlier conflict-oriented stages.

The final stage is the *adjourning* or dissolution stage. Some groups have planned endings. When these groups complete their tasks, they disband. Groups also end because of failure to accomplish goals or because of unanticipated problems that make continued group interaction impossible. The adjourning stage can be very stressful to group members because they might be ending the social relations that they have developed.

In some cases, groups do not have planned endings. Organizations can establish work teams that are designed to continue in operation indefinitely. Like all types of groups, they go through the initial development stages until they reach the performing stage. However, they do not continue performing at a high level forever. Teams can become unproductive. They can get caught in conflicts that they are unable to resolve, or they can drift back into former stages because of changes in their tasks, personnel, and/or processes (McGrew, Bilotta, & Deeney, 1999). Group members can enjoy being together, so they seek reasons to justify their teams' continued existence. In all of these cases, it often is difficult for team members to recognize that it is time to end their teams. Research on work teams suggests that there might be a point, after a few years, when longevity no longer is a benefit to performance (Guzzo & Dickson, 1996).

| PROJECT DEVELOPMENT PERSPECTIVE

An alternative view of group stages is based on the characteristics of projects rather than on the development of group processes. These theories are based on research on work teams, whereas the previously discussed group development theories often are based on therapy or learning groups. For example, McIntyre and Salas (1995) present a model of team development based on the skills that team members develop while trying to complete a project. In their model, a team works on role clarification during the early stages, moves on to coordinated skills development, and finally focuses on increasing the variety and flexibility of its skills as a team. This model uses the changing relationship between the team and the project as the driver of change throughout the stages.

McGrath (1990) proposes a model of how project groups operate over time. There are four types of functions that a group performs: inception (selecting and accepting goals), problem solving, conflict resolution, and execution. Each of these functions has implications for how the group operates, how group members are affected, and how group relations are influenced. For example, during the *inception* stage, the group is focused on planning activities and collaborating. During the *conflict resolution* stage, social relations are strained because the group is dealing with conflict. The *problem-solving* and *execution* stages focus on coordinating the ideas or actions of the group members.

In McGrath's (1990) model, a group does not necessarily need to perform all of these functions to complete its goals. For example, on simple problems, the group may go directly from inception to execution without the middle functions. For very complex problems, the group may have to recycle through the four functions a number of times.

The amount of time available to a group affects the way in which it operates. The more time that is available, the more time that a group will spend analyzing a problem and developing its social relations. Therefore, giving a group sufficient time to complete its tasks tends to lead to better quality projects and a better developed group. Over the long term, a group that always is dealing with crises tends to produce lower quality decisions and to have poorer group processes.

Ancona and Caldwell (1990) present a model of group development for new product teams. The three stages of development are based on the changing nature of the tasks that a team performs. In addition, rather than focusing solely on the internal processes of the group, the model highlights the changing emphasis on internal and external relations.

During the first stage, *creation,* a team's activities are a mixture of internal and external processes. The team is developing new ideas and creative solutions while organizing the work team. External relations include gathering information from the organization, understanding the organizational context of the project, and building links with relevant organizational units. During the *development* stage, the team's focus is primarily internal. The project's idea has been approved by the organization, and the team is focused on mastering the technical details of the project. Motivation and coordination of activities are the central focus, and the team leader often tries to isolate the team from the organization so as to encourage these internal processes. The final stage is *diffusion,* where external relations become the primary focus of the team. The project is nearly complete, and coordinating its transfer to manufacturing and marketing is the focus of the team's activities. Ownership of the project shifts from the team to these other parts of the organization. Internal processes often are strained, and the leader has to work on keeping the team members together and motivating them to complete the final stages of the project.

| ALTERNATIVES TO STAGE THEORIES

Although stage theories of group development are popular, not all groups seem to follow these patterns. Some groups skip stages, others get stuck in certain stages, and still others seem to travel through the stages in different routes. The boundaries between the stages often are less clear-cut than the theories suggest.

Rather than emphasizing a sequence of stages, some group theorists believe that groups go through cycles that can be repeated throughout the groups' lives. For example, Bales's (1966) *equilibrium model of group development* views groups as balancing the needs for task completion and relationship development. Groups go back and forth between these two concerns depending on the needs of their members.

Gersick (1988) developed a theory of *punctuated equilibrium* from her research on project teams. Each team had its own pattern of development, but all of the teams experienced periods of low activity followed by bursts of energy and change. In addition, each team had a midpoint crisis where its members realized that half of their time had been used but the project still was in its early stages of completion. This led to a period of panic, followed by increased activity as the team focused on completing the task.

| IMPLICATIONS OF TEAM DEVELOPMENT STAGES

Understanding the stages that teams typically go through can help team members to better recognize what is happening to the team and how to manage it. Stage theories explain why most of the team's work gets done at the end of the project and why it is important to build social relations and team norms at the beginning of the project. However, it is important to remember that stage theories of team development do not always apply. A team's life often is a roller coaster of successes and failures. Some teams get stuck at one of the stages or even break up; they never get to the performing stage because they have not worked through their earlier problems.

There are several lessons that are important here. First, emotional highs and lows for a group are a normal part of group development. Second, developing the group is important. Time needs to be spent developing social relations and socializing new members, establishing goals and norms, and defining the project. Third, the group may go through periods of lower task performance as it tries to resolve conflicts about relationship and task issues; this is a normal part of group development as well.

GROUP SOCIALIZATION

Group socialization refers to the process by which a person becomes a member of a group. An individual goes through a series of role transitions—from newcomer to full member—during the socialization process. At each step of this process, the individual is evaluating the group and deciding on their level of commitment (Moreland & Levine, 1982). Evaluation is the judgment of whether the benefits of participation in the group outweigh the costs. Commitment describes the desire to maintain a relationship with the group. These processes are mutual. The individual evaluates the group and decides on a level of commitment, and the group evaluates the individual and decides how committed it is to him or her.

Evaluation and commitment usually are positively related. People who evaluate their groups positively usually are more committed to their groups. However, a positive evaluation does not always lead to commitment. There may be many groups that people are interested in joining, so people might not necessarily join groups that they evaluate positively or might evaluate groups positively but be excluded from membership. In addition, people may become committed to groups that they do not evaluate positively. A work group might be undesirable, but individuals feel committed because of the desire to retain their jobs. A highly demanding work group might not be enjoyable, but high levels of involvement by the other members often will encourage involvement and commitment.

The socialization process starts with the *investigation* stage, where each side searches for information. The group is attempting to recruit the individual while the individual engages in reconnaissance to decide whether he or she wants to join the group. This stage ends when the individual decides to join the group.

The *socialization* stage determines how the individual will be integrated into the group. The individual must learn about the norms and practices of the group and must accept its culture. This process of assimilation into the group is matched by the group's accommodation to fit the newcomer's needs. This stage ends when the individual has been accepted as a full member of the group.

During the socialization stage, the newcomer spends time seeking out what is expected of him or her by the group, and the group members provide information through both formal and informal orientation activities (Wanous, 1980). At the beginning, the newcomer often is anxious about his or her role in the group, so the newcomer tends to be passive, dependent, and conforming. This style actually increases the newcomer's acceptance by established group members (Moreland & Levine, 1989). The newcomer is a threat to the team because he or she brings in a fresh and objective perspective that can be unsettling to existing members. The passive approach adopted by many newcomers helps to reduce the potential threat of criticism of the team and, thereby, encourages acceptance of the new members.

During the *maintenance* stage, the individual is fully committed to the group. Even though the individual is a full member of the group, there is an ongoing process of negotiating his or her roles and position in the group and the group's goals and practices. Although many members stay in this stage until they leave the group, in some cases members may diverge from the group and reduce their commitment because of conflicts between their personal goals and those of the group.

During *resocialization,* the former full member has become a marginal member of the group. The individual either can reconcile his or her differences with the group and go through the process of assimilation or accommodation or can leave the group. If the individual decides to leave the group, then the former member and the group go through a period of *remembrance.* The former member reminisces about his or her participation in the group, while the group reviews its history and traditions by examining the impact of membership changes.

TEAM GOALS

Group goals are "a desirable state of affairs members intend to bring about through combined efforts" (Zander, 1994, p. 15). It is important for a group to have goals that reflect common agreement that is publicly stated so as to support collaboration. The development of group goals is viewed as one of the primary tasks during the first stage of many models of team development.

A clear understanding of a group's objectives through well-articulated goals is the most common characteristic of successful teams (Larson & LaFasto, 1989). Research on work teams shows that clear project goals help to improve team performance and internal team processes (McComb, Green, & Compton, 1999). A team with shared goals is more likely to achieve its goals on time. Goals also have a positive effect on the internal team functions. When a team agrees on a set of goals, the amount of internal conflict is lessened.

Goals are only one way in which a team can define its purposes. Teams often create mission statements or charters that, in general terms, define their purposes and values. A mission statement articulates a team's values, but it does not say how the team's purposes will be fulfilled. A team's goals must be consistent with the mission statement, but goals should be objective, defining the accomplishments that need to be completed for success. A team also can create subgoals or objectives that serve as signposts along the way to completing the team's goals.

Group goals can be oriented to many different types of performance. They may focus on quantity, speed, quality, service to others, and so forth. It is clear that specific goals, regardless of form, improve performance better than do no goals or ill-defined goals. However, the improvement is directly related to the form of the goals (Guzzo & Dickerson, 1996). Goals for quantity improve quantity but not necessarily other aspects of the group's performance.

| VALUE AND CHARACTERISTICS OF GOALS

The value of team goals is to provide direction or vision to the team and motivation for the team members. Good team goals are clear and specific so that team members understand them and can relate the goals to their performance (Locke & Latham, 1990). Goals should be moderately difficult, that is, motivating but not impossible to achieve. To gain acceptance and support for the group's goals, goal setting should be done as a participatory process that seeks to obtain mutual agreement and commitment to the goals from all team members. Team goals work best when the task is interesting and challenging and requires that team members work together to succeed.

Goals serve a variety of functions for a team. Table 3.2 lists several of these functions. Goals help to direct and motivate the team and its members,

TABLE 3.2
Functions of Team Goals

1. Serve as a standard that can be used to evaluate performance.

2. Motivate team members by encouraging their involvement in the task.

3. Guide the team toward certain activities and encourage integration of team members' tasks.

4. Provide a criterion to evaluate whether certain actions and decisions are appropriate for the team.

5. Serve as a way in which to inform outside groups about the team and establish relationships with them.

6. Determine when team members should be rewarded or punished for their performance.

SOURCE: Adapted from Zander (1994).

but they also serve functions outside the team. They help to establish relationships with other groups and to establish criteria for evaluation from the surrounding organization.

Zander (1994) believes that the three most important characteristics of group goals are accessibility, measurability, and difficulty. Accessibility refers to the probability of completing the goals. This relates to the group's knowledge of how to complete the task and meet the goals. For example, research and development teams might set goals that turn out to be impossible to meet, or management teams might not know how to implement a task once the goals are formed. These situations are quite different from that of a production team needing a little guidance and a lot of motivation to complete its task.

Measurability refers to the ability to quantify whether the team is reaching its goals. If progress toward the goals is not measurable, then the team cannot receive adequate feedback about its performance. The research on process improvement teams shows that measurable goals are necessary for a team to improve its performance. Without measurability, one might as well tell the team to "go out and do your best"—a nice motivational expression that does not lead to improved performance.

The final characteristic of good goals is difficulty. The goals need to be at least moderately difficult to encourage and motivate performance so that the team feels a sense of accomplishment when it reaches the goals. However, care should be taken not to establish goals that are too difficult. When a team repeatedly misses its goals, members become embarrassed, begin to blame each other and outside factors for performance problems, and might refuse to commit to goals in the future (Zander, 1977).

It is important to note that the team is not always free to set its own goals. Teams have relationships with outside groups, such as customers, that depend on the team's efforts and influence its goals. Teams also set goals relative to the performance of comparison groups such as other organizations. Goals are influenced by the opinions of outside onlookers such as the media. Finally, team goals are strongly influenced by their organizational and managerial contexts. With the exception of top management teams, most teams have goals that are defined by their organizations.

Although goals can play an important role in providing direction and motivation for a team, this does not always happen. Often, a team is faced with a situation where the goals are unclear or where team members have different views of the team's goals. For a project team, sometimes understanding the problem it is trying to solve (i.e., defining the goals of the project) is more difficult and time-consuming than developing a solution. Improving the quality of a team's goals through goal-setting activities is a solution to these problems and is discussed later in Chapter 17.

| HIDDEN AGENDAS

Group goals provide a number of valuable functions, but they also can be a source of problems. Problems arise from the conflict between individual goals and group goals that often develops as a result of hidden agendas. In essence, hidden agendas are unspoken individual goals that conflict with overall group goals.

The most basic type of hidden agenda relates to the motivational aspect of goals. Although the team might decide to commit itself 100% to doing a high-quality job on a project, some team members might not feel that the team's activities are very important. They might decide to slack off and spend more time and effort on other activities. Their goal is to help the team succeed with the least amount of effort on their part.

A second type of hidden agenda relates to the directional aspect of goals. Some team members might not agree with the goals of the team or might have individual goals that are not compatible with the team goals. For example, in an organization budget committee, team members must deal with the sometimes conflicting goals of doing what is best for the organization versus doing what is best for the departments they represent.

These differences between individual and group goals can create conflict within a group. It is a difficult conflict to resolve because it is hidden. A low-motivated team member will create excuses rather than tell the team that he or she is unwilling to work hard on the project. A team member with conflicting loyalties will hide this conflict, leading other team members to distrust what is being said. The overall effect of hidden agendas is to break down trust within the team. Over time, this reduces communication, creates conflicts, and makes conflicts more difficult to resolve.

Dealing with hidden agendas can be difficult. By the time one is aware that this is the team's problem, the team probably already is suffering from conflicts and distrust. Directly confronting people about hidden agendas often does not work. It forces them to be defensive and to deny that this is the problem. Hidden agendas often are better dealt with indirectly (Johnson & Johnson, 1997). Rather than confronting team members directly about their hidden agendas, the team can strengthen its group goals or improve its communication processes.

Focusing on the group's goals is an indirect approach for dealing with hidden agendas. Can the group adopt a set of goals that team members can agree to support? Spending time evaluating and modifying the group's goals so that they are acceptable to all members reduces the problem of hidden agendas. An alternative approach is to deal with the communication problems created by hidden agendas. Conducting group activities that encourage honest communication and help to build trust among team members is useful. Open and trustworthy communication helps the team to better manage its conflicts and may allow team members to discuss goal conflicts in a safe manner.

GROUP NORMS

Group norms are the ground rules that define what is appropriate and inappropriate behavior in a group. They establish expectations about how group members are to behave. These rules can be explicit (e.g., 51% majority needed on all votes for a decision) or implicit (e.g., group members take turns when talking). Although most groups do not formally state their norms, members typically are aware of the rules and follow them.

There are four main functions of group norms (Feldman, 1984). First, group norms express the group's central values, which help to give members a sense of who they are as a group. Second, norms help to coordinate the activities of group members by establishing common ground and making behavior more predictable. Third, norms help define what appropriate behavior is for group members; this helps people avoid embarrassing or difficult situations and thereby encourages active participation in the group. Fourth, norms help the group to survive by creating a distinctive identity; this identity helps group members understand how they are different from others and gives them criteria to evaluate deviant behavior within the group.

There are a number of factors that affect the power of group norms to control group members' behavior (Shaw, 1981). Conformity to group norms relates to the personality characteristics of members. For example, people with low self-confidence are more likely to obey group norms. The more clear and specific a norm is, the more members will conform to it. If most group members accept and conform to the norms, then others are more likely to conform. The more cohesive a group is, the more conformity there is to group norms.

Groups can have norms that are central to or peripheral to their operations (Schein, 1988). Studies show that groups tend to tolerate more deviance from norms that are peripheral than from norms that are central to their operations. For example, technical experts who are important contributors to a team's project might be allowed to violate peripheral norms concerning dress codes or social etiquette rules. Most team norms relate to the task of the team (Hayes, 1997). These norms encourage behavior that coordinates the integrated activities of the team members, and they recognize that different types of contributions are needed to complete the team's task. Rather than promoting rejection of team members who are deviant, team norms often recognize the need for multiple perspectives and different types of contributions according to skills.

| HOW NORMS ARE FORMED

Group norms often develop unconsciously and gradually over time. Norms develop as members align their behavior with the behavior of other members in the group. In other words, they are created by mutual influence and develop through the interactions of the group members. Even though people obey these norms, they might not be able to articulate them. In addition, group members typically obey norms even when there is no external pressure, such as threats of punishment, for doing so. This shows that they have accepted the norms and use them to guide their own behavior.

Group norms come from a variety of sources. Groups can develop norms based on those from other groups to which they have belonged. Norms can be based on outside standards such as the ways in which other groups in society or the organization operate. Norms also are strongly influenced by what happens early in the group's existence, and they are most likely to develop in situations where people are unsure of how to behave. For example, when a group is having problems with people showing up late for meetings, the group is likely to develop explicit norms about attendance.

Many teams simply ignore the notion of group norms. They assume that everyone knows how to behave in a group, so there is no need to take time to create explicit norms. It is not until a team starts to have problems that it becomes aware that team members are operating under different sets of norms. The team benefits from discussing and establishing explicit group norms. This prevents the development of inappropriate norms (e.g., it is okay to be late in submitting one's part of the project) and makes everyone aware of the types of behavior that are expected.

| IMPACT OF GROUP NORMS

There are both positive and negative aspects to group norms. Because they control the group's interactions, norms can allow more fair communication, help to keep people respectful of others, and distribute power to weaker members of the group. Strong norms are a benefit to the internal workings of the group. However, norms also can enforce conformity, and this can be a problem from the organization's perspective.

The Hawthorne studies of teamwork showed the benefits of and problems with group norms. In this factory setting, group norms controlled the amount of work that people performed. When the team had high performance norms, norms were a benefit because they kept the laggards in line and encouraged workers to help each other. However, when the team had low performance norms, management had a limited ability to change the team's behavior because group norms were resistant to outside influence.

APPLICATION: JUMP-STARTING PROJECT TEAMS

Organizing people into teams to complete projects often leads to initial drops in performance (Katzenbach & Smith, 1993). As we have seen, it takes time for groups to develop their internal social processes. Teams that have been working together often are more productive than new teams. Part of this difference relates to the shared knowledge that develops among team members; this shared knowledge is known as the transactive memory system (Wegner, 1986). Team members develop a shared knowledge base about how to perform a task. Each team member learns about the knowledge and skills of the other team members by working together on a project. This shared knowledge improves coordination of activities and increases team performance (Moreland, Argote, & Krishnan, 1996).

However, when new teams are formed to complete projects, there are techniques that can be used to help speed their development. Teams can learn to operate better, and this experience can help them to better manage their projects, improve performance, and reduce the stress of finishing up their projects in a hurry. Improving teamwork requires efforts at the beginnings of projects. The aim is to improve social relations, develop useful group norms, and better define projects.

TEAM WARM-UPS

One of the problems with teams is the tendency to focus on their tasks almost exclusively. It is important to recognize the value of developing the social relations within a team. Many of the stages of group development explain that developing social relations precedes the group's performance stage. Approaches to developing social relations among team members also help in the socialization of new team members. This makes it important to focus on the development of social relations early in the team's existence.

Team warm-ups are social "icebreakers" that are conducted at the beginnings of team meetings (Scholtes, 1988). They are very important at the first team meetings and should be used during the early stages of team formation so as to develop social relations within the team. Warm-ups are social activities designed to help team members get to know each other. This helps to improve communication during the team project. Warm-ups can be as simple as spending 5 minutes sharing favorite jokes or talking about what team members did over the weekend. Table 3.3 contains several common team warm-up exercises that are useful during the early stages of a team's life.

PROJECT DEFINITIONS

Teams often jump into projects and then later have to back up to earlier stages when problems arise. In the rush to try to complete a task, a team

TABLE 3.3
Team Warm-Up Exercises

1. Team introductions	The team members take turns going around the table introducing themselves. Besides just saying their names, team members can be asked to tell things about themselves, such as where they grew up, their favorite jokes, and their favorite movies. This exercise can be repeated at later team meetings by adding other types of information about each team member.
2. Team name	By yourself, write down five names that you think would be good for your team. Then, have each team member state his or her five names. Have the team create a new list of team names that does not overlap with the existing list. Try to select a name for your team from the second list. The selected name should be supported by all of the team members.
3. Conversation starters	It often is useful to spend 5 or 10 minutes having a group discussion about social and personal topics. The following list contains some useful conversation starters, but you can create your own:

- What types of work activities do you like and dislike?
- What things do you like most and least about team projects?
- What values are most important to you?
- What do you do when you want to relax?
- What types of things make you feel uncomfortable?

SOURCE: Adapted from Scholtes (1988).

might not spend enough time understanding the assignment (Pokras, 1995). It is important to make sure that everyone on the team has the same understanding of the assignment and that this understanding is the same as the organization's understanding. Many professional teams find the project definition stage of a team to be the most difficult and important stage.

There are many reasons why teams try to skip over the project definition stage. Team members might feel socially uncomfortable at the beginning, so they want to quickly focus on performing the task. Task assignments often are ambiguous, and this ambiguity causes discomfort. Making quick decisions to clear up this problem is emotionally satisfying. For a larger project, a team might feel overwhelmed by how much is unknown about the project. By starting off in one direction, the team is managing this sense of being overwhelmed. These actions might help to deal with the emotional aspects of the problem, but they often result in a team heading off in a wrong direction that will lead to conflict and time delays later in the project.

As discussed later in Chapter 11, there are a number of techniques that a team can use to improve its ability to define a problem and understand its underlying causes. The team should use these techniques at the beginning of its project to better understand its assignment.

| CREATING NORMS

Early in a team's existence, it should establish ground rules for operating meetings, how team members will interact, and what types of behavior are acceptable. These ground rules are part of the group's norms. The team should have an open discussion of ground rules and reach agreement on what is acceptable and unacceptable behavior. The team should form ground rules early and review them periodically, especially if there are compliance problems.

There are a number of signs that a group is having problems with norms. If topics are avoided and irrelevant conversations keep recurring, no one acknowledges or follows the norms, and/or there is conflict over the meaning of group norms, then the group needs to do something about its norms. Table 3.4 presents some issues to consider when establishing group norms for team meetings.

SUMMARY

Groups develop through a series of stages, from forming to adjourning. These stages may be due to the time needed to develop the groups' internal processes or the changing demands of their tasks. This team development perspective shows the different types of challenges that groups face during their existence. Groups often encounter conflict during the early stages of projects. Rather than a smooth progression, groups go through periods of low activity followed by bursts of achievement. Understanding these stage

TABLE 3.4
Norm Issues for Team Meetings

Decisions	How should decisions be made? Must everyone agree for consensus? Does anyone have veto power?
Attendance	What are legitimate reasons for missing meetings? How should the team encourage regular attendance?
Assignments	When assignments are made, what should be done when team members do not complete them or when they complete them poorly?
Participation	What should be done to encourage everyone to participate?
Meeting times	When do meetings occur? How often should the team meet? How long is a team meeting?
Agendas and minutes	Who is responsible for these activities? What other roles should be set up?
Promptness	What should be done to encourage promptness?
Conversational courtesies	How can the team encourage members to listen attentively and respectfully to others? Does the team need rules to limit interruptions or to prevent personal criticisms?
Enforcement	How should the team enforce its rules?

SOURCE: Adapted from Scholtes (1988).

theories helps to explain why groups do most of their productive work during the later stages of projects.

The group socialization process describes the changing relationship between a group and its members. The group and its members evaluate each other so as to determine the respective levels of commitment. The socialization process proceeds through a series of stages, from investigation to remembrance. Each stage is marked by a role transition that marks the changing level of commitment that members have to the group.

Goals define the purpose and values of a group and are an important factor in the success of the group. Goals often are divided into objectives that are linked to actual performance criteria. Effective group goals are accessible to the group, measurable so that they provide feedback on performance, and moderately difficult to achieve so as to motivate performance. One common goal problem for the group is hidden agendas. Hidden agendas occur when group members have individual goals that conflict with the group goals. These can create conflict and distrust in the group and must be managed carefully.

Group norms define what is appropriate behavior for group members. They help the group to operate more smoothly and to create a distinctive identity. Norms often evolve gradually over time. However, the group should formally establish operating norms. The impact of group norms can be both positive and negative. Norms help the group operate better internally, but they might make the group more resistant to change by the outside organization.

One of the values of viewing the ways in which groups change over time is that doing so illustrates the problems that teams have at the beginnings of projects. Teams must deal with the problems of undeveloped social relations, ill-defined projects, and ambiguous norms before they can focus on performing their tasks. The operation of teams can be improved by focusing on these problems at the beginnings of team projects.

ACTIVITY: OBSERVING TEAM NORMS

Objective. Norms define the rules for appropriate and inappropriate behavior. Although team members often follow them, most teams do not develop a formal set of norms. Teams can have norms that cover a variety of issues. Norms can be enforced by official sanctions (e.g., a fine for violating them) or by informal pressure from the leader or team.

Activity. Observe a team meeting and, using Activity Worksheet 3.1, try to note the norms that are being used to make decisions, manage participation, and encourage conversational etiquette. For example, does the team use voting to make decisions? Does everyone have to participate before a decision is made? Are there rules to prevent people from interrupting each other?

Analysis. After developing a set of norms that the team is using, note how well the team follows them. Do the team members consistently follow them? Are there examples of people violating the norms? How does the team respond to these violations?

Discussion. Does the team you observed have effective norms? Are the norms explicit or implicit? If you were asked to provide advice to the team, would you recommend that it develop formal norms? What norms do you think the team should formally adopt? Why?

ACTIVITY WORKSHEET 3.1
Observing Team Norms

Decision-making norms:
Participation norms:
Conversation etiquette norms:

Chapter 4

UNDERSTANDING THE BASIC TEAM PROCESSES

Motivation, group cohesion, role assignment, and performing both task and social behaviors are the basic building blocks of successful team performance. Working in a team should help motivate its members, but often individual effort decreases when performed in a group. This phenomenon is called *social loafing*. Developing challenging tasks that require interdependent actions, improving the reward system, developing motivating goals, and increasing commitment to the group can help to reduce social loafing and motivate the group.

Beyond motivating a group, successful performance depends on other factors. Group cohesion is the bond that ties the members together. Cohesive groups generally perform better, but cohesion also can cause performance problems. Like the roles in a play, people perform roles in a group. Poorly defined roles can lead to stress, whereas clear roles can help groups to operate more efficiently. Although task behaviors typically dominate in work teams, social behaviors also are necessary to build relationships among group members. Groups sometimes suffer from a lack of activities aimed at building relationships among members.

➤➤ LEARNING OBJECTIVES

1. What factors cause social loafing in a group? How can social loafing be prevented?
2. What encourages a group to be more motivated?
3. What factors encourage the development of group cohesion?
4. How does cohesion affect group performance?
5. What are the causes of role ambiguity and role conflict?

6. What are the formal roles that teams often use?
7. What are the main task and social behaviors that are performed in a group?
8. Why is it important for a team to enact social behaviors?
9. What is the value of group process observations?

MOTIVATION

The potential of teamwork is that the whole is greater than the sum of its parts; the collective work of a group of people is more than the individuals could accomplish separately. Group synergies, the creativity of conflicting ideas, the motivating impact of team spirit, and other sources should give a team an advantage over a collection of individuals, but it does not always work out this way. In some circumstances, working together causes a decrease in motivation. This can be due to social loafing. Understanding this motivation problem suggests the ways in which teams can increase group motivation.

SOCIAL LOAFING

One of the biggest motivation problems for teams is social loafing, which is the reduction of individual contributions when people are working in groups rather than alone (Latane, Williams, & Harkins, 1979). Imagine a simple experiment to demonstrate social loafing. Record the volume of people who are asked to shout as loud as they can when they are alone. When asked to do the same task in pairs, the volume is 66% of two individuals shouting alone. When asked to perform in six-person groups, the volume is 36% of six individuals. Social loafing occurs in a wide variety of tasks for both genders and in all cultures.

Social loafing is related to several other group phenomena. People can become "free riders" who perform little in a group because they do not believe that their individual efforts are important and they know that they will receive their share of the group's reward regardless of their efforts (Sweeney, 1973). There also is the "sucker effect" (Johnson & Johnson, 1997). Good performers often slack off in teams because they do not want others to take advantage of them. This can lead to all group members reducing their contributions to the task.

There are a variety of factors that contribute to social loafing (Karau & Williams, 1993). The tasks that the team is performing sometimes are just a collection of individual tasks, so there might be no need for the team to perform in a coordinated way. This can reduce motivation because of the lack of a perceived need to work as a team so as to complete the task. Individual performance can be hidden in the team's collective effort, so members reduce their effort because they no longer are concerned about what others will think about their performance. Finally, team members might be unaware of how much effort others are putting into the task, so they do not know whether they are doing their fair share. Unfortunately, people tend to overestimate the extent of their contributions to the group.

One of the best ways in which to understand social loafing is to look at one place where it almost never occurs—a championship basketball game. In basketball, only the team's score counts to determine the winner. However, everyone's individual participation is observable and measurable. The task is motivating by itself and becomes more motivating through the social aspects of performing it. The task also requires an integrated and coordinated performance. One player cannot win the game by him- or herself, so each player is dependent on the coordinated efforts of the team to win. Winning is important, so success is highly rewarded. There is no social loafing in basketball or in other tasks that have these characteristics.

Research on work groups shows that these sports principles apply to work. When work teams are given challenging tasks, when they are rewarded for group success yet have identifiable individual performance, and when there is commitment to the team, social loafing does not occur (Hackman, 1986).

| INCREASING GROUP MOTIVATION

The discussion of the impact of social loafing on a group helps to identify the factors that will encourage motivation in the group. Increasing a team's motivation relates to the task it performs, how performance will be evaluated and rewarded, the goals of the team, and the team members' sense of commitment or belonging.

Task

A team is more motivated when the task that it performs is interesting, involving, and challenging. Probably the best description of how to create this type of task comes from the job characteristic model (Hackman & Oldham, 1980). A satisfying job creates three critical psychological states: experienced meaningfulness, responsibility for outcomes, and knowledge of results. The *meaningfulness* of a task comes from being able to use a variety of skills, completing a whole piece of work from beginning to end, and having the job affect others. The experience of *responsibility* comes from autonomy or having the freedom to design, schedule, and carry out the job as desired. *Knowledge of results* comes from feedback about the effectiveness of one's performance.

However, a good team task is more than just a good individual task. A good team task requires task interdependence; the members of the team need to work together so as to successfully complete the task. Task interdependence is an additional factor that can be added to the job characteristic model (Van der Vegt, Emans, & Van de Vliert, 1998). It is a shift from individual responsibility to experienced group responsibility for outcomes. To be successful, team members need to feel responsible for both their own work and the work of the other team members.

Task interdependence can come from the distribution of skills among team members and the work processes of the team. It is one reason why action teams (e.g., sports teams) and cross-functional teams (e.g., design teams where members have different skills) often are more successful than student project teams. In a sports team, the players need each other to succeed. In a cross-functional team, working together is the only way in which to complete a project. However, in a student team, the students typically all have the same skills and knowledge, so they do not need each other to complete the task.

Interdependence helps to motivate team members in several ways. To the extent that team members depend on each other to complete a task, power is shared among the members (Franz, 1998). The more the team members need each other to complete a task, the more power each team member has over the group. Task interdependence is an important moderator variable in studying team effectiveness (Langfred, 2000). Interdependence affects how factors such as conflict, cohesiveness, work norms, decision-making approach, and autonomy relate to group effectiveness. When teams are highly interdependent, these variables have a more powerful effect on how well teams perform. Interdependence also encourages members to believe that their contributions to the group are indispensable, unique, and valuable, thereby making them more willing to put effort into the group's task (Kerr & Bruun, 1983).

Evaluation and Rewards

Interdependence relates to both the task and the outcome of the team's work. The task might require coordinated effort, but team members might feel that their evaluations and rewards are primarily based on individual performance rather than on the success of the team's effort. Research shows that a belief in outcome interdependence is important because it helps to motivate members to work together (Van der Vegt et al., 1998).

Only when team members feel both individual and group responsibility will they work in a cooperative way. Group goals and reward systems linked to them encourage this dual sense of responsibility. For example, managerial teams often do not perform well because managers are more concerned about what happens in their respective departments than in the organization as a whole. One of the values of company-wide profit-sharing programs is to make organizational success an important goal that is rewarded for each member of the managerial team. This encourages the managers to think about what is good for the organization rather than only about what is good for their departments.

There needs to be a balance of individual- and team-based rewards to encourage both a commitment to the team and an incentive for individual performance (Thompson, 2000). Finding the right balance can be difficult for an organization. In addition, the performance evaluation system must fairly identify both team success and an individual's contribution to it. When individual contributions to the team are identifiable and linked to the performance evaluation and reward system, motivation is increased (Harkins & Jackson, 1985). (The topic of evaluating and rewarding teams is discussed in more detail in Chapter 17.)

Goals

As was discussed in Chapter 3, team goals help to provide direction and motivation for the team. Clear goals support motivation by leading to increased effort, better planning, better performance monitoring, and increased commitment to the group (Weldon, Jehn, & Pradhan, 1991).

Goals also have an impact on team members' sense of efficacy, which is the belief that, through effort, one will succeed. Self-efficacy often is reduced in a group because members do not feel that their contributions are important or valuable. This reduces motivation toward the team's task. Increasing a sense of collective efficacy can help to increase motivation. The more confident about success an individual is, the more motivated the individual is. Collective effort is determined by the expectation about reaching a goal and the value of the goal (Karau & Williams, 1993). So, setting goals that are challenging but attainable increases the motivation of all team members.

Commitment and Cohesion

The more that people value membership in the group, the more motivated they are to perform. The increased sense of commitment and attraction to a group is called *group cohesion*. Cohesive groups are less likely to experience social loafing (Karau & Williams, 1997). Group cohesiveness includes a commitment to the task that the group is performing. In a highly cohesive group, group members like the task that the group is performing, enjoy working together on the task, have personal involvement in the task, and take pride in the group's performance. Research shows that highly cohesive groups have more commitment to their tasks and perform better (Wech, Mossholder, Steel, & Bennett, 1998). Because group cohesion has other important effects besides motivation, a more complete discussion of it is presented in the next section.

GROUP COHESION

Group cohesion refers to the interpersonal bonds that hold a group together. Cohesion is a multidimensional concept that relates to several different factors. To many theorists, the feeling of belonging or social identity is the core of group cohesion. Members of a cohesive group have a shared social identity. Membership in the group is personally important, so they define themselves as members of the group (Hogg, 1992). Others view cohesiveness as a type of social attraction (Lott & Lott, 1965). Members of a cohesive group like each other and feel connected because of this relationship. Cohesiveness also can come from the group's task. The joining together to work as a team creates a sense of cohesiveness (Guzzo & Dickson, 1996). The more interdependent the members need to be so as to complete the task, the greater the likelihood that they will feel like part of a cohesive group.

The sense of identification with the group that occurs in cohesive groups has important implications (Hayes, 1997). A group is better able to manage stress and conflict among its members if it has a firm sense of itself as a distinctive group. The creation of a sense of insiders and outsiders to the group causes people to view the members of the team as more similar to and different from members of other groups. In work teams, members might have very different skills, professions, and even statuses, but that does not prevent development of a cohesive team.

HOW COHESION AFFECTS THE GROUP'S PERFORMANCE

Group cohesion has a number of effects on the group. People who are part of cohesive groups are more satisfied than are members of noncohesive groups (Hackman, 1992). Group cohesion also helps to reduce stress because members are more supportive of each other. The interpersonal effects of group cohesion are generally positive, but the effects on a group's performance are mixed.

Group cohesion has a generally positive impact on group performance (Mullen & Copper, 1994). This is especially true for smaller groups. This relationship goes in both directions. When a group is successful at performing its task, its level of cohesiveness increases. Cohesion that is based on commitment to the task has a bigger impact on performance than does cohesion that is based on group attraction or unity. The effects of cohesion are more important when the group's task requires high levels of interaction, coordination, and interdependence.

Members of a cohesive group are more likely to accept the group's goals, decisions, and norms. The increased interpersonal bonds among the group members increase the pressure to conform to the group's norms. As was seen in the discussion of group norms, norms can either support or hamper group productivity. Effective work teams have norms that support high-quality performance and a level of group cohesiveness that provides social support to its members. However, cohesive teams without good performance norms might not be effective and might be highly resistant to change (Nemeth & Staw, 1989).

Cohesiveness affects a group's social interactions, and this can affect performance and decision making. Low levels of group cohesiveness might limit the team's ability to work together, whereas high levels of cohesiveness might impair decision-making ability. Sometimes, group members will agree to a decision only because they do not want to upset the group's relationships rather than because they agree with the decision (Janis, 1972).

An important aspect of group cohesion relates to conflict resolution and problem solving. A team with poor social relations will try to avoid dealing with problems until they disrupt the team's ability to perform the task or threaten its existence as a team. A team with good social relations is better equipped to handle problems when they arise. The team can do this because its more open communication allows team members to manage conflicts constructively. This is why it is important to develop group cohesion and good social relations early in the team's life. Forming good social relations early means better ability to solve problems and manage conflicts throughout the team's project.

| BUILDING GROUP COHESION

Research on organizations has identified a number of factors that encourage cohesion in work teams (McKenna, 1994). Team members in a cohesive group tend to have more similar attitudes and personal goals. They have spent more time together, and this increases their opportunity to develop common interests and ideas. When the team is isolated from others, it can help to produce a sense of being special and different. A smaller team tends to be more cohesive than a larger team. Having strict requirements to join a team increases cohesion. Finally, when incentives are based on group performance rather than on individual performance, the team becomes more cooperative and cohesive.

There are several approaches to increasing the amount of cohesion in a work team (Wech et al., 1998). Training in social interaction skills, such as effective listening and conflict management, can help to improve communication and cohesion. Training in task skills, such as goal setting and job skills, improves the team's ability to work successfully. Team success, and being rewarded for it, improves cohesion. The team leader can help to increase cohesion by promoting more interactions among team members, reducing status differences, making sure that everyone is aware of each other's contributions, and creating a climate of pride by building the confidence of team members and recognizing successful accomplishments.

TEAM ROLES

Roles are another one of the basic building blocks of successful team performance. Roles are sets of behaviors that are typical of people in certain social contexts. Roles within a group are similar to roles in a play. They describe what people are supposed to do and how their parts relate to what others in the group are doing. Group members can negotiate the roles they want to play, and they have a certain amount of freedom in how the roles are performed.

A group can deliberately create roles for members to perform. These roles are related to the task and allow the group to operate more efficiently. Even without deliberately creating formal roles, group members assume informal roles within the group. Informal roles emerge over time as the group interacts. These roles can be task related (e.g., expert, facilitator) or socially related (e.g., supporter, clown).

The selection of who should fulfill a role can occur in a variety of ways. The selection of roles can come from the organization, team, or individual. For example, upper management in the organization can assign the team leader, the team can elect its leader, or the team can have no official leader (but an informal leader eventually will emerge in the team). The type of role also affects the selection process. The team often selects members to perform skill-based tasks, whereas social roles often emerge by self-selection.

The definitions of the activities in a role also vary. The group explicitly defines some role behaviors, whereas the person filling the role defines other behaviors. For example, the recorder is the person who takes notes so as to write up the minutes, but whether these are funny or detailed depends on the particular recorder fulfilling the role.

| ROLE PROBLEMS

The roles that people perform in a group sometimes can be a cause of stress. Role ambiguity and role conflict cause this stress. Because roles often emerge in the group without formal definitions, the responsibilities of the roles often are ill defined. A person fulfilling a role might not understand what the other group members expect of him or her. This creates uncertainty in the person performing the role and sometimes hostility from the other group members because the role is not being performed the way in which they desire.

Group members also occupy several roles at a time, and these roles may involve conflicting demands. Inter-role conflict occurs when a person occupies several roles that are incompatible with each other. For example, when someone is promoted, the individual often experiences conflict between being a manager and being a friend with his or her former co-workers. Conflicts also can occur within a single role (i.e., intra-role conflict). In a task force that includes team members from different parts of an organization, the team members may experience a conflict between doing what is good for the team and doing what is good for their organizational areas.

Role ambiguity and conflict have a negative impact on people in an organization. Research shows that people with these role problems have higher levels of stress, decreased satisfaction and morale, and increased job turnover (Kemery, Bedeian, Mossholder, & Touliatos, 1985). Role problems also decrease commitment to the organization and reduce involvement and participation in the group's interactions (Brown, 1996).

For a project team, role problems often appear to get worse near the end of the project. As team members are rushing to complete their assignments, they become more aware of the different expectations that members have about who will do what. These different expectations, which are about what roles members should be performing, lead to conflicts at a time when the team already is stressed about the project deadline.

A team can do several things to help deal with role problems. It can make explicit the important roles in the group so that people know what is expected of them. The tasks that the group is performing can be prioritized so that group members know how to decide what to do when there are conflicts among tasks.

| TYPES OF TEAM MEETING ROLES

Team meetings are an example of how roles are useful for a team, and assigning meeting roles will help to make the time the group spends together more productive. Meetings operate more efficiently when the major task roles are explicitly defined and team members are assigned to fulfill them (Kayser, 1990). One of the main meeting roles is the leader or facilitator. The leader is responsible for structuring the team's interactions to ensure that the team can complete its goals. The leader manages the structure, but not the content, of the meeting. The primary activities of the leader are to (a) develop the agenda to help structure the team's meetings; (b) ensure that information is shared, understood, and processed by the team in a supportive and participative environment; and (c) remove internal problems that hinder the team's operations.

The recorder takes notes on key decisions and task assignments (i.e., who agreed to do what). The minutes focus on the main points rather than trying to capture all of the discussion. Having good documentation of the team's actions is important because it makes information available for future use, provides a fixed point of reference for later, and provides evidence of the analysis process used.

Sometimes, the recorder also acts as the team's scribe. The scribe notes the comments of team members on a blackboard or flip chart during a discussion. After the discussion is completed, the recorder notes the conclusions that the team has reached. Some groups assign the role of scribe to another person or let the leader do this.

Another role is that of the team's timekeeper. When the agenda is presented at the beginning of the meeting, the amount of time for each section can be identified. When the team has used up the time for a particular agenda item, the timekeeper points this out to the team. The team can continue on that topic, but it needs to recognize that to do so will make the meeting longer than planned.

These team meeting roles should be recognized and filled at the beginning of a team's existence. However, it is not important that team members be permanently assigned to these roles initially. It often is better to rotate people through roles, giving everyone a chance to try them out, before the team assigns permanent roles (Kayser, 1990). This has several benefits. Every team member gets practice with the roles. This is a good learning experience, and members might have to fulfill other roles later due to team absences. In addition, the team gets a chance to see how everyone performs. After team members have tried out roles for several meetings, the team is better able to select who should fill them on a more permanent basis.

TASK AND SOCIAL BEHAVIORS

There are two basic types of behaviors that are performed in a group: task behaviors and social behaviors. *Task behaviors* are focused on the group's goals and task and on members' support of each other while performing the task. *Social behaviors* focus on the social and emotional needs of the group members. They help to maintain the social relations among the members and sometimes are called *group maintenance behaviors*. Groups need both task and social behaviors so as to function effectively. Table 4.1 shows the primary task and social behaviors that occur during group interactions (Benne & Sheats, 1948).

The optimum balance between task and social behaviors depends on the characteristics of the group (Benne & Sheats, 1948). For a task-oriented group such as a work team, task-oriented behaviors will dominate the

TABLE 4.1
Types of Group Behaviors

Behavior	*Function*
Task behaviors	
Initiator/contributor	Proposes new ideas or new ways for the group to act
Information giver	Provides data and facts for decision making
Information seeker	Requests more information to help in decision making
Opinion giver	Provides opinions, values, and feelings
Opinion seeker	Requests the opinions of others to help in decision making
Coordinator	Shows relationships of ideas to organize the discussion
Energizer	Stimulates the group to continue working
Evaluator/critic	Questions the group's ideas and procedures
Social behaviors	
Encourager	Supports and rewards others
Harmonizer	Mediates conflicts among members
Compromiser	Shifts members' position so as to reduce conflict
Expediter	Facilitates communications from others
Standard setter	Evaluates quality of the group's interactions
Follower	Accepts ideas of others
Group process observer	Observes and comments on the group's processes

SOURCE: Adapted from Benne and Sheats (1948).

group's interactions. A study of engineering teams found that more than 90% of a group's interactions were task oriented (Levi & Cadiz, 1998). When technical teams are under a lot of time pressure, they might not have time to devote to group process issues. Under these conditions, teams may fall back on traditional management methods rather than using teamwork to get the job done (Janz, Colquitt, & Noe, 1997). This limits the ability of the team to fully use its resources.

The right mix of task and social behaviors also depends on the maturity level of the group. When groups are in the forming stage, they need to engage in more social-oriented behaviors so as to develop the social relations of the group. Groups in the performing stage will be dominated by task-oriented behaviors. When a work team develops good social relations early in a project, the team is better able to handle the time pressure that occurs at the end because it has developed the working relationships it needs to complete the project.

| VALUE OF SOCIAL BEHAVIORS

A team tends to focus on the task and ignore the social or relationship aspects of teamwork. Not only does the team fail to promote social relations in the group, but many team members do not even believe that they are necessary. It is important to recognize that a team needs a balance. Social behaviors are important for building trust in communication, encouraging the team to operate smoothly, providing social support, and rewarding participation. When a team runs into problems, it often blames individual team members and does not recognize that these problems may be caused by weak social relations in the team.

Although there is a need for a balance of task and social behaviors, there is no formula for the right percentage of each. Some teams operate well when most of their behaviors are task oriented. A team is out of balance when emotions or personality conflicts become disruptive to the team's operations. These types of behaviors indicate a breakdown in social relations.

Observation studies on task teams show that one of the deficits of team communication is the lack of praise, support, and positive feedback (Levi & Cadiz, 1998). All team members are responsible for this lack of positive communication. People are quick to criticize another member's idea if they do not like it, but they are somehow reluctant to praise a team member for a good idea or even for good performance. Increasing the amount of positive support that team members provide each other greatly helps to improve social relations within the team and to increase team effectiveness.

One of the values of using a team to perform a task is that groups help to reduce stress by providing social support to their members. The types of social support provided by groups are shown in Table 4.2. Stress can disrupt a team's ability to perform and can encourage members to leave the team.

TABLE 4.2
Types of Social Support Provided by Groups

Emotional support	Rewarding and encouraging others
	Listening to problems and sharing feelings
Informational support	Giving ideas, advice, and suggestions
	Explaining and demonstrating how to perform a task
Task support	Helping another with a work task
	Providing supportive actions
Belonging	Expressing acceptance and approval
	Demonstrating belonging to the group

SOURCE: *Group Dynamics*, 3rd ed., by D. R. Forsyth. Copyright © 1999. Reprinted with permission of Wadsworth, a division of Thomson Learning.

| IMPROVING TEAM INTERACTIONS

Group process observation and analysis can be used to improve a team's interactions. The group process observer provides valuable support to the group by observing and commenting on how the group is operating. In many team-building programs, outside group process observers are used to evaluate the group's interactions and provide advice on how the group could improve its performance. Although this is a valuable function, it is better if the members of the group do this themselves (Dyer, 1995). Developing group process observation skills among the members allows the group to work on its problems when they occur rather than waiting for an outside consultant to provide this service.

When a team analyzes its group process, a number of common problems emerge (Hayes, 1997). In most cases, the team uses only a limited range of the behaviors that are available. For example, team members might frequently give their opinions but only rarely provide support for the ideas of others. Team members also can become stuck in behavioral patterns rather than responding to the needs of the team. For example, someone might become the team's critic and rarely provide information to help decision making. The team's performance improves when people are more flexible, with behaviors more related to the needs of the team than to their personal behavioral styles. The use of group process observations can help the group members to see what is lacking in their interactions and can encourage team members to adjust their personal styles to help the team operate more effectively.

Group process analysis has been used to develop team-building programs and to analyze the characteristics of effective teams (Belbin, 1981). An effective team needs a balance of task and social behaviors, and the right balance depends on the nature of the task. The team must learn how to shift its emphasis depending on its current needs. Because some team members probably will use only a limited range of behaviors because of their personalities, the team requires people with different interpersonal skills so that all of the behaviors will be performed. The team cannot effectively use its technical expertise without a balance of task and social behaviors.

SUMMARY

Motivation is a problem for many groups. Working in a group can encourage social loafing, which is the reduction in individual effort that occurs when performing in a group. Free riders and the sucker effect are related motivation problems. These motivation problems can be caused by tasks that do not require coordinated efforts, the inability to identify individual contributions to the group's work, and the false belief that individual members are doing their fair share.

Improving group motivation requires countering the negative effects of social loafing. The group's task should be involving and challenging and should require coordinated efforts to be completed. The group needs an evaluation and reward system that recognizes and rewards both individual and group performance. The group's goals should create the belief that motivated effort will lead to success. Finally, strengthening commitment to the group by increasing cohesion helps to increase group motivation.

Group cohesion is the interpersonal bond that forms within a group. It can be caused by feelings of belonging, social identification, interpersonal attraction, or commitment to the group's task. In most cases, a cohesive group performs better because of improved coordination and mutual support. However, high levels of group cohesion sometimes can encourage conformity and impair decision making. One of the main ways of developing group cohesion is to improve communication within the group.

Roles are sets of behaviors that people perform in groups. They can be deliberately created and filled or can operate on a more informal basis. Ill-defined roles (i.e., role ambiguity) and conflicts among roles can create stress for group members. There are formal team roles (e.g., leader, recorder, timekeeper) that help a team to operate more efficiently.

Group members perform task and social behaviors. Task behaviors help the group perform its task, whereas social behaviors help maintain the group's interpersonal relationships. Work teams often ignore the importance of social behaviors, leading to a reduction in the amount of interpersonal support in the team and an increase in the amount of stress. Team interactions can be improved by bringing the types of behaviors performed more into balance. Also, team members need to learn how to act as process observers to help develop the team's interactions.

ACTIVITY: OBSERVING TASK AND SOCIAL BEHAVIORS

Objective. A team needs both task and social behaviors to operate effectively. Task behaviors help the team to complete its goals. Social behaviors help to foster communication and maintain the social relations in the team. Team members often vary in how much they participate and in the types of behaviors they perform.

Activity. Observe the various communication in a team and, using Activity Worksheet 4.1, note whether each communication is task oriented or social oriented. Record each communication that occurs by noting the frequencies of task communication and social communication contributed by each team member.

Analysis. How does the amount of task communication compare to the amount of social communication? Was there a good balance between these types of behaviors? How is the use of task communication and social communication distributed among team members? Are there people who are primarily task oriented or social oriented? Is the leader primarily task oriented or social oriented?

Discussion. What is the right balance between task behaviors and social behaviors in a team? What factors cause this balance to change? What type of behaviors should the leader perform?

ACTIVITY WORKSHEET 4.1

	Team Members					
Task Behaviors	*1*	*2*	*3*	*4*	*5*	*6*
Gives suggestions, opinions, or information, or asks questions.						
Organizes the discussion, or helps the decision process.						
Social Behaviors						
Shows support, satisfaction, or acceptance.						
Encourages communications from others and tries to reduce tension.						

Chapter 5

COOPERATION AND COMPETITION

Cooperation is necessary for teams to operate smoothly and effectively, and a cooperative atmosphere also offers many benefits for team members. However, many team members find themselves in mixed-motive situations that include both cooperation and competition. Team members may be competitive for cultural, personal, and organizational reasons. Cooperation can be encouraged through strategies focused on group goals, communication, and interpersonal actions. However, if teams become too cooperative, then overconformity and poor decision making can result. Competition also can create negative effects on the team, even when the team is successful.

▶▶ LEARNING OBJECTIVES

1. What is the impact of being in a mixed-motive situation?
2. Why do people act competitively in teams?
3. How are cooperators, competitors, and individualists different?
4. How does competition hurt a team?
5. How does competition between groups affect a team?
6. What are the benefits of cooperation?
7. What problems are created by too much cooperation?
8. How can a team deal with the negative impacts of competition?

TEAMWORK AS A MIXED-MOTIVE SITUATION

The essence of teamwork is the cooperative interactions of team members. Cooperation is limited by competition, especially when the goals cannot be shared. Team members should be working together toward a common goal. However, competition causes team members to work against each other because their individual goals become more important than the team goal. In a competitive relationship, one's goal is to do better than others. When this occurs within a team, it prevents the team from focusing on its common goals.

Being a member of a team should encourage people to act cooperatively, but often team members find themselves in a mixed-motive situation. Consider the following examples:

- You are the member of a budget committee who has to allocate funds to various departments within an organization. As a committee member, you want to do what is best for the organization, but you also want to make sure that your department gets more than its fair share.
- As a student working on a group project, you want to do a good job so that you can get a good grade. However, you have other classes and demands on your time. What you really want is to put in the least amount of effort and still get a good grade.
- As a basketball player, only the team's score counts to determine the winner. You should be focused on coordinating your plays with the other team members. However, there is a scout in the audience, and being the game's high scorer will get you the attention you want.

These are examples of the all-too-common mixed-motive situations in which team members find themselves. Rather than being cooperative or competitive situations, they are both at the same time. They create "social dilemmas" for the participants. Each member wants to maximize his or her rewards and minimize his or her costs. Selfish behavior might be the best strategy for each individual, but the team and everyone in it would be better off if people acted cooperatively instead.

Unfortunately, many people decide to be competitive in a mixed-motive situation. Once they start acting competitively (or putting in reduced efforts for the group), others respond in the same way. The end result is poor group performance. This is one of the reasons why students complain that the worst problem with group projects is that not everyone does his or her fair share (Wall & Nolan, 1987).

Cooperation in a mixed-motive situation is encouraged by several factors. When team members believe that their contributions to the team are valuable and important, they are more likely to contribute (Kerr & Bruun, 1983). Members are more likely to act cooperatively if they believe that others are likely to cooperate (Dawes, 1988). Smaller groups are more likely to be cooperative than are larger groups (Kerr & Bruun, 1983). Finally, the more members trust each other and believe that they will work for the group, the more committed they become (Parks, 1994).

WHY ARE PEOPLE IN TEAMS COMPETITIVE?

Even though working cooperatively on a team should prevent competition, competition can occur anyway. Team members can misperceive the situation and turn a cooperative situation into a competitive one. People sometimes choose to act competitively even when it is in their best interests to act cooperatively. Why do people misperceive a cooperative situation and turn it into a competitive one? The main explanations for this phenomenon relate to culture, personality, and organizational rewards.

| CULTURE

One way in which to view cultural differences is along an individualist-collectivist dimension (Hofstede, 1980). Individualists tend to be more competitive with their co-workers. The United States has an individualist culture that promotes competition. Our emphasis on individualism, freedom, capitalism, and personal success all support the value of competition. Although we are not anti-cooperation, we glorify the winners in a competition. To some Americans, saying that competition is bad is un-American.

Clearly, this cultural value affects the ways in which people respond to situations. Some Americans even have a negative attitude toward teamwork because they believe that the individual is more important than the group. To them, a focus on the group means a loss of individual freedom and autonomy.

From a cultural and business perspective, the Japanese have developed a good approach that combines cooperation and capitalism (Slem, Levi, & Young, 1995). Their collectivist culture encourages cooperation. Cooperation is highly encouraged and rewarded, and commitment and loyalty are the keys to success, within Japanese corporations. At the same time, Japanese business workers have a keen competitive sense. They believe that they are in a competitive fight for survival with other organizations. The key to this struggle is to band together to overcome these external forces.

PERSONALITY

Some people are more competitive than others and act more competitively regardless of the situation. They misperceive situations and redefine them as opportunities to act competitively. This individual difference can be explained as a personality difference. Researchers have identified three personality types that can be used to explain why some people are competitive (Knight & Dubro, 1984). These personality types affect the ways in which people interpret the situations they are in and how they define success. Figure 5.1 shows how these personality types relate to their concerns.

Cooperators focus on the group. They are concerned with both their own outcomes and the outcomes that everyone will receive. They attempt to make sure that the group is successful and that rewards are distributed equitably among the group members.

Competitors view a situation as an opportunity to win. They define success not in terms of their individual goals or the group's goals but rather in terms of their relationships with others. To a competitor, success means performing better than others are performing. Whether they succeed or the group succeeds is less important than whether they do better than the other members of the group.

Individualists define success relative to their own personal goals. Unlike competitors, they do not evaluate their performance relative to others. They may or may not care about the success of the group. The group's success is important only if they have adopted the group's goals for themselves.

REWARDS

In many organizations, the shift to teamwork has been disrupted by the human resources practices of the organizations. Although managers and leaders say that they want all employees to work as a team, organizational practices often do not encourage or reward this. In most organizations, one's performance evaluation is based on individual performance and one is evaluated relative to the performance of the other employees. Employees find themselves facing a mixed message: Do what the leader says is important (teamwork) or do what you will get rewarded for (standing out as superior to

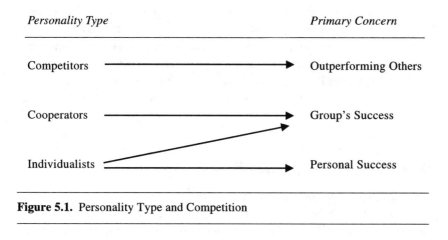

Figure 5.1. Personality Type and Competition

your coworkers). It does not take a psychologist to figure out how most employees will respond to this mixed message.

The inability to share rewards probably is the biggest problem that encourages unhealthy competition within organizations (Hayes, 1997). It affects both individual employees and organizational units. For example, departments within an organization often act competitively because they believe that they must fight for their share of the organization's resources. Working interdependently to succeed should encourage cooperation over competition (Cheng, 1983). However, many employees are worried that what is good for the overall organization might not be best for them.

Do managers actually model teamwork to their subordinates? In many organizations, upper-level managers are the most competitive employees. They act in highly political ways so as to succeed (Gandz & Murray, 1980). This demonstrates to everyone in these organizations that competition is the key to success. With this kind of message, it is very difficult to argue that employees should act cooperatively.

Although culture, personality, and organizational rewards all encourage competition when it is not appropriate, the most important of these factors is the organizational reward system. One can blame American culture, but there are many examples of successful team-oriented organizations in the United States. Obviously, it is not impossible to have a corporate culture that supports teamwork. By definition, personality differences are stable and enduring traits that are difficult to change. Explaining competition as being caused by personality implies that there is nothing the organization or team can do to change this. However, organizational and team rewards can be changed. There are approaches to performance evaluation that reward teamwork and discourage individual competition. Because this explanation provides one way in which to change the situation, it is the most useful one to consider. For example, managers who evaluate employees who participate in teams could incorporate cooperation into the evaluation process (e.g., by including feedback from other team members) to demonstrate to employees the importance of team cooperation.

PROBLEMS WITH COMPETITION

What is wrong with competition? Why should competition not help to motivate a team? The problems with competition occur at both the individual and group levels. Individual competition disrupts the group from focusing on its common goals. Group competition also creates problems regardless of whether the group is successful. Understanding the dynamics of competition can help to explain when and where competition is appropriate in an organization.

| COMMUNICATION AND GOAL CONFUSION

When individuals or teams within an organization compete against each other, several changes occur that prevent the team from being successful (Tjosvold, 1995). Individual competition creates confusion about goals. Eventually, this creates distrust that reduces the amount of communication within the team.

A successful team has members who work together to reach a common goal. This common goal provides a focus for the team. However, when team members compete against each other, individual goals come into conflict with the team goal. There is a conflict between doing what is best for the individual to succeed (by being better than the others) and doing what is best for the team. This goal conflict creates confusion about the goals of the team. Team members start to distrust each other because they are uncertain about each other's motives.

The distrust created by mixed goals leads to reduced communication within a team. Communication requires trust; without trust, there is no reason to communicate with others. Over time, internal competition reduces communication within the team.

This goal confusion and breakdown in communication caused by competition can be seen at the organizational level. The managers in an organization must get together and decide on budget allocations. Should a department manager try to do what is best for his or her department, or do what is best for the organization as a whole? If the departments are competing for limited resources, then should the managers request what their departments need, or should they assume that all of the other departments are trying to get ahead so that they should aggressively bargain to get as much as they can? Is there any reason to trust the budget estimates from other departments? This question leads to budget battles in which false numbers are used to justify competitive positions.

| INTERGROUP COMPETITION

Just as individual competition within a team can create problems, intergroup competition can be a problem for the team. The classic research project on intergroup competition is Sherif's (1966) studies of boys at a summer camp. Researchers divided the boys attending a summer camp into two groups. For a few weeks, these groups of boys competed against each other in a variety of activities. The effects of this competition were negative for both groups. The boys who were arbitrarily divided began to see the members of the other group in negative terms. Prejudices were formed, that is, negative beliefs about the abilities of the other group and the personalities of its members. Conflicts became a regular occurrence and required intervention by the camp counselors.

The problem of competition leading to conflict and hostility is more pronounced in the intergroup situation. Groups are more likely to act competitively with each other than are individuals (Insko et al., 1994). One explanation for this effect relates to *social identity theory* (Tajfel & Turner, 1986). According to this theory, people's sense of self-worth is connected to the groups to which they belong. Consequently, it is important to view one's groups as adequate and superior. This leads to an in-group bias, where one views his or her own group in overly positive terms and views out-groups in overly negative terms. When other groups challenge the superiority of one's group, members rally to support their group and attack the out-group. The conflict can escalate easier because group behavior is more anonymous and there is less trust and interpersonal connections with people outside one's group.

The Sherif (1966) studies demonstrate a number of important points about the effects of competition. Their main focus was to show that competition led to prejudice. However, they also were able to show the effects of external competition on a team. When a team enters a competition, there is an increase in cohesion and group spirit. The team members become more task focused and tolerate more autocratic leadership. As the competition continues, more loyalty and conformity are demanded from the team members. In the short run, these changes can increase productivity and efficiency. However, in the long run, there are problems for the team regardless of whether it is successful.

A team in a competition focuses on the task, to the exclusion of dealing with social and emotional issues within the team. Over time, ignoring these issues can lead to the breakdown of the team. Demanding loyalty and conformity from team members can hurt the team's ability to adapt to change. Creativity and innovation can be stifled by competition.

These negative effects of competition occur for both the winners and the losers. When the groups compete, the winners attribute their success to their own superiority (Forsyth & Kelley, 1996). This causes the winners to ignore their problems, so they do not improve over time. The losing teams often enter into a period of blaming and scapegoating (Worchel, Andreoli, & Folger, 1977). They first try to blame the situation to explain their losses, and then team members blame each other. Eventually, if they survive the internal emotional turmoil, the losing teams are able to recognize their problems and then are able to improve.

One of the amazing things about the Sherif (1966) studies is how easy they are to replicate. In a couple of hours in a workshop, a group of people can be divided into teams and placed into competition with each other. All of the negative emotional effects of competition (e.g., prejudices, conflicts, and misperceptions that disrupt performance) can be demonstrated. This occurs regardless of whether one is studying boys at camp or executives in training programs (Blake & Mouton, 1969). People easily fall into these negative behavior patterns and even accept the negative impacts of a competition if they win.

| WHEN IS COMPETITION APPROPRIATE?

Competition is the basis of capitalism because competition encourages innovation, lower prices, and motivation. How can this be a true statement given the negative impacts of competition? It is important to recognize the difference between internal competition and external competition. Capitalism is based on competition between organizations, not within organizations. It is useful to have Ford compete against General Motors to produce high-quality, low-cost automobiles. It is not useful to have the accounting and manufacturing departments within Ford compete to become more important within the organization.

To understand how competition affects teamwork, one needs to make this distinction between what occurs within and outside of the team. Competition between organizations can help to improve productivity (Hayes, 1997). The operation of one's competitors provides motivating goals and feedback about performance to the organization. However, competition within an organization can be devastating. It does not matter if the marketing department of General Motors does not give accurate information to Ford; Ford does not expect it. However, when departments within an organization lie to each other to get ahead, the negative impact can be substantial.

Competition sometimes can successfully occur within an organization. This happens when jobs are independent rather than interdependent. For example, an organization may run competitions among its sales staff that reward the best performers. This is okay when salespeople do not depend on each other to make sales (and when there are rules that separate customers to prevent the sabotaging of sales by others). However, most jobs within an organization are interdependent. This is especially true when the organization uses teams. Internal competition among teams within an organization can lead to sabotaging others' work, unjustified criticism, and withholding information and resources (Tjosvold, 1995).

BENEFITS OF AND PROBLEMS WITH COOPERATION

Competition, and especially internal competition, creates problems for teams. Cooperation provides many benefits to both the team and its members. However, in some situations, too much cooperation can be a problem that disrupts a team's performance and decision-making abilities.

| BENEFITS OF COOPERATION

Cooperation provides benefits both to individuals and to the entire team. Cooperative relationships encourage team members to support each other. This mutual support helps to create a motivated and cohesive team.

Effects on Individuals

Competition is good for the winners. In other words, for the majority of the people in a competitive situation, competition is not a good thing. When the members of a group compete, the winners are motivated by the competition. Some of the other members who believe that they have a chance of winning also are motivated. However, over time, most of the group members (about 90%) stop believing that they will win, so they stop being motivated by the competition.

Besides reducing motivation, competition has other negative effects on the individuals in a group. Competition reduces communication and cooperation, so team members are less willing to help each other. This disrupts the group's ability to function because communication is necessary for coordination of task activities. It also hurts the social aspects of the group because people become less willing to provide emotional support to other members of the group.

Cooperation has the opposite effect on team members. In a cooperative team, all the team members are motivated by the team's goals. This motivation is reinforced or encouraged by the other group members. Team members help each other and learn from each other. Not only does the team perform better, but most of the individuals also perform better.

The research on the effects of cooperative education shows the benefits of cooperation versus those of competition (Johnson, Maruyama, Johnson, Nelson, & Skon, 1981; Slavin, 1985). In cooperative education classrooms, the best performers still perform at a high level, but the performance of the average and lower performers improves. The high performers spend time helping others, and they learn from this experience. Overall, the groups have higher performance, better social relations, higher self-esteem, and a better attitude toward school.

Effects on Teams

The benefits that accrue to individuals in a cooperative situation also have positive impacts on teamwork. Cooperation encourages supportive, rather than defensive, communication (Lumsden & Lumsden, 1997). Team members are more willing to talk to each other, and this encourages more communication. The increased communication helps to improve coordination on tasks, satisfaction with working together, and overall team performance (Cohen & Bailey, 1997).

The benefits of cooperation at work partly depend on the tasks. Cooperation is more important when the tasks are ambiguous, complex, or changing (Tjosvold, 1995). These types of tasks require substantial information sharing to determine the best way in which to perform them. Cooperation also is more important when the tasks are interdependent because this requires coordination. Most professional and managerial work meets these task requirements.

Cooperation provides the foundation for the social relations that the group members have with each other. Cooperative work groups have less tension, fewer conflicts, and fewer verbal confrontations (Tjosvold, 1995). Cooperative groups have a stronger sense of team spirit and greater group cohesion.

| PROBLEMS WITH COOPERATION

Cooperation has its own problems. A team can be too cooperative. It can become too focused on maintaining its internal social relations and lose sight of the goals of the team. The problems with cooperation affect both performance (conformity) and decision making (unhealthy agreement).

Conformity

Highly cooperative groups tend to become highly cohesive. Over time, the team members become socially and emotionally connected to each other. This can be one of the benefits of teamwork because it makes communication and coordination easier. However, it also can create problems because the team becomes too oriented toward itself.

A highly cohesive team is self-rewarding. It rewards contributions to the team and discourage any behavior that is not aligned with the team. This means that the team demands conformity from its members. Conformity can help the team to operate, but it also can make the team resistant to outside influence and changes in the ways in which it operates (Nemeth & Staw, 1989).

When a group is functioning well and has good performance norms, conformity is a benefit. However, this conformity can make it difficult to influence the team and change its direction. Even a poorly performing team can be highly cohesive and cooperative. Sometimes, a work group has norms about not doing too much work (e.g., some of the work groups in the

Hawthorne studies). These norms are enforced by the team and can be resistant to change from the organization.

Unhealthy Agreement

Another negative impact of cooperation involves a team's ability to make decisions. Decision making should be focused on making the best decision given the constraints of the situation. Cooperation can help decision making by establishing trust, which encourages open communication. However, because a cooperative group is cohesive, members' liking for each other sometimes can disrupt the decision-making process.

The Abilene paradox describes a problem with group decision making that is caused by trying to be friendly and cooperative (Harvey, 1988). This situation occurs when group members adopt a position because they believe that other members want it. The members do not challenge each other because they want to avoid conflict or want to achieve consensus. In the end, they support a proposal that no one really wants because of their inability to manage agreement. For example, a project team might continue working on a design strategy that no one thinks will work. However, everyone believes that the other team members support this approach, so no objections are raised against it during team meetings.

The Abilene paradox is an example of unhealthy agreement within a group (Dyer, 1995). This occurs when the team's desire to reach agreement on an issue becomes more important than its motivation to find a good solution. Team members look for the first acceptable solution, or just go along with the leader's solution, so as to avoid disagreements and conflict. This search for quick solutions and avoidance of conflict can lead to poor decisions that cause a lot of problems and time delays later in the project. The problem is that the team is suffering from unhealthy agreement.

Following are some symptoms of unhealthy agreement:

- Team members feel angry about the decisions that the team is making.
- Team members agree in private that the team is making bad decisions.
- The team is breaking up into subgroups that are blaming others for the team's problems.
- People fail to speak up in meetings and communicate their real opinions.

Unhealthy agreement in a team can have a variety of causes other than cooperation. Domineering team leaders can discourage team members from stating their true opinions. High levels of stress or a lack of time can encourage members to try to find solutions too quickly. Nonassertive members might be reluctant to state their true opinions in team meetings. Finally, the desire to maintain friendly relations among team members might discourage members from criticizing others' ideas.

APPLICATION: ENCOURAGING COOPERATION

The central issue in cooperation is the beliefs that team members have about the goals of the team and its members (Tjosvold, 1995). Cooperation is based on mutual goals that encourage trust and the ability to rely on others. This encourages the team members to combine and integrate their efforts, thereby promoting successful teamwork. Incompatible goals create suspicion and doubt about other team members, thereby leading to a breakdown in communication. Once team members start to compete against each other, the other team members tend to respond in kind (Youngs, 1986).

Encouraging cooperation within a team requires counteracting the negative effects of competition. Whereas competition leads to confusion about the goals of team members and a breakdown in communication, strategies for dealing with these effects need to focus on developing common goals and rebuilding trust and communication (Figure 5.2). In addition, once a team has established a competitive relationship, team members need to develop a strategy to negotiate cooperation in the future.

Common Goals

Research on race relations shows that equal-status interactions can help to reduce a sense of competition between groups but that contact is not sufficient by itself. The groups need to have some reason to work together so as to break down competitive situations. One approach to forming bonds between groups is through the use of superordinate goals (Sherif, 1966). A superordinate goal is a common goal that all of the groups accept as important. By working together on this common goal, prejudice and conflicts between the groups decrease. In the Sherif summer camp studies, the boys were brought together to work on common problems that affected the entire

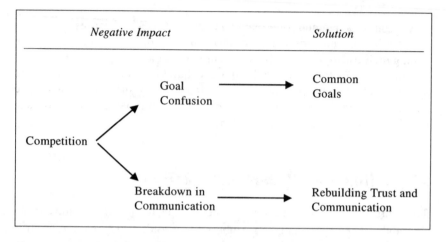

Figure 5.2. Dealing With the Negative Impacts of Competition

camp. Companies focus on the competitive threat from outside as one way in which to get the various parts of their organizations to work together.

Working together cooperatively encourages cooperation in the future. Cooperation encourages a redefinition of the group. Rather than viewing the situation as composed of competing parts, people come to believe that they all are part of the same group or team. However, this works only when the cooperative activity is successful. Failure leads to blaming and scapegoating, thereby furthering the competitive relationship among the group members (Worchel et al., 1977).

Rebuilding Trust and Communication

Cooperation is encouraged by trust, and competition leads to a breakdown in trust (Smith, Carrol, & Ashford, 1995). Trust has both cognitive (is someone telling the truth?) and emotional (do I feel that I can trust this person?) components (McAllister, 1995). Cooperation primarily relates to the emotional part of trust. People telling the truth, the number of interactions that team members have with each other, and the number of helping experiences that they have all will lead to more trust among team members. (Approaches to building trust in a group are presented in Chapter 6.)

Cooperation encourages constructive controversy, whereas competition reduces communication and encourages avoidance (Tjosvold, 1995). Constructive controversy allows for open feedback, the raising of questions, and increased communication. Cooperation improves decision making because it increases task-related conflict. People are able to express a conflict openly without creating social problems within the group. By contrast, conflict is avoided in competitive situations because it is too destructive to social relations. Table 5.1 presents a set of communication rules to foster constructive controversy within a team.

Negotiating Cooperation

Research on the negative effects of competition has examined the various strategies that can be used to encourage cooperation with one's opponent. There is an entire research field that uses simulation gaming, such as the prisoner's dilemma, to explore the various options. This research has found a fairly simple strategy for encouraging cooperation (Axelrod, 1984).

The problem for people in a competitive situation is how to make the transition to cooperation. Once competition starts within a team, it tends to continue. If a member tries to threaten the competitors, then they will become defensive and more hostile. If a member tries to act consistently cooperative toward the competitors, then they will exploit him or her. An effective strategy must resolve these dilemmas.

The most effective strategy has two rules. First, when the opportunity arises, a team member should signal his or her desire to form a cooperative relationship by acting cooperatively. The team member always should start by acting cooperatively and creating opportunities to start over again during transition points in the team's existence. Second, the team member always should respond in-kind to his or her competitors' moves (i.e., the tit-for-tat rule). If the competitor acts cooperatively, then the member should respond cooperatively. However, if the competitor acts competitively, then the member should respond competitively. This is necessary because always acting cooperatively can lead to exploitation.

SUMMARY

Cooperation is the essence of teamwork. However, team members often find themselves in mixed-motive situations that are a combination of cooperation and competition. This is caused by the conflict between individual goals and the team's goals.

People in teams become competitive for three reasons. First, our culture emphasizes the value of competition. Second, people might be competitive,

TABLE 5.1
Rules for Constructive Controversy

1. Establish openness norms.	Encourage all team members to express their opinions and feelings. Do not dismiss ideas because they appear to be too impractical or undeveloped at first.
2. Assign opposing views.	Assign a person or subgroup the role of critically evaluating the group's current preferences.
3. Follow the golden rule of controversy.	People should discuss issues with others the way in which they want issues discussed with them. If you want others to listen to you, then you should listen to them.
4. Get outside information.	Search for information from a diverse set of outside sources to help the group make a decision.
5. Show personal regard.	Ideas can be criticized, but do not attack a person's motivation or personality.
6. Combine ideas.	The team should avoid either/or thinking and should try to combine ideas to create alternative solutions.

SOURCE: Adapted from Tjosvold (1995).

rather than cooperative or individualist, for personality reasons. Third, the organization might reward competition among team members. Although all these reasons encourage competition, the organization's reward system is the most important reason.

Competition hurts a team by creating goal confusion. Team members use both individual and group goals to guide their behavior. This leads to distrust, which eventually disrupts communication within the team. Competition with other teams also can create problems. It can lead to hostility and conflict. Although competition with outside organizations can be appropriate, internal competition can be destructive to the team and organization.

Cooperation provides benefits to both individuals and the team. Individuals are motivated and supported in cooperative situations. Cooperation encourages communication and interpersonal support in the team. However, cooperation also can cause problems. A cooperative team has high levels of conformity, and this can reduce performance and creativity. It also can lead to unhealthy agreement, where team members make bad decisions so as to preserve group harmony.

A team have several tactics that it can use to deal with the negative impacts of competition and to build a cooperative environment. A commitment to common goals can help to unite the team members' orientations. Trust-building activities can be used to help rebuild the breakdown in a team's communication. Finally, there are negotiation tactics that can be used to respond to inappropriate competitive behavior in the team.

ACTIVITY: ARE TEAM MEMBERS COOPERATORS, COMPETITORS, OR INDIVIDUALISTS?

Objective. Teamwork should be a cooperative activity. However, team members sometimes act cooperatively, competitively, or individually. Cooperators are concerned with both their own outcomes and the outcomes that everyone will receive. Competitors view the team situation as an opportunity to do better than others. Individualists define success relative to their own personal goals.

Activity. Observe the interactions of team members in a meeting. Are they acting cooperatively, competitively, or as individualists? Classify each team member. Using Activity Worksheet 5.1, write down examples of cooperative, competitive, and individualist behaviors that you observed. It might be useful to have the team you are observing be assigned a task that requires distributing resources, salaries, or awards among members.

ACTIVITY WORKSHEET 5.1
Observing Cooperation, Competition, and Individualism

	Team Member					
	1	*2*	*3*	*4*	*5*	*6*
Cooperators						
Competitors						
Individualists						

Cooperative behavior: _____

Competitive behavior: _____

Individualist behavior: _____

Analysis. Overall, was the team acting cooperatively or competitively? Were there differences among the people on the team? Was personality or social reasons the primary cause of competition in the team? What are some examples of competitive behaviors that disrupted the team's performance?

Discussion: How does competition disrupt a team's ability to operate successfully? What can the team do to reduce the amount of competition among team members?

Chapter 6

COMMUNICATION

Central to any team's actions is communication, which can occur in a variety of patterns. The communication process is affected by the characteristics of the sender, the receiver, and the message. The communication climate also affects the willingness of team members to participate, so optimizing communication in a team requires managing this climate. Improving communication requires building trust within the team, facilitation of team meetings, and developing good communication skills.

➤➤ **LEARNING OBJECTIVES**

1. How does the credibility and attractiveness of a communicator affect a communication?
2. How do the different backgrounds of members affect communication in a team?
3. What factors lead to miscommunication in a team?
4. What are the differences between centralized and decentralized communication networks?
5. What are the characteristics of positive and negative communication climates?
6. What biases does a team have when processing information to make a decision?
7. How can one build trust within a team?
8. What are some of the important activities of the facilitator of a meeting?
9. What are the basic communication skills that are useful to facilitate a team meeting?

COMMUNICATION PROCESS

Communication is the process by which a person or group sends some type
of information to another person or group. This definition highlights the
three basic parts of a communication: sender, receiver, and message.

| SENDER

The characteristics of the sender or communicator affect the amount of
influence that a communication will have on the audience. How the audience perceives the communicator affects how the audience interprets the
message, how much attention the audience pays to it, and how much impact
it will have on the audience's beliefs. The two primary characteristics of the
sender are his or her credibility and attractiveness.

The more credible the communicator, the more the audience will believe
the message. Credibility relates to the perceived amount of expertise and
trustworthiness of the communicator. A credible speaker knows what he or
she is talking about and has no motive to deceive. Saying smart things, being
introduced as having credentials, and speaking confidently create perceived
expertise. Perceived trustworthiness is affected by the belief that the communicator is not trying to persuade the audience and will not personally
benefit from the communication (Eagly, Wood, & Chaiken, 1978).

Although credibility is a characteristic of the sender, it often depends on
the audience's evaluations of the speaker. The sender may believe that he or
she is an expert without bias, but the receiver might not acknowledge this.
For example, a college professor may be considered an expert in his or her
field of study, but students might not believe that the professor is an expert
on various social or political topics. A highly credible communicator can be
very persuasive, whereas a communicator with very low credibility actually
can cause the audience to believe the opposite of the message (sometimes
called the *boomerang effect*).

The attractiveness of the communicator also increases the amount of influence of the communication (Chaiken, 1979). Attractiveness relates not
only to physical appearance but to other factors as well. We tend to find
more attractive people who are similar to us in appearance, background, attitudes, and/or lifestyles (Wilder, 1990). We also find attractive high-status
people and other people whom we want to be like.

Is attractiveness more important than credibility? The answer depends
on the issue being examined. If the issue is about objective facts, then credibility is more important. However, if the issue is about subjective values or

preferences, then similarity with the communicator is more important than credibility (Goethals & Nelson, 1973).

| RECEIVER

The receivers or audiences of communication can vary in a number of ways that affect the amount of influence of the communication. For example, there are personality characteristics of receivers such as intelligence, language skills, and self-esteem that affect communication. Intelligence and language issues relate to how a communication needs to be worded for the audience. Credible communicators more easily influence people with low self-esteem.

Teams often are composed of members with different professional backgrounds. All professional specialties have specialized languages or jargon, thereby making communication across fields difficult. The development of jargon is inevitable. It helps to foster communication among people within a specialty area by allowing easier sharing of complex ideas. However, it can lead to miscommunication and feelings of being left out by recipients who do not know the jargon (Kanter, 1977). This creates communication barriers within teams. To avoid this, language needs to be clear and simple in mixed audiences.

Receivers also differ in their relationships to messages. It is easy to communicate to someone who already basically agrees with the message. However, if the audience is skeptical or antagonistic, then the communicator needs to be more careful about how he or she frames the message. Low levels of disagreement between the sender and the receiver produce discomfort, and this discomfort often encourages people to change their opinions. High levels of disagreement may cause the receiver to view the sender as not credible and to discount the message. So, people are more open to arguments that are within their range of acceptability (Zanna, 1993). However, highly credible sources can get away with advocating unpopular positions.

| MESSAGE

The impact of various characteristics of the message interacts with the characteristics of the receiver. Messages can vary in sophistication, emotionality, and aesthetics. Whether these differences influence the audience depends on how they are perceived.

The basic requirement of a message is that it must be understood so as to have an effect. Messages with too much jargon, highly sophisticated language, or complex arguments might be ineffective with an audience incapable of appreciating them. However, the communicator can oversimplify a persuasive communication. One-sided messages that ignore the existence of alternative arguments are not more effective than two-sided messages if the audience will hear other arguments later or is aware of other positions (Jones & Brehm, 1970).

Rational arguments do have an impact, especially for better educated audiences (Cacioppo, Petty, & Morris, 1983). Emotionally arousing messages, especially fear-arousing messages, also can be persuasive. However, the communicator needs to be careful that the audience does not attempt to block or manage the emotion rather than the situation. The sender should provide a way for the audience to act on its emotions so as to work through them.

| COMMUNICATION WITHIN TEAMS

Characteristics of the sender, receiver, and message are the foundations of successful communication but also create the opportunity for miscommunication. The sender can fail to send a message or not be trusted to send a useful message. The receiver can distort or misperceive the message. Or, the message can be inaccurate or distorted. There are a number of problems that can disrupt communication within a team.

Senders typically tailor the messages to their audiences, so messages may be shorter or longer depending on assumptions about what the receivers know. For example, when people give directions, they give longer directions to people who are unfamiliar with an area (Krauss & Fussell, 1991). In a team, senders often send briefer messages than are needed because they overestimate how familiar the receivers are with the information. Research also suggests that senders often are poor at perspective taking. They act as if the receivers have more background information on topics than they really do (Keysar, 1998). This lack of perspective taking is one reason why technical professionals such as engineers have difficulty sharing specialized knowledge in a team. They assume that the receivers have sufficient background information to make sense of brief messages.

Messages also get distorted within team discussions. All team members have a bias to present information that will be positively received (Higgins, 1999). This causes the team to ignore its problems because unpleasant topics never are addressed. Team members also often believe that the reasons behind their statements are obvious, so they do not fully explain issues (Gilovich, Savitsky, & Medvec, 1998). This leads to an illusion that there is clear communication when, in fact, it does not exist.

One of the best examples of clear communication comes from military teams. Miscommunication in a military team can be fatal, so the military has developed strict rules about how team members should communicate and support each other. Successful teams perform the following actions: performance monitoring, feedback, closed-loop communication, and backing-up behaviors (McIntyre & Salas, 1995). Members of successful teams monitor the performance of other team members and step in to help out when needed. During formal debriefing sessions, all team members give feedback to each other to help improve performance. Internal communication is closed-loop; in other words, senders and receivers acknowledge and make sure that the meanings of messages have been correctly received. Finally, team members back each other up; they are not solely focused on their individual tasks and are trained in each other's jobs so that they are capable of replacing each other when needed.

COMMUNICATION NETWORKS, CLIMATES, AND INFORMATION PROCESSING

When people talk in a group, patterns of communication develop. In most situations, evenly distributed communication patterns where everyone participates are better for the team. However, patterns created by organizational networks control where information flows. Communication climates influence the amount and style of communication within a team. Finally, interpersonal processes influence team members' willingness to share information in team discussions.

| COMMUNICATION NETWORKS

Communication networks are patterns that dictate who may communicate with whom. The nature of these communication linkages has an important impact on group functioning (Shaw, 1978). There are two basic types of networks: decentralized and centralized (Figure 6.1). *Decentralized* networks include the circle and open models, whereas centralized networks include the Y, wheel, and chain. *Centralized* networks require any communication to pass through certain members before going to other members.

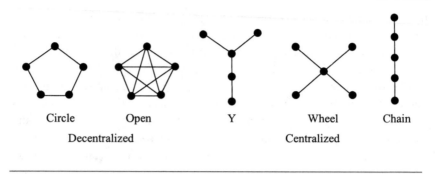

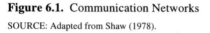

Figure 6.1. Communication Networks
SOURCE: Adapted from Shaw (1978).

People in decentralized networks have equal access to information, whereas centralized networks create unequal access to information.

Centralized networks provide faster and more accurate information flow on simple tasks, whereas decentralized networks work better on complex tasks (Forsyth, 1999). This is due to limits of processing information when flow is restricted. On complex tasks, the key links in the centralized communication networks can suffer from information overload, which reduces their ability to function well.

Most people prefer working in decentralized networks. These networks have more equal-status interactions. The peripheral members of centralized networks may feel powerless and unappreciated, so they become dissatisfied with the group's communication.

These differences in communication networks often are only temporary because people find ways in which to work around the networks to complete their tasks and influence the operation of the group (Burgess, 1968). Informal communication networks operate around the formal networks, thereby mitigating some of their effects.

COMMUNICATION CLIMATES

Members of high-quality work teams have strong feelings of inclusion, commitment, pride, and trust in their teams. These feelings are developed by a communication climate that is open, supportive, inclusive, and rewarding. Gibb (1961) shows how climates develop through communication acts and emotional responses. Supportive climates encourage people to focus on the message. Supportive climates encompass diverse ideas and expressions of both agreement and disagreement. Every member feels like part of the group. Because of their emotional comfort, team members are better able to focus on the task. Negative climates are characterized by defensive behaviors. They are closed, alienating, blaming, discouraging, and punishing.

The communication climate develops in cycles (Lumsden & Lumsden, 1997). When team members take a chance and communicate, they could receive supportive responses. These responses encourage trust and openness, and this increases their willingness to communicate again, thereby further increasing trust and helping to create a supportive climate. When communication receives defensive responses, such as negative evaluations and sarcastic comments, this decreases trust and leads to self-protection. This creates a defensive climate, which in turn leads to conflict or withdrawal.

Table 6.1 shows the types of communication behaviors that occur in supportive and defensive climates. In supportive climates, messages are facts or opinions rather than negative evaluations or criticisms of others. There is a focus on problem solving and discussing the issues rather than on controlling the team's communication and winning. Communication is open and expressive, with a free flow of ideas and opinions rather than guarded statements that reflect concern about power issues. Members test out their ideas with the team rather than trying to close off discussion by drawing overconfident conclusions.

Both defensiveness and supportiveness can escalate. When a supportive climate escalates, it builds openness, trust, and empathy. These elements are interrelated. When a defensive climate escalates, it leads to conflict or withdrawal.

| PROCESSING INFORMATION WITHIN THE TEAM

The use of teams creates the potential to make better decisions because members can pool information from different backgrounds and experiences. This benefit from using teams occurs only if the members share the unique information they have with the team. However, studies of team communication show that the team spends most of its time reviewing common information and discussing what everyone already knows rather combining the unique knowledge and perspectives of the members (Gigone & Hastie, 1997). This is why the information held by most team members before a discussion has more influence on a decision, regardless of whether this information is accurate. The focus on common information rather than on unique

TABLE 6.1
Supportive Versus Defensive Communication Behaviors

Supportive	Defensive
Description	Evaluation
Problem orientation	Control
Spontaneity	Neutrality
Equality	Superiority
Provisionalism	Certainty

SOURCE: Adapted from Lumsden and Lumsden (1997).

information also explains why teams often overlook technical information. This latter information is likely to be known to few team members, so the team rarely discusses it.

The biases in the ways in which a team processes information can prevent the team from making good decisions because important information that one team member holds often is ignored by the group (Stasser, 1992). Consider the example of a design team with members from engineering, marketing, and finance. They should be sharing their unique perspectives and sources of information to create the best design. The engineer should be discussing new technical ideas, the marketing person should be presenting the latest results from marketing surveys, and the finance person should be examining new options for reducing costs. However, the team's discussion is more likely to focus on the members' common knowledge and perspectives rather than on new or unique information. This reduces the creativity of the design and can lead to designs with problems that could have been identified in advance.

Avoiding these problems often requires that the team leader actively facilitate the team's communication (Larson, Foster-Fishman, & Franz, 1998). The leader has the ability to ask questions and emphasize technical information so as to focus the team's attention on it. The team should take a problem-solving approach during a discussion that focuses on encouraging team members to provide factual evidence and not just opinions on the topic. When it is time to make a decision, each alternative should be analyzed in turn so as to encourage members to discuss the unique information that relates to only that alternative. When technical information is needed, the leader should ask for the opinions of the technical members of the team. Finally, the leader needs to build trust so that members feel free to contribute to the discussion.

BUILDING TRUST

The key to good communication within the team is trust. Trust is the expression of confidence in the relationship, that is, the confidence one has that other team members will honor their commitments (Thompson, 2000). It is built on past experiences, understanding the motives of others, and a willingness to believe in others. If team members trust each other, then they will be willing to open up and state their beliefs and feelings about the team's issues. The absence of trust destroys the ability of a team to operate. Teams with low trust levels have decreased communication, less cooperation, and more conflicts that are harder to resolve.

The experience of trust evolves from people's values, attitudes, and emotions (Jones & George, 1998). We tend to trust people who share our values, and people who are trustworthy tend to trust others more. Trust also is based on the attitudes that people form about each other. For example, are people who work in the organization generally trustworthy or honest? Finally, trust is affected by people's emotions. Often, the decision to trust someone is based primarily on one's feelings rather than on some concrete behaviors. When trust is broken, it is hard to regain for emotional reasons.

Trust also can be based on social networks or social embeddedness (Uzzi, 1997). People's interactions take place as a result of their social relations. It is these relationships that create the basis for trust. People make investments to develop and maintain their relationships. These embedded ties among people encourage cooperation and the development of trust.

At the beginning of a social encounter, people do not assume that the other person is trustworthy, but they suspend suspicion about the other person. They take a chance by interacting while observing the response of the other person to decide how much trust to put into the relationship. The experience of future trust is determined by what happens in the relationship. Trust is built over time through the sharing of feelings and thoughts. Trust is established when both parties have confidence in the trustworthiness of each other, have favorable attitudes toward each other, and have had positive experiences together.

Trust has a direct relationship to interpersonal communication, cooperation, and teamwork. However, it also has a number of indirect relationships

(Jones & George, 1998). When teams have high levels of trust, a number of other favorable behaviors occur that support teamwork. When trust is high, people are more willing to help others in a variety of situations. Trust encourages the free exchange of information and increased participation in the team's activities. People are more willing to commit to group goals (and to ignore personal goals) when trust is high. Finally, people are more willing to become involved in the team's activities when trust is high.

Building trust in a group requires performing two types of behaviors: being trusting and being trustworthy (Johnson & Johnson, 1997). *Being trusting* relates to one's willingness to be open with information and to share with others by providing help and resources. *Being trustworthy* relates to acceptance of the other group members' contributions, support for their actions, and cooperation in assisting them.

Although building trust is a slow process, destroying trust is quick and easy. Trust can be destroyed by a single incident and can be very resistant to change. Reestablishing trust after it has been broken can be difficult. The following are some techniques to help rebuild trust after it has been broken:

- Apologize sincerely for actions that destroyed trust in the group.
- Act trusting and demonstrate your support for others in the group.
- Promote cooperation in the group.
- Review the group's goals and gain commitment to common actions.
- Establish credibility by making sure that one's actions match one's words.

FACILITATING TEAM MEETINGS

Team meetings often have a structure that controls the communication. The model presented in Figure 6.2 was developed for professional business meetings (Kayser, 1990). The meeting starts with a review of the agenda and warm-up activities designed to get people talking socially. The main body of the meeting focuses on managing the communication process and making the team's decisions. The meeting ends with a summary of decisions and assignments and an evaluation of how well the team is operating.

Although the team leader is the primary facilitator of meetings, all of the team members have a responsibility to help facilitate team meetings (Kayser, 1990). The following is a description of the five main communication activities of the facilitator.

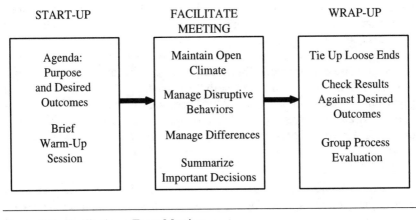

Figure 6.2. Facilitating a Team Meeting
SOURCE: Adaped from Kayser (1990).

Maintain an open and collaborative climate. When discussing the topics of the meeting, the discussion should focus on the issues, not on people's personalities or behaviors. Focusing on the behaviors of individuals rather than on issues can make the team members defensive and reduce communication. Discussions can be encouraged by the leader in a number of ways such as asking open-ended questions, organizing discussions around specific issues to help focus the team, and asking questions that help to clarify the situation. When the discussion is going well, the leader should acknowledge this and verbally praise the active team participants. If the discussion gets too personal and individuals are verbally attacked, the leader needs to intervene and help focus the discussion on the issues.

Manage disruptive behaviors. When team members are being disruptive, the leader needs to be firm but friendly in confrontations. Disruptive team members may be dominating the discussion, overly talkative, or rude to other team members. All team members share responsibility for handling difficult members; it is not just the job of the leader to maintain the flow of the meeting. The leader should acknowledge and verbally reward acceptable behaviors. If problem behaviors persist, then the leader should talk privately with repeat offenders. If none of these approaches works, then assistance from outside the team (e.g., from a manager who is responsible for supervising the offender) might be needed.

Manage differences. Differences can be a constructive force because they can encourage critical thinking, creativity, and healthy debate. Differences are constructive when issues (and not people) are attacked, team spirit is increased, understanding is enhanced, and achievement takes place. Differences also can be a destructive force. They can create winners and losers, group polarization, and unproductive sessions. Differences are destructive when there are personal attacks, repeated negative statements, misinterpretations of people's positions, and stubborn resistance to reconsidering positions. Differences can be managed by clarifying the various points of view, defining areas of agreement and disagreement, and taking steps to resolve differences through problem-solving techniques and consensus decision making.

Summarize important decisions. The leader needs to keep the team members focused on the agenda topics. To help keep the group process flowing, the leader should stop after major agenda items and summarize the team's conclusions. This allows for a check on whether all team members agree with what has happened at the meeting.

Evaluate the group process. The leader should hold a group process evaluation at the end of each team meeting to discuss how the meeting operated and areas for improvement. These group process evaluations provide feedback to the team about its performance. This helps to deal with problems before they get emotionally out of hand. (The topic of group process evaluations is discussed in detail in Chapter 17.)

COMMUNICATION SKILLS FOR TEAM MEETINGS

There are many communication skills that are useful for team members to have and use. This section reviews four of these skills: asking questions, active listening, giving constructive feedback, and managing feelings.

| ASKING QUESTIONS

There are many types of questions that are useful for promoting team discussions (Hackett & Martin, 1993). In general, open-ended questions encourage discussion, whereas closed-ended questions (e.g., yes/no questions) tend to limit discussion. It is better to ask the team to discuss the pros and cons of an idea rather than to just ask team members whether they agree or disagree with it. After someone has answered a question, it often is useful to ask follow-up questions to clarify the issues. When questions are addressed to the leader, they often should be redirected back to the team to promote discussion.

Being asked a direct question by the leader can be a threatening experience that reduces discussion. Leaders should try to ask questions of the entire team whenever possible. After asking a question, the leader should remember to give the team members sufficient time to respond. The leader should reward participation by acknowledging responses. If no one responds, the leader should try rewording the question or going around the room and having everyone comment on it. A lack of response might mean that the question has a bias or is putting some of the team members on the defensive.

| ACTIVE LISTENING

The goal of active listening is to provide feedback to the sender of a communication so as to clarify the communication and promote discussion (Johnson & Johnson, 1997). A good listener communicates his or her desire to understand the message and improve his or her understanding.

The largest barrier to effective listening is evaluation. People often spend time evaluating a communication rather than listening to what really is being said. This constant evaluation makes the sender defensive and decreases further communication.

Active listening is one approach to improving communication. In this approach, the listener paraphrases what he or she has heard and asks the sender if this is correct. The paraphrasing should convey the listener's understanding of the communication and not be a simple parroting of the message. This sends a message that the listener cares about understanding the message, and it allows the sender to clarify the communication if needed. Although this is a useful technique, it can become tiresome if used all the time.

| GIVING CONSTRUCTIVE FEEDBACK

Everyone needs feedback to improve his or her performance. However, receiving feedback (especially negative feedback) can be an uncomfortable experience. Improving one's ability to give constructive feedback is an important teamwork skill (Scholtes, 1994).

The first step in learning how to give constructive feedback is to recognize the need for it. Remember that it is important to give both positive and negative feedback. Before giving feedback, one should examine the context to better understand why the behaviors occurred. If a situation is emotional, one should wait until things calm down before trying to give constructive feedback. When giving feedback, one should describe the situation accurately, try not to be judgmental, and speak for him- or herself. When receiving feedback, one should listen carefully, ask questions to better understand, acknowledge receiving the feedback, and take time to sort out what one has heard.

If someone is giving only negative feedback, then that person is not being constructive. Expressing only negative feedback about the performance or ideas of other team members makes people defensive and discourages communication. It is better to try to reward the ideas and behaviors one wants than to try to punish the ideas and behaviors one does not want. When giving negative feedback to a team member, one also should offer corrective alternatives. Also, negative feedback should be given privately to avoid embarrassing the recipient.

| MANAGING FEELINGS

When emotions become disruptive to the operation of the team, it is important to manage them effectively (Kayser, 1990). One cannot prevent people from becoming emotional, nor would one want to try. When emotional issues are related to the team's task, the issues should be addressed in the team meeting. Emotional conflicts that relate to personal issues might need to be handled in private. All team members should learn how to handle emotional interactions in the team. The following is an approach to managing feelings during team meetings:

1. *Stay neutral:* People have a right to their feelings. The team should encourage and acknowledge the expression of feelings.
2. *Understand rather than evaluate feelings:* All team members should be sensitive to verbal and nonverbal messages. When dealing with emotional issues, one should ask questions and seek information to better understand the feelings.
3. *Process feelings in the group:* When the team's operation is disrupted by emotions, one should stop and be briefly silent to cool down. Then, the task-related issues should be discussed as a group.

This approach to managing emotions is useful when the emotional issues are related to task issues. Team norms that encourage open communication of emotions increase the beneficial impact of task-related conflict on performance (Jehn, 1995). However, norms that encourage open communication about relationship-oriented conflict have a negative impact on the team. When emotions are about personal or relationship issues, it is not a benefit to process them with the team.

SUMMARY

Communication is one of the central activities of a team. The effectiveness of a communication depends on the characteristics of the sender, the receiver, and the message. Senders are more effective if they are credible and attractive to the audience. Teams often contain members from different backgrounds, so the message must be made understandable to this mixed audience. The basic requirement of a message is that it be stated in a way that the audience understands it. Unfortunately, miscommunication is a common occurrence in teams because of a lack of awareness of the perspectives of others.

The communication network, the team's communication climate, and the way in which teams process information influence team communication. Communication networks define the linkages among team members. Although centralized networks are more efficient for simple problems, most team communication should use decentralized networks. The team's communication climate can be either supportive or defensive, and this has a strong impact on the willingness of team members to participate. Teams should be able to pool the knowledge of each member to make better decisions. However, this does not occur because of the tendency to focus on common, rather than unique, information in the team.

Trust is one of the key factors underlying team communication. Trust evolves from the relationships among team members and supports both communication and cooperative behaviors. Developing trust takes time, but destroying trust can happen quickly. Once trust has been broken, it is difficult to rebuild.

Team meetings operate more effectively if a facilitator structures the communication. The role of the facilitator is to maintain an open and collaborative climate, manage disruptive behaviors, manage differences, summarize important decisions, and evaluate the group process.

There are a number of important communication skills that are useful for team members to learn and perform. Learning to ask open-ended, nonthreatening questions can help to foster better team interactions. Active listening helps to clarify the communicator's meaning and acknowledge its importance. Giving constructive feedback is a technique that helps team members to learn how to improve on how they perform. Teams can be disrupted by emotions, and learning how to process these emotions in a group is an important skill.

ACTIVITY: OBSERVING COMMUNICATION PATTERNS IN A TEAM

Objective. Communication within a team often develops into patterns and networks. Team members can either speak to the entire team or speak to individual team members. By observing the communication patterns, one can see whether the team is working collaboratively together, developing subgroups, or forming hierarchies.

Activity. During a team meeting, note whenever a team member speaks and to whom he or she speaks. The member can either speak to another individual or speak to the team as a whole. Using Activity Worksheet 6.1, record the team's communication pattern by drawing arrows connecting the various communications.

ACTIVITY WORKSHEET 6.1
Communication Graphic

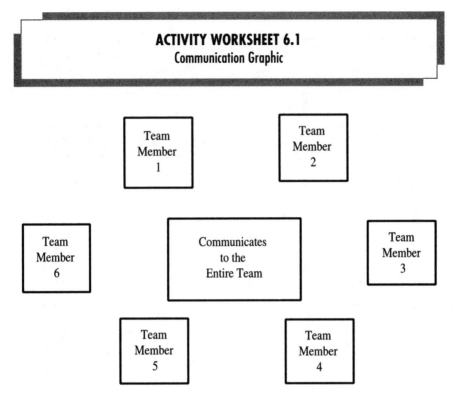

Analysis. Was most of the team's communication to the team as a whole? Did you notice any patterns of communication? Were certain team members more likely to address the team as a whole? Can you determine who is the team leader by observing this communication pattern? How would you describe the communication pattern of the team (i.e., centralized or decentralized)?

Discussion: What should the team leader do to facilitate more equal participation in the team's discussions?

PART III

ISSUES TEAMS FACE

Chapter 7

MANAGING CONFLICT

Conflicts of various types are a natural part of the team process. Although we often view conflict as negative, there are many benefits to conflict if it is managed appropriately. People handle conflict in their teams in a variety of ways, depending on the importance of their desire to maintain good social relations and develop high-quality solutions.

Managing team conflict can be done through negotiation or with the help of outside assistance in mediation and arbitration. Developing a solution to a conflict requires open communication, respect for the other side, and a creative search for mutually satisfying alternatives.

» LEARNING OBJECTIVES

1. Why is the lack of conflict a sign of a problem in a team?
2. What are the healthy and unhealthy sources of conflict?
3. When is conflict good or bad for a team?
4. How does the impact of conflict vary depending on the type of team?
5. What are the different approaches to conflict resolution?
6. Which approach to conflict resolution is best? Why?
7. How is negotiation different from mediation and arbitration?
8. What are the pros and cons of third-party interventions in a conflict?
9. What should a team do to create an integrative solution to a conflict?

CONFLICT IS NORMAL

Conflict is the process by which people or groups perceive that others have taken some action that has a negative effect on their interest. Conflict is a normal part of a team's life. Unfortunately, people have a number of misconceptions about conflict that interfere with how they deal with it. These misconceptions include the following:

- Conflict is bad and should be avoided.
- Conflict is caused by team members not understanding each other.
- All conflicts can be resolved to everyone's satisfaction.

In a dynamic team, conflict is a normal part of the team's activity and is a healthy sign. If a team has no conflict, then that might be a sign of a problem. A team without conflict might be suffering from unhealthy agreement, have a domineering leader who suppresses all conflict and debate, or be performing its task in a routine manner and not trying to improve how it works.

Teams often do not handle their conflicts very well. Rather than trying to manage their conflicts, they try to ignore or avoid them. This is called *defensive avoidance*. To avoid a conflict, everyone becomes quiet when a controversy occurs. Decision-making problems, such as the Abilene paradox, are partly caused by the desire to avoid controversy. Team members accept what the leader or most aggressive person says so as to avoid conflict. The consequences of this are poor decision making and more problems later in the group's life.

The causes of team conflicts change during the team's development (Kivlighan & Jauquet, 1990). During the initial stage, there is little conflict because team members are being polite and trying to understand everyone's positions. This gives way to team conflicts about norms and power issues as the team sorts out its roles and rules. Once the team becomes task oriented, conflicts arise about how task issues should be defined and resolved. Often, the final stages of a project have little conflict because team members are focused on implementing the decisions they have made earlier.

It sometimes is better to talk about conflict management than about conflict resolution. Conflict is a normal part of a team's operation, and some conflicts cannot be fully resolved. When negotiating and resolving a conflict, the type of conflict makes a difference in the ways that it can be resolved. If the conflict is about task issues, then the solution is an agreement. Typically, once the agreement is made, it continues to operate. If the conflict is about relationship issues, then an agreement, periodic checks on how well the agreement is working, and opportunities to redefine the agreement are needed. This is because agreements about relationship issues can change as the relationships change.

SOURCES OF CONFLICT

Conflict can arise from many sources including confusion about people's positions, personality differences, legitimate differences of opinion, hidden agendas, poor norms, competitive reward systems, and poorly managed meetings. The problem is determining the source to identify whether this is a good conflict that is healthy for the team or the sign of a hidden problem that needs to be uncovered and addressed. If the conflict is about legitimate differences of opinion or disagreements about the team's task, then it is considered a good conflict. The team needs to acknowledge the source of conflict and manage the decision-making process necessary to resolve it. However, often a conflict only appears to be about the team's task and, in reality, is a symptom of an underlying problem. The team needs to diagnose the source of the conflict before trying to resolve it. Finding the root cause of the conflict is important because the team does not want to waste time dealing with only the symptoms of the conflict. Table 7.1 presents a list of healthy and unhealthy sources of conflict.

Legitimate conflicts can be caused by a variety of factors. Differences in values and objectives of team members, differing beliefs about the motives and actions of others, and different expectations about the results of decisions all can lead to conflicts about what the team should do. These differences create conflicts, but from these conflicts come better team decisions.

Hidden conflicts that are not really about the team's task also can come from many different sources. They may be due to organizational, social, and personal reasons.

Organizational causes of conflict include competition over scarce resources, ambiguity over responsibilities or jurisdiction, power differentials among team members, and competitive reward systems. One of the most common types of organizational conflict in a team is the conflict between the team's goals and the goals of the other groups to which team members belong. This is especially true for a cross-functional project team that is made up of representatives from different parts of an organization or different organizations (Franz & Jin, 1995). Hidden agendas (i.e., the hidden personal goals of team members) can lead to conflict in the team that can be dif-

TABLE 7.1
Sources of Conflict

Healthy	Focused on task issues
	Legitimate differences of opinion about the task
	Differences in values and perspectives
	Different expectations about the impact of decisions
Unhealthy	Competition over power, rewards, and resources
	Conflict between individual and group goals
	Poorly run team meetings
	Personal grudges from the past
	Faulty communications

ficult to identify and resolve. Gaining agreement about the overall goals of the team can help with this problem.

Conflict can be due to social factors within the team. A team with a leader who has poor facilitation skills can have poorly run meetings that have a lot of conflict. Poor group norms often show up in poorly managed meetings. When meetings are unproductive, conflict can arise because team members are dissatisfied with the team process. Spending time evaluating and developing appropriate norms will help decrease this type of conflict.

Conflicts can arise from personality differences or poor social relations among team members. These may be due to grudges coming from past losses that can persist, faulty attributions about why someone is doing something, faulty communication such as inappropriate criticism, or distrust. These often are called *personality differences,* but typically their source is interpersonal. Although team members are disagreeing about issues, the root cause of the conflicts is an unwillingness to agree. However, it can be difficult to determine whether someone has a legitimate disagreement about an issue as opposed to disagreeing for personal reasons. To deal with these sources of conflict, team building and other approaches to improving social relations are important.

IMPACT OF CONFLICT

Conflict can have both positive and negative effects on a team. It can help the team to operate better by exploring issues more fully, but it also can lead to emotional problems that hurt communication in the team. Studies on conflict in work teams show that the impact of conflict depends on both the type of conflict and the characteristics of the team.

| BENEFITS OF AND PROBLEMS WITH CONFLICT

Although people often view conflict as a negative event, conflict in teams is both inevitable and a sign of health. Teams are organized so as to gain the benefits of multiple perspectives. Team members with these multiple perspectives will view issues differently and learn from each other in the process of resolving their differences. Conflict is an integral part of the team process. Conflict becomes unhealthy for the team when it is avoided or viewed as an opportunity to beat one's opponent.

There are a variety of benefits that can come from conflict. Conflict helps the team reduce conformity and unhealthy agreement, solve problems better, and overcome obstacles to group progress. Also, conflict is a sign that the team is using its resources and acknowledging different perspectives, and it encourages group creativity. These benefits come from a team that recognizes the source of the conflict and resolves it successfully.

The benefits of conflict are that it encourages the team to explore new approaches, motivates people to understand issues better, and encourages new ideas (Robbins, 1974). Controversies bring out problems that have been ignored and open up issues for discussion that can encourage debate and foster new ideas. When opposing views are brought out into the open and are fully discussed, the team makes better decisions and organizational commitment is enhanced (Cosier & Dalton, 1990). When conflict is dealt with constructively, it stimulates greater team creativity. For this to happen, team members must be willing to participate, and the team leader must facilitate the participation of everyone.

Conflict also can have negative effects on the team by creating strong negative emotions and stress, interfering with communication and coordination, and diverting attention away from the task and goals. Conflict is negative when it prevents the group from completing its task, interferes with the group's ability to make decisions, and threatens the social relations in the group. Conflicts can destroy team cohesion, damage social relations, reduce communication, and create winners and losers who will be a source of conflict in the future. When the conflict is with an outside group, it often can encourage a shift to authoritarian leadership, negative stereotyping of others, an emphasis on group loyalty, and an increase in conformity (Fodor, 1976).

Whether conflicts are productive or unproductive relates to how the team tries to solve its conflicts (Witeman, 1991). Productive conflicts are about issues, ideas, and tasks. The team typically tries to solve productive conflicts in a cooperative manner. Unproductive conflicts are about emotions and personalities. The team typically tries to solve these by one side trying to win. When conflict is productive, team members try to depersonalize the situation and focus cooperatively on solving the issues.

| CONFLICT IN WORK TEAMS

Whether conflict has a beneficial or detrimental effect on a work team depends on the type of conflict and the structure of the team (Jehn, 1995). Both relationship conflict and task conflict have negative effects on team members' satisfaction and liking of the group. In a team performing a routine task, disagreements about the task hurt group functioning. By contrast, in a team performing a nonroutine task, conflicts about the task have a positive effect on the team.

Management and professional project teams are examples of teams performing nonroutine tasks. For this type of decision-making or creative team, conflict is a sign that diverse opinions are being focused on the task. The team benefits from the airing of these diverse opinions, and conflict helps to improve the quality and creativity of decisions. However, even for this type of team, when conflict become very intense, it can be detrimental to the team. Conflict is important for the quality of decisions, but it may reduce the team's ability to reach consensus and may hurt emotional acceptance of the team and its decisions (Amason, 1996).

For a production or service team, the impact of task-related conflict depends on the type of task the team is performing (Cohen & Bailey, 1997). Task conflict disrupts performance on a routine task. However, it can improve performance on a nonroutine task. When this type of team is performing a routine task, task conflict is a sign that its jobs are poorly defined or that team members are unwilling to cooperate and work together. Conflict among team members in this situation usually is not productive. However, when the team is performing a nonroutine task, such as evaluating how to improve quality, conflict is a natural part of the problem-solving process.

Relationship conflict is detrimental regardless of the type of task that a team is performing (Jehn, 1995). Although relationship conflict creates dissatisfaction for the team, it often does not overly disrupt the team's performance. In many cases, team members try to avoid working with members with whom they do not get along personally. Consequently, relationship conflict hurts performance only when the task requires interdependent actions.

Unfortunately, cognitive and emotional conflicts often occur together (Amason, 1996). When team members disagree about an issue, the debate sometimes can turn personal. What starts out as conflict about an issue turns into personal and political conflict.

CONFLICT RESOLUTION APPROACHES

The conflict resolution approaches available to teams vary depending on the team members' desire to be assertive and cooperative. Because team members have long-term relationships with each other, they should try to use a collaborative approach to conflicts whenever possible.

| TWO DIMENSIONS OF CONFLICT

There are several ways in which people and teams can try to resolve conflicts. The approaches they take depend on their personalities, their social relations, and the particular situational contexts. The types of conflict resolution approaches can be analyzed using the following two dimensions: *distribution* (concern about one's own outcomes) and *integration* (concern about the outcomes of others) (Rahim, 1983; Thomas, 1976; Walton & McKersie, 1965). In other words, people in a conflict can be assertive and try to get the most for themselves, or they can be cooperative and concerned about how everyone fares. These two dimensions are independent and lead to the creation of five different approaches to conflict resolution (Figure 7.1):

1. *Avoidance:* This approach tries to ignore the issues or deny that there is a problem. By not confronting the conflict, team members hope that it will go away by itself.
2. *Accommodation:* Some team members may decide to give up their position so as to be agreeable. They are being cooperative, but it costs the team the value of their opinions and ideas.

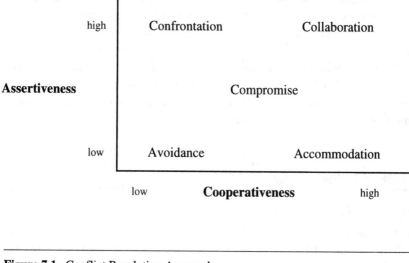

Figure 7.1. Conflict Resolution Approaches
SOURCE: Adapted from Rahim (1983).

3. *Confrontation:* Acting aggressively and trying to win is one way in which to deal with a conflict. However, winning can become more important than making a good decision.
4. *Compromise:* One way in which to balance the goals of each participant and the relations among the teams is for everyone to "give in" a little.
5. *Collaboration:* When both sides of a conflict have important concerns, the team needs to search for solutions that satisfy everyone. This requires both cooperativeness and respect for each other's position.

COMPARING DIFFERENT APPROACHES TO CONFLICT RESOLUTION

Although all these approaches can be used to resolve conflict, there are problems with the use of these styles. Avoidance, accommodation, and confrontation all can work to resolve the conflict, but these approaches create winners and losers. Teams that use these styles often have trouble implementing decisions, so they find themselves having to deal with the same issues later. Compromise works somewhat better because everyone wins a little and loses a little. A compromise promotes equity or fairness but usually does not result in optimal decisions.

When possible, teams should try to use a collaborative approach to conflict resolution. In collaboration, team members search for the alternative solution that allows everyone to win. Although trying to find a collaborative solution might be time-consuming and difficult, it has many benefits. Collaboration encourages creativity and stimulates performance, builds mutual support and morale within the team, leads to greater commitment and support for decisions, and helps improve the ongoing relationships among the team members (Pruitt, 1986).

In their study of conflict in work teams trying to make decisions, Farmer and Roth (1998) found that teams tended to use collaboration and accommodation. These two strategies reflect a high concern about others or a cooperative orientation. The least-used strategies were avoidance, compromise, and competition.

Members of work teams have long-term concerns about their relationships that go beyond specific situations or conflicts. Teams that have shared goals and long-term commitments are likely to show more concern about other team members' welfare and interests when conflicts arise. Conflicts arise from different perspectives and conflicting interests, but the shared goals encourage being concerned about the perspectives of others. Because the relationships will continue, team members want to be viewed in a positive light by other members, so they are more willing to cooperate with other members.

Although collaboration may be the best approach in general, it cannot always be achieved. A good conflict manager is able to change styles and use the one best suited to the situation. There are occasions when different conflict resolution approaches are best. For example, in a conflict with an emotionally upset boss, a good short-term strategy for the conflict is to be accommodating. In an emergency situation, people are more likely to accept a confronting style because they value a quick resolution. Collaboration is the best approach when the power relationships among team members are relatively equal and there is time to work through a solution. Other approaches may be better when there are large differences in power and a quick resolution is needed.

NEGOTIATION, MEDIATION, AND ARBITRATION

When a conflict becomes intense, sometimes the team is not able to resolve it alone. When teams have conflicts with each other, resolving the conflicts is difficult because there might not be a personal connection that encourages cooperation. In these cases, outside help might be needed to resolve the conflicts. For example, when Boeing was building the 777, it had numerous design teams working on various parts of the jet. To help resolve the inevitable differences among these teams, it established a set of "integration" teams whose function was to help mediate the differences among the design teams (Zaccaro & Marks, 1999).

| NEGOTIATION

Negotiation or bargaining is the process by which the two sides in a dispute exchange offers and counteroffers in an effort to find a mutually acceptable agreement. One of the most important dimensions in understanding how a negotiation will resolve a conflict is whether the participants have a win-win versus a win-lose perspective (Walton & McKersie, 1965). A win-lose perspective is based on the beliefs that what is good for one side is incompatible with what is good for the other and that the other side puts the same importance on issues that one's own side does (Thompson & Hastie, 1990). With a win-win perspective, the participants believe that it is possible to find a solution that satisfies both sides. A negotiation can either adopt a win-lose approach and try to find a compromise or adopt a win-win approach and search for an integrative solution.

In a win-lose approach, there are two types of tactics that participants can use successfully. The first approach is to stand tough and be firm (Siegel & Fouraker, 1960). The *stand tough* approach works well, especially if there is time pressure or other external pressure to make a deal. However, the stand tough approach can lead to a stalemate or to no solution because participants may walk away from the situation. In the second approach, called *GRIT* (graduated and reciprocal initiative in tension reduction), the participants initiate small concessions, reward reciprocal concessions, and build a relationship based on reciprocal trading (Osgood, 1962). This approach is especially useful if the parties in the conflict will need to work together in the future.

The win-win approach, called *integrative bargaining,* looks for a creative solution that satisfies the needs of both sides (Pruitt, 1981). Compared to the compromise approach, people are more satisfied and the relationship is better with the integrative solution. However, the integrative approach is more difficult to apply and often requires skillful negotiating.

For example, a budget committee might have limited resources available to allocate to two programs. Supporters of each program will forcefully argue for their positions because the overall amount of money available is fixed. A compromise (splitting the money equally) might leave each program with less money than it needs to expand. An integrative solution may combine the programs' administrative activities to reduce costs so that there is enough resources to expand both programs. However, developing this integrative solution is not an easy task within the context of an emotional conflict.

| MEDIATION AND ARBITRATION

Negotiation is when two parties bargain to try to resolve a conflict. Mediation and arbitration are when a third (outside) party intervenes to help resolve a conflict. Mediation is a third-party intervention in which the intervener does not have authority to impose a solution; the intervener acts as a facilitator. Arbitration is a third-party intervention in which the intervener can impose a solution; the intervener acts as a judge.

The advantage of third-party mediation is that it enables conflicting parties to make concessions in a negotiation and save face (Pruitt, 1981). The main tactic is to help the parties reframe the situation from a win-lose orientation to a win-win orientation. This allows them to focus on what they really want from the conflict rather than thinking about how to beat the other side (Thompson & Hastie, 1990). One of the advantages of using a mediator is that the mediator has the skills to help both sides work through the issues.

Mediators operate by gaining trust among the participants, managing hostilities, developing solutions to the conflicts, and gaining commitment to the solutions from the participants. They use a variety of tactics to do this. Some of the tactics focus on the emotional or relationship aspects of situations, whereas others are more oriented toward problem-solving and task aspects. Mediators may search to develop creative win-win solutions, or they may focus on pressuring the parties into, or rewarding the parties for, accepting compromise solutions. The tactics that mediators select depend on the perceived likelihood that agreements can be reached and their concerns with the parties meeting their goals (Carnevale, 1986).

Third-party approaches can work, but there also are problems with using them rather than negotiation. Mediation often does not work because it requires voluntary compliance to be effective. One cannot force both parties to accept using a mediator. If either of the parties in a conflict does not want to use a mediator or does not want to settle the conflict, then the mediator is unlikely to be successful (Hitrop, 1989). The success of mediation rests on the skills of the facilitator and the sincerity of the participants.

Arbitration can reduce commitment to try to negotiate differences voluntarily. Sometimes, the threat of arbitration encourages participants in a conflict to reconcile their differences. However, if the differences between two sides are substantial, then the threat of arbitration may cause each side to harden its position in preparation for the arbitration (Pruitt, 1986). People sometimes prefer not to use arbitration because they lose control over the solution. If participants suspect that the arbitrator is biased, then they might become reluctant to agree to arbitration. Commitment to arbitrated agreements often is less than commitment to negotiated ones (Thomas, 1992).

Whether mediation is better than arbitration depends on the situation (Pruitt & Carnevale, 1993). Arbitration is better when there is time pressure and the issues are very complex. Mediation is better when there is an ongoing relationship among the parties that will continue in the future.

MANAGING TEAM CONFLICTS

The goal of managing team conflicts is to develop integrative agreements in which both sides benefit. These collaborative agreements are better than compromises in which each side has to give up part of what it wants. Integrative agreements are more rewarding and help to improve the ongoing relationships among the parties (Pruitt, 1986). The keys to developing integrative agreements are focusing attention on interests rather than positions and developing trust and rapport between the conflicted parties.

When a team becomes involved in a conflict, members often form coalitions based on positions toward the conflict. Rather than focusing on the issues of interest to them, they focus on whether others are for or against their positions. Thompson and Hrebec (1996) found that 50% of people in a conflict failed to realize when they had interests completely compatible with each other and that 20% failed to reach agreement even when their interests were compatible. One of the reasons for this failure is that they did not exchange information about their interests and they overlooked areas of common interest (Thompson & Hastie, 1990).

Successful conflict management also requires developing trust and rapport among the participants (Ross & Ward, 1995). If one trusts members of the other side and believes that they want a just solution, then one is much better able to negotiate a solution to a conflict. Many conflict reduction approaches are designed to help build trust among the parties in a conflict. For example, in a study of bargaining through e-mail, allowing the participants to engage in a "get acquainted" telephone call before the bargaining session increased the chances of reaching an agreement by 50% (Nadler, Thompson, & Morris, 1999).

Imagine being on a committee whose goal is to reduce violence in local high schools. As the committee begins to search for solutions, a conflict arises over whether the schools should use electronic surveillance technology. Committee members divide into sides over this issue, and all future ideas are evaluated by whether they support or oppose this position. Over time, the debate within the committee becomes increasingly hostile, and new ideas are rejected because of who expressed them rather than being evaluated on quality.

The solution to this conflict is to find an integrative agreement that addresses the committee's goal (i.e., to improve safety in the schools) but does not depend on either position. The participants need to step back from their emotional involvement supporting their positions and must start to understand what is really important to them. There are many alternatives that can help to reduce violence without decreasing privacy in the schools. Some examples include training students in conflict management approaches, using students to monitor compliance with safety rules, and providing teachers with training to help them deal with aggressive incidents.

The search for an integrative solution can be difficult. It often is useful for a team to either use an outside facilitator for a major conflict or receive training in how to facilitate conflicts. The following steps (adapted from Fisher, Ury, & Patton, 1991) can help to structure the negotiation of a conflict:

1. Separate the people from the problem.
    - Negotiations must deal with both the issues and the relationship, but these two factors should be separated.
    - Diagnose the cause of the conflict. What goals are in conflict? Identify what each side in a conflict wants and make sure that each side has a clear understanding of the issues.

- Encourage both sides to recognize and understand their emotions about the conflict. Encourage them to view the conflict from the other side's perspective and to practice active listening.

2. Focus on the shared interests of all of the parties.
   - Focus on the issues, not on each side's position.
   - Identify how each side can get what it wants. Identify the issues that are incompatible between the two sides. Recognize that both sides have legitimate multiple interests.
   - Have each side identify and rank its goals in the conflict. This often shows that the important goals of each side are different, thereby helping each side to see how to trade off unimportant goals to get what it really wants.

3. Develop many options that can be used to solve the problem.
   - Creatively try to generate alternatives that provide mutual gains for both sides. Separate the process of generating ideas from the selection of alternatives.
   - Look for areas of shared interest. Invent multiple solutions as well as solutions to parts of the problem.
   - Practice viewing the problem from alternative perspectives.

4. Evaluate the options using objective criteria.
   - Develop objective criteria that can be used as a basis for decisions. Define what fair standards and fair procedures are for resolving the conflict. Agree on these principles before agreeing on a solution.
   - Talk through the issues so as to eliminate unimportant issues. Talk through important differences, searching for the common points on each side.
   - Focus on solutions to which both sides can agree. Do not give in to pressure.

5. Try again.
   - Creative solutions are difficult to develop. If one does not succeed at first, then one should keep trying.
   - Teams do not always resolve their conflicts, but they do try to manage conflicts while they work through their various tasks.
   - Establish monitoring criteria to ensure that agreements are kept.
   - Discuss ways in which the team can deal with similar issues in the future. How can the team improve its ability to manage conflicts?

SUMMARY

Conflict is a normal part of a team's existence. It is a sign of healthy team interactions. Unfortunately, teams often do not handle conflict very well. They make bad decisions so as to avoid conflict rather than learning how to manage it effectively.

Conflict can be analyzed in terms of its sources and types. Conflicts that are healthy for a team come from disagreements about how to address task issues. Conflicts that are unhealthy for a team originate from organizational, social, or personal sources. The type of conflict affects the way in which it should be managed. When conflicts are about misunderstandings and task issues, they can be managed using negotiations to develop acceptable agreements. When conflicts arise from social or personal sources, they often require team building to develop social skills and improve social relations.

Conflict provides both benefits and problems for a team. Conflict helps the team to perform its task by fostering debate over issues and stimulating creativity. Conflict hurts the team when it creates strong negative emotions, damages group cohesion, and disrupts the team's ability to operate.

Approaches to resolving conflicts vary depending on how assertive the participants are about getting their way and how cooperative the participants want to be. Team members use different conflict resolution approaches depending on the situation, but collaboration typically is the most effective approach. Collaboration attempts to identify an alternative solution that satisfies both parties. Although they may be more difficult and time-consuming to achieve, collaborative solutions encourage acceptance and support for the solutions.

When a conflict persists, a team might need to use a more formal approach to conflict resolution. A team typically tries to resolve conflicts through negotiation or bargaining. One of the most important factors in bargaining is whether the participants view the situation as a win-lose or a win-win scenario. Mediation and arbitration involve the use of a third party to help resolve a conflict. These approaches can be useful for conflicts that are difficult to resolve, but the third party must be accepted by all of the participants to be effective.

Improving a team's ability to manage conflicts can be achieved in several ways. Developing trust provides a foundation for resolving team conflicts. Learning how to fight constructively also is a useful skill. Conflict mediation facilitators have developed helpful approaches for structuring the negotiation process.

ACTIVITY: OBSERVING CONFLICT RESOLUTION STYLES

Objective. Team members use one of the following five styles to handle conflicts and disagreements. Avoidance means trying to ignore the issue or deny that there is a problem. Accommodation means giving up one's position so as to be agreeable. Confrontation means acting aggressively and trying to get one's way. Compromise means seeking a balance so that all parties get some of what they want. Collaboration means trying to search for a solution that satisfies everyone.

Activity. Observe a team and note what happens when there is a conflict or disagreement. Classify the team members' responses to each conflict or disagreement using the conflict resolution styles just listed. Using Activity Worksheet 7.1, write down an example of each type of conflict resolution style you observe.

Analysis. Which conflict resolution style did the team use most often? Did certain team members adopt a similar style for each conflict? Did the team handle its conflicts in a constructive manner?

Discussion. How could the team handle conflicts better? What could be done to encourage more use of collaboration as a conflict resolution style?

ACTIVITY WORKSHEET 7.1
Observing Conflict Resolution Styles

	Team Member					
	1	2	3	4	5	6
Avoidance						
Accommodation						
Confrontation						
Compromise						
Collaboration						

Chapter 8

POWER AND SOCIAL INFLUENCE

Groups use their power to influence people's behaviors by providing information about how to behave and exerting pressure to encourage compliance. Team members gain power from personal characteristics and their positions and use a variety of power tactics to influence other members. The dynamics of power in teams has a major influence on leaders' behaviors, how team members interact, the impact of minorities, and the amount of influence members have on each other.

Empowerment is at the core of teamwork where members have been given power and authority over a team's operations. Within the team, members need to learn how to use their own power to work together effectively. Learning how to act assertively, rather than passively or aggressively, encourages open communication and effective problem solving.

➤➤ LEARNING OBJECTIVES

1. How do conformity and obedience influence people's behaviors?
2. What are the different bases of power?
3. How does one decide which influence tactics to use?
4. How does having power change the power holder?
5. How does unequal power affect a team's interactions?
6. What makes a minority influential?
7. What is empowerment?
8. What problems does an organization encounter when trying to empower teams?
9. How do passive, aggressive, and assertive power styles affect a team and its members?

DEFINITIONS OF POWER AND SOCIAL INFLUENCE

Social influence refers to attempts to affect or change other people. Power is the capacity or ability to change the beliefs, attitudes, or behaviors of others. We often think about power in terms of how individuals try to influence each other, but a group also has collective power. Conformity occurs through influence from the group caused either by providing information about the appropriate way in which to behave or through implied or actual group pressure. In addition, obedience occurs through influence from the leader or high-status person in the group.

It is important to recognize that what becomes influenced or changed depends on the situation. There is an important distinction between compliance and acceptance. Compliance is a change in behaviors due to pressure or influence but is not a change in beliefs or attitudes. Acceptance is a change in both behaviors and attitudes due to social pressure. However, if a person is influenced to repeatedly change his or her behaviors, then the person often internalizes it by creating a justification for his or her new way of behaving. Therefore, changing behaviors often changes attitudes as well.

Why do people change due to social influence? Social psychologists provide two main reasons for social influence effects: normative influence and informational influence (Deutsch & Gerard, 1955). *Normative influence* is change based on one's desire to meet other people's expectations and to be accepted by others. *Informational influence* is change that is based on accepting information about the situation from others.

Social psychologists have conducted several classic studies on power that demonstrate the basic characteristics of social influence and show some of the factors that affect the influence process. These studies show how a team influences the behaviors of its members and the power that team leaders have over the members.

| CONFORMITY

Asch's (1955) conformity studies show that even with merely implied social or group pressure, people are willing to make bad judgments. The participants in these experiments were asked to select which line was the same length as a target line. When working alone, people rarely made mistakes. However, when participants were in a room with people who gave the wrong answers, the participants gave the wrong answers 37% of the time. Only 20% of the participants stayed independent and did not give in to group pressure. The others conformed to group pressure even though there was no obvious pressure to conform (i.e., no rewards or punishments).

Follow-up studies using this approach to study conformity helped to explain why people gave in to the group even though there was no direct pressure. For many of the participants, the influence was informational. They reasoned that if the majority were giving answers that obviously were wrong, then the participants must have misunderstood the instructions. Other participants went along with the majority for normative reasons. They feared that the group members would disapprove of them if their answers were different. Later studies showed that nonconformists were rated as undesirable group members.

Research also examined the effects of group size and unanimity on conformity. A group of about five people shows most of the conformity effects. There is not much difference in conformity by using larger groups (Rosenberg, 1961). Unanimity is very important. Many of the conformity effects are greatly reduced with limited support for dissenting (Allen & Levine, 1969). It is difficult to be a minority of one person but not of several people.

These studies show the power that a team has over its members. In these experiments, temporary groups set up in psychology laboratories were able to change what people believed and how they behaved. The impact of a team, where members have ongoing relationships with each other, can create much stronger conformity effects. This is especially true when the team has a high degree of group cohesion because cohesive groups have more power to influence members (Sakuri, 1975).

| OBEDIENCE

The Milgram (1974) obedience studies show that people are obedient to authority figures even when the requested behaviors are inappropriate. In these obedience studies, the participants believed that they were part of a learning experiment. They were asked to give an electric shock to a learner whenever the learner made a mistake. They also were told to increase the level of shock with each mistake. Nearly all participants were willing to administer mild shocks, and most (65%) continued to administer shocks even after they were informed that the learner had a heart condition, the learner had stopped responding, and they could see that the level of shocks being administered had increased to dangerous levels.

The amount of obedience in these studies was influenced by several factors. The more legitimate the authority figure, the more likely people were to be obedient. They were more likely to obey when the authority figure was in the same room monitoring their performance. Whenever possible, the participants did not shock the learner and lied to the authority figure about it. The closer the participants were to the victim (and could see or hear the victim's pain), the less obedience there was. Finally, when there was a group of people running the shock machine, the participants were less obedient if one other person refused to obey.

The important issue to note in the Milgram studies is that obedience occurs even when the authority figure does not have power to reward or punish the participants. In most teams, the team leaders are given only limited power by their organizations. For example, team leaders usually do not conduct performance evaluations of the members; evaluations usually are done by outside managers. Even without this source of power, team members' tendency to obey authority figures gives team leaders considerable power over how teams operate.

TYPES OF POWER

In addition to conformity and obedience, team members use various types of power to influence each other and the team. The types of power that members possess can be examined in several ways. The study of bases of power is concerned with the sources of the power, whereas the study of influence tactics examines how various power tactics are used.

| BASES OF POWER

There are two types of power that an individual can have in a group or an organization: personal or soft power and positional or harsh power (French & Raven, 1959; Raven, Schwarzwald, & Koslowsky, 1998). *Personal or soft power* comes from an individual's characteristics or personality. It includes expert, referent, and information power. *Positional or harsh power* is based on one's formal position in an organization. It includes legitimate, reward, and coercive power. Definitions for these bases of power are provided in Table 8.1.

The types of power are highly related to each other and often used together (Podsakoff & Schriesheim, 1985). For example, the more one uses coercive power, the less one is liked, so one has less personal or soft power.

TABLE 8.1
Types of Power

Personal or soft power	
Expert	Power based on one's credibility or perceived expertise in an area
Referent	Power based on another's liking and admiration
Information	Power based on the knowledge or information one has about a topic
Positional or harsh power	
Legitimate	Power based on the recognition and acceptance of a person's authority
Reward	The ability to reward behavior that one wants to occur
Coercive	The ability to threaten or punish undesirable behavior

SOURCE: Adapted from French and Raven (1959).

The more legitimate power one has, the more reward and coercive power one typically also has.

The use of the personal sources of power often is more effective than that of the positional sources of power (Kipnis, Schmidt, Swaffin-Smith, & Wilkinson, 1984). One of the reasons for this is that the targets of influence are more likely to resist the use of positional power and are less satisfied with its use. Because of this, leaders typically prefer using expert power the most and coercive power the least. However, the use of expert power is limited. The fact that someone is an expert in one area does not make that person an expert at everything.

Reward and coercive power can be used to influence people to do what is desired, but people do it only because of the reward or fear of punishment. The result is compliance but not acceptance. These strategies are useful for changing overt behaviors but not for changing attitudes and beliefs; the influencer has to monitor the behaviors to make sure that the results are occurring (Zander, 1994).

Teamwork should rely on the personal power of the team members. Group decision making is better when the discussion is dominated by people who are most expert or have the relevant information to add, rather than by people who have authority to make decisions. Cooperation is more likely to be encouraged by the use of personal power sources than by the use of threats of punishment by team leaders. When team leaders rely on positional power to get their teams to comply with their requests, members are likely to feel manipulated and may resist.

| INFLUENCE TACTICS

There are a variety of social influence tactics that team members can use to influence each other. Descriptions of these tactics are presented in Table 8.2. The use of these tactics depends on who one is trying to influence (e.g., subordinate, peer, superior) and the objective (e.g., assign task, get support, gain personal benefit) (Yukl & Guinan, 1995).

These power tactics vary by directness, cooperativeness, and rationality. Direct tactics are explicit and overt methods of influence (e.g., personal appeals and pressure), whereas indirect tactics are covert attempts at manipulation (e.g., ingratiation and coalition tactics). Cooperative tactics encourage support through rational argument or consultation, whereas competitive tactics attempt to deal with resistance through pressure or ingratiation (Kipnis & Schmidt, 1982). Finally, some tactics are based on rational argument or the exchange of support, whereas inspirational and personal appeals rely on emotion.

People prefer direct and cooperative strategies. The most effective tactics are rational argument, consultation, and inspirational appeals (Falbe & Yukl, 1992). These are the more socially acceptable tactics and are useful in most situations. However, status differences in a group affect which tactics are used. Leaders often use pressure and legitimating tactics on subordinates, whereas team members often use rational argument, personal appeals, and ingratiation to influence leaders.

POWER DYNAMICS

The use of power has a number of impacts that change the dynamics of the group process. Unequal power changes how the leader treats other team members and how members communicate with each other. Subgroups that disagree with the majority can have a substantial influence on how the team operates. The amount of interdependence among team members changes the power they have over each other.

TABLE 8.2
Social Influence Tactics

Rational argument	Use logical arguments and factual information to persuade.
Consultation	Seek a person's participation in the decision.
Inspirational appeals	Attempt to arouse enthusiasm by appealing to a person's ideals.
Personal appeals	Appeal to a person's sense of loyalty or friendship.
Ingratiation	Use flattery or friendly behavior to get a person to think favorably of you.
Exchange	Offer to exchange favors later for compliance now.
Pressure	Use demands, threats, or persistent reminders.
Legitimizing tactics	Make claims that one has the authority to make the request.
Coalition tactics	Seek the aid and support of others to increase power of request.

SOURCE: Adapted from Yukl and Guinan (1995).

STATUS AND THE CORRUPTING EFFECT OF POWER

Power is rewarding, so people with power often want more of it (Kipnis, 1976). It has a corrupting influence; people with more power often give themselves a higher share of rewards. It is easy for someone with power to give commands rather than use requests; this really becomes an unconscious act. Because powerful people get mostly positive feedback from subordinates, they begin to care less about what subordinates say and have a high view of their own worth.

Kipnis (1976) demonstrates the corrupting nature of power in studies on groups in business organizations and families. He documented a cycle of power in which having power leads to a desire to increase one's power. Table 8.3 shows how the cycle operates.

One of the problems with this effect is that its impact often is unconscious. Over time, powerful leaders believe that their subordinates are externally controlled and, therefore, must be monitored and commanded for the leaders to get them to do anything. It is a cycle that reinforces itself. A team can try to deal with this problem by rotating the person who is the team

---

TABLE 8.3
Cycle of Power

- Access to power increases the probability that it will be used.
- The more power is used, the more the power holders believe that they are in control.
- As power holders take credit, they view the target as less worthy.
- As the target's worth is decreased, social distance increases between them.
- The use of power elevates the self-esteem of the powerful.

SOURCE: Adapted from Kipnis (1976).

---

leader. When the leader knows that he or she eventually will become just another team member, the leader is less likely to use controlling power tactics.

UNEQUAL POWER IN A TEAM

Groups vary in the ways in which power is distributed. When groups have unequal power levels among members, there tends to be more mistrust, less communication, and more social problems than with more egalitarian groups. Groups with powerful leaders tend to have less communication and more autocratic decision making, thereby reducing the quality of team decisions.

Unequal power often is caused by status differences among the participants. These status differences have an impact on team communication (Hurwitz, Zander, & Hymovitch, 1953). High-status or more powerful people talk more and are more likely to address the entire group. People communicate with high-status people and pay more attention to what they say. Low-status people often talk less, fear the opinions of high-status people, and are unwilling to state their true opinions if they differ from those of high-status people. Consequently, when high-status people speak, people either agree or say nothing, so high-status people have more influence in group discussions. This type of communication pattern does not lead to good decision making or to satisfied and motivated team members.

In theory, a team should have only equal-status communication, but this is not always the case. The team leader may view him- or herself as an equal and encourage equal-status communication, or the leader may assume a higher status than the other team members. A team sometimes is composed of members who have different levels of status within the organization. Team members should leave their external status positions at the door so that everyone on the team has equal status in the team context. However, this is not always the case. It is difficult to interact as an equal with someone in one situation and be deferential in other situations.

When power is unequal due to status or other factors, a team can try to improve the situation by using group norms that equalize the presentation of power and help to control communication. Norms level the playing field in a group. They can help equalize power by putting constraints on the behaviors of powerful people. For example, the norm of majority rules or democratic decision making limits the power of the leader. The group can have other types of norms that encourage open and shared communication, prevent the use of intimidation or threats, and value free and independent thinking. All of these help to reduce the impact of power differences in the group.

| MINORITY INFLUENCE

Most of this discussion of power has focused on the impact of powerful people or pressure from the group majority. However, a group can have individuals or subgroups that resist group pressure. The minority groups resist the leader and group pressure and eventually can be influential in changing the group (Moscovici, 1985). The ability of minorities to influence the majority group depends on their consistency, self-confidence, belief that they are autonomous, and relationship to the overall group.

Minorities become influential by sticking to their positions (Nemeth, 1979). When minorities are consistent, they cause the majority to think about its position. A group can put quite a bit of pressure on minorities to change, so it takes self-confidence to resist this pressure. Minorities must appear to be autonomous and able to make their own choices to be influential. If the minorities are viewed as being supported, rewarded, or influenced by an outside group, then their impact is reduced. Finally, minorities must appear to be part of the group. Minorities are less effective if they reject the group or are always seen as being dissenters (Levine, 1989).

One of the most important values of a minority to a team is to stimulate members to view an issue from multiple perspectives (Peterson & Nemeth, 1996). When a minority disagrees with the team's view of a situation, it causes the team to rethink its position and encourages the generation of more alternative views. The overall effect of this is to encourage more flexible and divergent thinking, thereby increasing creativity and innovation. The minority might not get its way per se, but over time it has a substantial impact on how the team thinks and acts.

IMPACT OF INTERDEPENDENCE

Task interdependence is the degree to which completing a task requires the interaction of team members. Teams with high levels of interdependence are more likely to be effective if they have autonomy or the power and authority to control how they operate (Langfred, 2000). In highly interdependent teams, autonomy allows the team members to work together more efficiently, to control their own interactions, and to increase internal coordination. These actions help to improve performance. In teams with low levels of interdependence, the team members are accustomed to working independently, so increases in communication and coordination do not help to improve performance.

Interdependence can help a team to perform better by changing the amount of power that team members have over each other (Franz, 1998). Dependence in a relationship is one of the bases of power. To the extent that team members depend on each other to complete a task, power is shared among the members. Heightened levels of overall task interdependence are associated with increased personal power. The more team members need each other to complete a task, the more power each team member has over the group.

EMPOWERMENT

Empowerment in a workplace refers to the process of giving employees more power and control over their work. It is the shifting of power and authority from managers to employees. The goal is to give team members more control over their own fates and a share in influencing the way in which the team operates. The success of empowerment programs depends on the organization's willingness to share information and power with its employees (Hollander & Offerman, 1990).

In one sense, empowerment is the core notion of teamwork. A team needs to have the power to control how it operates. This is what makes a team different from a work group. A team cannot operate successfully if a manager controls its internal operation or if its external relationships are completely controlled by an organization.

Empowerment can be a benefit both to the individuals and teams that are empowered and to their organizations. Employees who work in empowered jobs have increased motivation and job satisfaction (Ford & Fottler, 1995). Empowerment increases employees' confidence in their ability to perform a task. Empowered teams have access to more information that improves communication, problem solving, and decision making. The power and freedom to change the way in which employees work encourages continuous improvements and innovation (Burpitt & Bigoness, 1997). Organizations benefit by having teams that function more effectively, are able to make improvements in quality, and show increased acceptance of change.

| DEGREES OF EMPOWERMENT PROGRAMS

There are a variety of approaches for promoting empowerment. These can range from simple changes (e.g., suggestion boxes or employee surveys to receive input from employees), to work teams, to fully empowered self-managing teams (Lawler, 1986). Although these programs have a number of commonalities, they differ on what is shared and the breadth of involvement activities.

The sharing of information is the minimum requirement for empowerment to occur. However, for a team to fully feel empowered, it also needs the power to make and implement decisions. Without some power to act, employees have little incentive to continue making attempts to improve the way in which their team operates.

A second dimension for analyzing empowerment programs concerns the breadth of empowerment activities. Most empowerment programs give team members control over their job content (i.e., the task and work procedure they perform) but not over job context (i.e., goals, reward systems, and personnel issues) (Ford & Fottler, 1995). For example, total quality management programs might allow employees to make changes to improve the quality of their work operations but might not allow employees to influence personnel decisions. By contrast, at the Saturn automobile plant that uses empowered work teams, team members control their work processes, deal with external customers, hire new team members, and conduct performance evaluations.

| SUCCESSFUL EMPOWERMENT PROGRAMS

Although research shows that empowerment can be effective, few organizations are willing to make the transition due to beliefs about power. If
power is viewed as a limited commodity, then giving power to a team reduces managerial power. This ambivalence about power makes managers
reluctant to empower teams (Herrenkohl, Judson, & Heffner, 1999). However, when teamwork programs are successful, everyone in the organization
gains in power.

Lawler and Mohrman (1985) identify two main problems with quality
circle programs that relate to other types of empowerment programs. First,
the middle managers who were responsible for implementing the programs'
recommendations were not part of the decision-making process, thereby reducing their commitment to the programs. Second, if the programs became
too successful and involvement increased, then the programs were perceived as a threat to the power of management. Other analyses of empowerment programs also point to problems created in middle management. Klein
(1984) found that although 72% of supervisors believed that empowerment
is good for the organization, only 31% believed that it is good for supervisors. Although some supervisors support empowerment, most are concerned about their loss of status, lack of support from upper management,
and the feeling that they are being bypassed.

Successful empowerment programs attempt to deal with these power issues. If the organizational culture does not support power sharing, then empowerment programs should begin with activities that share only information. Although these programs are not as effective, they are less threatening
and may increase the acceptability of other teamwork programs later. Initially, programs such as quality circles should be focused on special issues
within defined areas. Only when the organization is ready should empowerment programs be expanded.

Resistance from supervisors and middle managers can be handled in a
number of ways (Klein, 1984). Supervisors need to be involved in the design
of the empowerment programs. The roles of supervisors should be evaluated, and their new responsibilities and authority should be clearly defined.
Often, supervisors will need additional training in teamwork skills to prepare them for their new roles as team leaders. Additional training can have a
secondary benefit in that it demonstrates the organization's commitment to
the supervisors.

APPLICATION: ACTING ASSERTIVELY

People express power through their behaviors. They can act passively, aggressively, or assertively (Alberti & Emmons, 1978). Their emotional tones and the ways in which they confront problems define these power styles. The use of these power styles has important impacts on communication in teams. That is why assertiveness training is used as part of teamwork training programs (Cannon-Bowers & Salas, 1998). Table 8.4 presents an overview of these power styles, their impacts on teams, and situations in which they often are used.

When people talk about power styles, there is some confusion about whether the styles are part of someone's personality, a behavior, or something in between. Power styles are like personality traits because some people adopt preferred styles and use them in most situations. However, most people change styles depending on the situation, and people can be taught how to use particular styles. This suggests that power styles are behaviors rather than personality traits. It probably is best to view power styles as behavioral patterns that are related to both personalities and situations.

Nonassertive/Passive Style

The nonassertive or passive style is polite and deferential. A sweet, pleasant, or ingratiating emotional tone is added to one's communication. A person using the passive approach tries to avoid problems by not taking a stand or by being unclear about his or her position. By being evasive, a person using this approach tries not to upset or anger anyone by disagreeing. The person's desire to be liked by others is based on his or her personal insecurity or fear of the situation.

The goal of the passive approach is to win approval and be liked. Unfortunately, this style does not work out this way. Passive people often feel stressed and resentful, partly because problems never seem to go away. The receivers of passive communication often have mixed responses. On the one hand, they get their way; on the other, they are uncertain about the real beliefs of the passive communicators and lack respect for them.

There are situations in which the passive approach is appropriate. When a conflict becomes highly emotional, sometimes a passive response can help to defuse the situation. When interacting with a person of higher status, a passive response sometimes is expected from a subordinate. Acting

TABLE 8.4
Power Styles

	Styles	Impact	Use
Nonassertive/ passive	Polite and deferential Avoid problems	Resentment and confusion	Dangerous situations Unequal status
Aggressive	Forceful and critical Focused on winning	Satisfaction and withdrawal	Emergencies Unequal status
Assertive	Clear and confident Problem solving	Satisfaction and trust	Most situations Equal status

aggressively to one's boss can be an inappropriate or dangerous tactic. There are situations where being assertive is too risky.

Aggressive Style

The aggressive style is forceful, critical, and negative. A negative emotional tone is added to communication so that it appears to be more powerful. A person using the aggressive approach deals with problems and conflicts by trying to win and will not listen or compromise. The underlying feelings of the aggressive style are anger, insecurity, and a lack of trust. In some ways, this is similar to the passive style. That is why people sometimes swing back and forth between passiveness and aggressiveness without ever being assertive.

The use of the aggressive style often is rewarded. In many situations, people give in to people who are acting forcefully. This is partly due to a misapplication of the rule of reciprocity. People may let another person have his or her way if something is important to that person because they expect that they will get their way for things that are important to them. What the aggressive person does is to act forcefully in all situations. There is a cost to the aggressive style. People on the receiving end of the aggressive style feel resentment, act defensively, and try to withdraw from the situation.

There are some situations in which the aggressive style is appropriate. It might be needed in problem or emergency situations where forceful action is required. It also can be a valuable approach for dealing with blocked situations where no progress is being made. If there is resistance and if change is vital to the group, then aggressiveness might be the appropriate response.

Assertive Style

The assertive style uses clear and confident communication. No emotions are added to the messages. Assertiveness is communicating openly with concern for both others and oneself. It is taking responsibility for one's own communication. The assertive person takes a direct problem-solving approach to conflicts and problems. The goal is to find the best solution, so the person is willing to listen and compromise.

Although they are not always successful, assertive communicators generally are satisfied and relaxed about their performance. This style shows respect, encourages trust in others, and encourages open communication in a team. High self-esteem and trust in the group underlie the use of the assertive style.

The assertive approach is appropriate in most situations in which people are interacting on an equal basis. Therefore, it should be the most typical type of communication within a team. When it is not, that is a sign of unequal status differences that are disrupting communication or unresolved conflicts that are creating a defensive communication environment.

| USE OF POWER STYLES

Teams are more productive when their communication is primarily assertive (Lumsden & Lumsden, 1997). Both the passive and aggressive styles create resentment and inhibit open communication. Teams may adopt unproductive power styles for several reasons. For example, power styles trigger other power styles. An aggressive style triggers a passive response, whereas an assertive style triggers an assertive response. The use of a particular style also depends on the distribution of power and status in a team. Assertiveness is a power style used among people who have relatively equal power or status, whereas passiveness and aggressiveness are power styles used among people who have different amounts of power or status.

Differences in power styles often are attributed to personality, gender, or racial differences. This explanation rarely is true, and it gets in the way of improving team communication. For example, women often act more passively in business teams, thereby causing some men to assume that women are more passive. Kipnis (1976) shows that this has to do with organizational power, not gender. When men and women have equal power in a situation, there is not a tendency for women to act more passively.

Assertiveness is primarily a reflection of the distribution of power in a group. To encourage assertive problem-solving communication, the group needs to reduce power differences among its members. In an organization, people work in a hierarchy that gives everyone different amounts of power. However, when people are working in a team, they need to leave their organizational status at the door and treat their fellow team members as equals.

| ENCOURAGING ASSERTIVENESS

Assertiveness is the power style that is most appropriate for teamwork. The primary key to encouraging assertiveness is to equalize power among the team members. However, equalizing power might not be enough. People develop habits or patterns of communicating with others. It might be necessary to provide people with training in assertive communication (Alberti & Emmons, 1978). Assertiveness training programs use a number of techniques to encourage better communication in teams.

1. *Active listening:* Active listening is summarizing and repeating a speaker's message so as to ensure that it is understood. This technique clarifies the message, shows respect and attention, and encourages more communication.
2. *Positive recognition:* Learning how to give positive recognition to others can reduce the need for manipulative power tactics. Too often, high-status people criticize what they do not like but never acknowledge what they like. Positive recognition acknowledges someone's work and helps to encourage more of what one wants.
3. *Clear expectations:* Learning to state expectations clearly is another communication technique that encourages assertiveness. People often misinterpret behaviors as inappropriate or resistant when the behaviors really are caused by a lack of understanding of what is desired. Clarifying expectations lets everyone know what the issues are.
4. *Saying no:* For people who overuse the passive style, learning how to say no to inappropriate requests is an important skill to learn. Passive communicators often feel guilty when they turn down requests, thereby

encouraging them to agree to do something and then passively resist doing it.

5. *Assertive withdrawal:* Being assertive is not always the right response,
so people need to know when not to participate. When situations become
too emotionally heated or threatening, people need to learn how to give
clear messages of their desire to postpone or terminate conversations.

The use of these communication techniques helps to encourage assertive
communication. The power of teamwork comes from the ability of the team
members to communicate freely and work together. Assertiveness training
is one way in which to encourage this to happen.

SUMMARY

Power is the ability to change the attitudes, beliefs, and behaviors of others.
Groups have power because they can influence their members by providing
information that suggests how people should behave. Groups also exert social pressure to get members to conform to group norms. Group leaders have
the power to influence others through obedience to authority.

Power can be analyzed by examining where it comes from and the types
of techniques that are used. Group members gain power through personal
bases (e.g., being an expert) and positional bases (e.g., having authority
from the organization). Influence tactics can be based on encouraging others or trying to control others. People prefer to use their personal power
bases and cooperative tactics because these approaches are less likely to
create resistance.

The use of power by groups has several important dynamics. Having
power tends to corrupt the users. People who have power tend to use it and
take personal credit for the success of their groups, thereby encouraging
them to use power more often. Unequal power in teams, due to status differences among members, disrupts group communication. High-status people
talk more, people tend to agree with high-status people, and low-status people become reluctant to state their true opinions to the group. Minorities in
groups can be influential if they are consistent, self-confident, and autonomous. By resisting the influence of the majority, minorities focus their
groups' discussions on their positions. Interdependence among team members increases their power to influence each other.

One of the core notions of teamwork is empowerment. To be effective,
teams need to have power, authority, and responsibility to control their own

behaviors. Unfortunately, organizations often have trouble sharing managerial power with teams. Empowerment programs can range from the simple sharing of information with team members to the development of self-managing teams. Successful empowerment programs must deal with the perceived loss of power by supervisors and managers by incorporating them into the teams' activities.

Team members can act in a passive, aggressive, or assertive manner. These are personal power styles. Although there are situations in which acting passively or aggressively is appropriate, in most group situations assertiveness is the best approach. Assertiveness encourages clear communication and a rational approach to problems, but it is disrupted by unequal status in the group. There are several techniques to help train group members to act more assertively.

ACTIVITY: USING POWER STYLES—
PASSIVE, AGGRESSIVE, AND ASSERTIVE

Objective. There are three different power styles that team members can use. The nonassertive or passive style is polite and deferential. This approach tries to avoid problems by not taking a stand or by being unclear about one's position. The aggressive style is forceful, critical, and negative. This approach deals with problems and conflicts by trying to win. The assertive style uses clear and confident communication. The assertive person takes a direct problem-solving approach to conflicts and problems.

Activity. Observe the interactions in a team. Note whether team members are acting passively, aggressively, or assertively. Using Activity Worksheet 8.1, write down examples of passive, aggressive, and assertive behaviors that you observed. An alternative activity is to break into groups and take turns using the three power styles. Participants should analyze their own performance and that of others according to how each style feels and how people react to it.

Passive behavior: _____

Aggressive behavior: _____

Assertive behavior: _____

ACTIVITY WORKSHEET 8.1
Observing Passive, Aggressive, and Assertive Power Styles

	Team Member					
	1	*2*	*3*	*4*	*5*	*6*
Passive						
Aggressive						
Assertive						

Analysis. Which power style did the team use most often? Did certain team members adopt a similar power style for most communication? Was the team's various communication dominated by assertive communication or by passive/aggressive communication? Did the leader primarily use the assertive style?

Discussion. What triggers the use of a power style? Is it due to one's personality or to characteristics of the team? How could you encourage the team to have more equal-status assertive communication?

Chapter 9

DECISION MAKING

Decision making is one of the central activities of teams. One of the largest benefits of teams is their ability to bring together multiple skills and perspectives to make decisions. There are different approaches that teams can use to make decisions, from consultation to consensus. These approaches vary in speed, quality, and acceptance by team members.

Teams encounter a number of problems in trying to make good group decisions. Group polarization and "groupthink" are two examples of these problems. There are structured decision-making approaches that can help to improve the decision-making process. Although it might be difficult at first, learning how to make consensus decisions is an important skill for teams to develop.

➤ LEARNING OBJECTIVES

1. What are the main benefits of and problems with using groups to make decisions?
2. What factors cause group decisions to be superior to individual decisions?
3. How are consultative, democratic, and consensus decision making different?
4. What factors are useful for evaluating a decision-making approach?
5. How does the normative decision-making theory help teams to make decisions?
6. What factors disrupt the ability of groups to make good decisions?
7. How do group polarization and groupthink affect teams' decision-making process?

8. What are the benefits of and problems with structured decision-making techniques such as the nominal group technique?
9. How can teams improve their ability to achieve consensus decision making?

VALUE OF GROUP DECISION MAKING

Using groups to make decisions creates both benefits and problems for teams. Depending on the situation, group decisions may or may not be superior to individual decisions.

BENEFITS OF AND PROBLEMS WITH GROUP DECISION MAKING

A group brings more resources to a problem than are available to one person. Through group discussion, group members pool their knowledge. The interaction of group members leads to new ideas and insights that no single member would have developed (called *process gain*). Incorrect solutions are more likely to be identified and rejected. A group has a better memory of past facts and events, so it is less likely to repeat mistakes. Overall, group members combine different skills and knowledge to make higher quality decisions.

Group decision making also has motivational effects for the group members (Zander, 1994). Being part of a group encourages members to try to make a good decision and to try to perform better. They are more committed to a decision in which they participated, so they are more likely to support its implementation.

Group decision making affects the skills of the group members and the team as a whole. The members benefit by gaining a better understanding of the issues involved by participating in the discussion. These benefits are lost if decisions are forced on the group by the leader or an outside source. The team also benefits by learning how to make decisions. Over time, a team can become more efficient at decision making, thereby reducing many of the problems with group decision making.

The main problem with group decision making is that groups are less efficient at quick decision making because they suffer from process loss (Steiner, 1972). When groups enter into discussions, some of the discussions are about coordination and social issues. This "wasted" discussion time prevents groups from focusing solely on their tasks.

Groups also encounter many communication problems when trying to make decisions (DiSalvo, Nikkel, & Monroe, 1989). Group decision making requires skillful facilitation to be efficient, and some leaders and groups lack these skills. Decisions can get bogged down in emotional conflicts that waste time and hurt the morale of groups. Powerful team members or people who like to talk too much can dominate the discussions and disrupt groups' ability to make decisions. Finally, discussions can get sidetracked, get interrupted, or become disorganized.

One of the benefits of group discussions is the availability of information from the variety of experiences and skills of group members. However, group discussions are not necessarily good at incorporating this information. Analyses of group interactions show that information known by most of the group members is more likely to be discussed than is information held by specific individuals (Stasser & Titus, 1985). In other words, groups do not pool all of the knowledge available; they focus on the knowledge that is common to all of the members.

Finally, sometimes a group can work hard to make a decision when it is not really important (Zander, 1994). The group may be asked to make a decision, but it actually is only a recommendation, and the decision is to be made higher in the organization. This creates a sense of wasted time and effort in the group and may discourage future participation in the group.

| WHEN ARE GROUP DECISIONS SUPERIOR TO INDIVIDUAL DECISIONS?

Group decisions are better than individual decisions when there is successful pooling of resources to solve problems or make decisions. This successful pooling is affected by several factors. The first factor relates to group composition. Groups with heterogeneous members with complementary skills make for superior group decisions. Diversity of opinion is one of the major advantages of using groups (Wanous & Youtz, 1986). If a group is composed of similar members with identical skills and knowledge, then there is little benefit from making group decisions.

Second, successful group decision making assumes that good communication exists. Group decisions are better only if the discussion process successfully pools the knowledge and ideas of the group members. However, poor communication skills and problems with managing the group discussions can prevent groups from using their resources (DiSalvo et al., 1989).

A third factor relates to the need for groups to make decisions. Groups are needed for tasks that are too complex for one individual to perform or problems that are too difficult for one individual to solve. For a simple problem, the issue is whether anyone has the correct answer and whether the group will accept the correct answer. A simple problem does not require the group to spend time making a decision.

From these considerations, one can outline the types of situations in which individual decision making is better than group decision making. Individual decision making is better when the issue does not require action from most group members, the decision is so simple that coordination is not needed to implement it, or the decision has to be made quickly.

There also is another situation in which individuals often are superior to groups. On poorly structured tasks that require creative solutions, individuals often perform better than groups (Hill, 1982). The presence of other people can inhibit the creation of ideas and can distract people. (This creativity problem with groups, and how to solve it, is discussed in Chapter 12.)

APPROACHES TO GROUP DECISION MAKING

When thinking about how to make decisions, groups often decide to vote. However, this can be a problem. There are a variety of methods groups can use to make decisions, and it is important to use the type of decision-making process best suited to the problem. Not all problems need full participation and group decisions, and sometimes voting can create problems rather than solve them. For important decisions, groups might need to reach consensus.

The options that teams can use to make decisions may be viewed as lying along a continuum, from leader-based decisions to decisions made with full participation of the team (Johnson & Johnson, 1997). These options are shown in Table 9.1. Although there are many approaches that a team could use, teams typically use either consultative, democratic, or consensus decision making.

In *consultative* decision making, one person has authority to make the decision, but he or she may ask for advice and comments from team members before deciding. This style of decision making often is used in a team when a project is divided into parts and one person has responsibility to do a part. That person may ask for advice and might need to coordinate with others, but if it primarily affects his or her part of the project, then that person makes the final decision. The consultative approach also may be used in a work group when the leader has management authority and responsibility for the group's decision.

TABLE 9.1
Approaches to Group Decision Making

Leader-oriented	Leader decides
	Leader assigns expert to make the decision
	Consultative: Leader consults with team and then decides
Group technique	Mathematical techniques (averaging)
	Structured decision techniques (e.g., nominal group technique)
	Democratic: Voting with majority rules
Full participation	Consensus

The consultative approach uses only some of the resources of the team. Its disadvantages are that it does not fully develop commitment to a decision, does not resolve conflicts among team members, and may encourage competition among team members to influence the leader. However, it is a very efficient decision-making approach (it takes little time to complete), and it can provide the leader with crucial information to help make a decision.

In *democratic* decision making, voting to make a decision is the most popular style, but it is not really a good team approach. The problem with a democratic decision is that nearly half of the people could disagree, and they might be unwilling to support and implement the decision after it has been made (Castore & Murnighan, 1978).

One of the major advantages of the democratic approach is that it is a quick way in which to include the opinions of all team members. However, it can prematurely close discussion on an issue that has not been fully resolved. This can lead to a lack of commitment from the losing minority. Because there are winners and losers, voting can create resentment among team members. It can be useful for relatively unimportant decisions that have limited conflict and implementation issues.

The *consensus* approach to decision making requires discussion of an issue until all members agree to accept it. By acceptance, this does not mean that the decision is one's favorite alternative. It means that one is willing to accept and support the decision.

Consensus decision making might be time-consuming, but it is the best way in which to fully use the resources of the team. When successful, it also improves the operation of the team. The consensus approach should be used for important decisions that require the full support of the team for implementation. It takes time, energy, and skill to reach consensus, but consensus decisions have a greater likelihood of being implemented by the team.

In a sample of work teams in more than 100 companies, Devine, Clayton, Philips, Dunford, and Melner (1999) found that most (62%) of the teams used consensus decision making. In the other teams, decisions were made by the leaders or managers (25%) or by voting (13%). The use of consensus decision making was positively related to team effectiveness for all types of teams, whereas the use of leader-based decisions and voting was either neutral or negatively related to effectiveness depending on the type of team.

| EVALUATING GROUP DECISION-MAKING APPROACHES

The primary criteria for evaluating a decision-making approach are quality, speed, and acceptance or support (Johnson & Johnson, 1997). A good decision-making approach should use the resources of the team to make a high-quality decision. The decision-making process should reflect efficient time management. Once a decision has been made, the members of the team should be willing to accept it and support its implementation. The importance of these three criteria varies depending on the problem or situation. For example, in an emergency situation, time is very important and acceptance is less important because people often are willing to support any decision.

In general, decision-making techniques that include group discussion and participation lead to higher quality decisions. This is especially true if the problems are complex or unstructured or if the leaders do not have enough information to make good decisions. However, for some issues, good leaders can make high-quality decisions alone. The importance of quality as a decision criterion also varies. Some issues are relatively trivial, so high-quality decisions are not necessary. In these cases, having leaders make the decisions saves time for groups.

Group decision making is slower than individual decision making, but the importance of speed as a criterion varies. In many cases, the issue is not speed but, rather, prioritizing the decisions that a team needs to make. Some decisions are important and need to be made quickly, whereas other decisions should be put off until the team gathers more information. Teams often spend too much time on unimportant decisions and not enough time on the important ones.

The third factor is acceptance. To the extent that a decision requires the support and acceptance of the team members so as to implement it, the decision should include input from the team members (Murnighan, 1981). Teams often use decision-making techniques (e.g., voting, averaging) to speed up the decision-making process, but these techniques can limit the amount of acceptance of the decisions. When acceptance is important, teams should use either consensus decision making or a voting approach that requires more than the majority to adopt the decisions.

These three evaluation criteria are interrelated. The relationship between quality and speed is fairly obvious. When more time is available to make a decision, there also is more time for gathering information and analyzing it. Groups require more process time than do individuals, so the benefits of group decision making require more time than do those of individual decision making.

Speed and acceptance also are related. In comparing Japanese and U.S. decision making, one finds that the U.S. organizations make decisions faster. However, when implementation is considered, the U.S. organizations are both slower and more likely to fail. In Japanese organizations, final decisions are not made until the organizations have gained commitment to implement the decisions from all relevant participants. Once they make decisions, they are quickly able to implement them.

| NORMATIVE DECISION-MAKING THEORY

How should a team leader choose how to make a decision? There are both benefits of and problems with the consultative, democratic, and consensus approaches. It is difficult to sort out these factors and determine the best approach for a team. *Normative decision-making theory* addresses this problem (Vroom & Jago, 1988; Vroom & Yetton, 1973). It is a leadership theory that can be used by teams to help them with their decision-making problems.

Normative decision-making theory is based on the assumption that the best type of decision-making approach depends on the nature of the problem. The problem determines how important time, quality, and acceptance are in reaching a decision. Once the nature of the problem is understood, the best decision-making approach can be selected. This theory typically is used by the leader to analyze a problem to determine the best decision-making approach.

The analysis of the problem focuses on two issues: whether a quality decision is important and whether acceptance of the decision by subordinates is important. To predict the quality of the decision, the leader needs to understand whether a high-quality decision is important and whether the group members are able to make a good decision by themselves. To predict acceptance of the decision, the leader needs to determine whether acceptance by subordinates is crucial for implementing the decision and whether the group generally agrees with the approach of the leader. These considerations form seven questions that are used to analyze a problem (Table 9.2).

Once a leader analyzes the nature of a problem, a decision tree is used to tell the leader whether to use an autocratic, consultative, democratic, or consensus approach to decision making. In general, the leader should use more group-oriented approaches (e.g., democratic, consensus) when a high-quality decision is needed or when team acceptance is needed to implement the decision. Research testing the theory has been fairly supportive, although the results are dependent on the decision-making skills of the leader. (It does not work to tell a team leader to use consensus decision making if the leader does not have the skills to facilitate the decision-making process.)

The normative decision-making theory makes some important points about group decision making. When the decision is important and requires support to implement, the decision-making process should be group oriented. However, when the decision is trivial and just needs to be made, it is a waste of the team's time to discuss it. Often, people believe that democratic or consensus decision making is better for value reasons, but this can lead to a team wasting too much time on trivial issues. One important function of the team leader is to manage the situation. The leader handles the minor and administrative decisions so that the team has the time to focus on the important issues.

DECISION-MAKING PROBLEMS

There are many different types of problems that can disrupt a team's ability to make a good decision. Disagreement, time pressure, and external stress can cause these problems. Group polarization can affect a group decision by making the result more extreme due to interpersonal processes. Groupthink describes a number of group decision-making flaws caused by the group's desire to maintain good relations rather than to make the best decision.

TABLE 9.2
Questions for Analyzing a Problem

1. Is a high-quality decision required?
2. Do I have enough information to make such a decision?
3. Is the problem structured?
4. Is it crucial for implementation that subordinates accept the decision?
5. If I make the decision alone, is it likely to be accepted by my subordinates?
6. Do subordinates share the goals that will be reached through the solution of this problem?
7. Do subordinates disagree about the appropriate method for attaining the goals so that conflict will result from the decision?

SOURCE: Adapted from Vroom and Yetton (1973).

| CAUSES OF GROUP DECISION-MAKING PROBLEMS

Disagreements

Probably the most common group decision-making problem is premature closure, that is, trying to avoid disagreement by voting to make a quick decision. This technique works for making the decision, but it often leads to implementation problems later. Politics, a domineering leader, hidden agendas, poor norms, and other factors can cause disagreements. Many of these problems relate to the group process rather than to the topic of the decision. When the discussion of the decision gets disrupted by these problems, the group needs to focus on improving its internal communication.

Too little disagreement also can be a problem. Disagreement helps stimulate thinking and leads to better decisions. Research shows that group discussions with some disagreement lead to better decisions than do conflict-free group discussions (Schwenk, 1990). However, these constructive conflicts come at a cost. Group discussions with substantial disagreement are rated as less satisfying experiences by group members and reduce interest in continuing to interact with the group.

Time Pressure to Decide

Groups respond to time pressure by trying to make quick decisions. To do this, they often use decision-making approaches that are simple and inadequate (Zander, 1994). For example, a group may support the first useful suggestion and ignore or prevent further discussion of alternatives. A group may select a plan that has worked in the past without adequately examining whether it is applicable to the current situation. Finally, a group may delegate the decision to the leader or a group member, thereby forgoing the benefits of a group analysis and decision.

Outside Stress

Stress from outside a team can lead to poor decision making. This occurs when outside forces pressure the group for a decision. These outside forces could be external competition, upper management, or other parts of the organization. When a group experiences stress, it often becomes more cohesive. However, this can lead to groupthink or allowing the leader to make the decision. Stress disrupts the decision-making process by reducing the number of ideas generated and the amount of criticism and analysis of issues. It can cause a desire to make decisions more quickly so as to reduce uncertainty, thereby rushing the decision-making process. All of this leads to poor-quality decisions.

| GROUP POLARIZATION

Although one might expect that the outcome of a group discussion would lead to a decision that is close to the average of the group's initial position, this is not the case. The effect of a group discussion is to make the final decision more extreme than the average of the members. This can be either more risky or more cautious, depending on the initial inclination of the group. This phenomenon is called *group polarization.*

Original research by Stoner (1961) showed that groups made riskier decisions than did individuals. This was called the *risky shift* phenomenon. However, subsequent research showed that this actually was an intensification effect. Groups tend to move toward an extreme and become either more risk oriented or more conservative (Myers & Lamm, 1976). The group polarization effect occurs only when the group has an initial tendency, not when there are major differences of opinion among the members. There are several explanations for group polarization that examine the role of normative and informational influences.

Normative influence describes how the existing group norm affects the decision-making process. Group members want to create a favorable impression, so they compare their answers to the group's norm and then shift their positions to be more consistent with it (Myers & Lamm, 1976). The group norm shifts as members shift their positions in an attempt to be more typical of the group's position. The combined effect of these shifts is to move the group decision more to the extreme. This is especially important when the decision is primarily a matter of values or preferences.

Information influence is caused by the amount of exposure to information during a group discussion. When a group discusses an issue, most of the discussion is from the dominant position. Therefore, group members are more exposed to arguments supporting the dominant position, so they shift their opinions in that direction (Burnstein & Vinokur, 1977).

| GROUPTHINK

One of the most famous types of group decision-making problems is *groupthink,* a term coined by Janis (1972). Janis used the analysis of historical decisions, such as the Cuban missile crisis of the 1960s, to show how decision-making processes can go wrong. Groupthink occurs when group members' desire to maintain good relations becomes more important than reaching a good decision. Instead of searching for a good answer, they search for outcome that will preserve group harmony. This leads to a bad decision that is accompanied by other actions designed to insulate the group from corrective feedback. Since the initial identification of groupthink, researchers have expanded on the causes and implications of the phenomenon (Table 9.3).

Research has shown that there are three main factors that contribute to groupthink: structural decision-making flaws, group cohesiveness, and external pressure (Parks & Sanna, 1999). *Structural decision-making flaws* create bad decisions because they impair the group decision-making process. These flaws include the ignoring of input from outside sources, a lack of diversity in viewpoints within the group, the acceptance of decisions without critical analysis, and a history of accepting the decisions made by the leader. *Group cohesiveness* encourages groupthink by creating an environment that limits internal dissension and criticism. Pressure from the outside for a decision limits discussion time and encourages the group to support the first plausible option presented to the members. The *external pressure* that the group experiences leads to a set of symptoms that show

TABLE 9.3
Model of Groupthink

Antecedent conditions	Structural: Domineering leader and limited input from outside of the group Cohesiveness: Desire to maintain good relations is dominant Stress: Outside forces put stress on the group to make a decision
Symptoms	Illusion of invulnerability: Belief that the group's decision will work Collective rationalization: Group members support each other's ideas Belief in morality of the group: Belief that the group's actions are inherently right Direct pressure on dissenters: Suppression of negative comments in group discussion Stereotypes of out-groups: Overestimation of the group's superiority compared to others Self-censorship: Group members do not state their opinions if they differ from the group's position Illusion of unanimity: Belief that everyone agrees with the decision Self-appointed mind guards: Group members protect the leader and group from negative information about the decision
Decision defects	Group considers only a few alternatives when making a decision Group fails to examine the adverse consequences of its decision Alternatives are eliminated without careful consideration Group does not seek the advice of outside experts Group does not consider what to do if the decision does not work

SOURCE: Adapted from Janis (1972).

that groupthink is occurring. These symptoms indicate how the group convinces itself that it has made a good decision and that everyone in the group agrees with it. Consequently, there is pressure on the members not to voice their concerns and objections. The collective effect of these symptoms is a poorly selected decision that is made without considering alternative options or the longer term consequences of the decision.

A number of techniques have been proposed to prevent groupthink. A group can create the role of *critical evaluator* to comment on the group's decisions and processes. Group members can be asked to discuss the alternatives with experts outside the group, especially people who might not agree with the direction in which the group is going. After a decision has been made, the group should schedule another meeting to examine remaining doubts about it.

DECISION-MAKING TECHNIQUES

Several decision-making techniques have been developed to manage group decision-making problems. These techniques structure the decision-making process with a set of process rules. They are technically good approaches but sometimes appear like magic to the users. An answer appears that represents the group's opinion even though the group never has discussed the issues.

| NOMINAL GROUP TECHNIQUE

The *nominal group* technique is a decision-making technique that allows a group of people to focus on the task of making a decision without developing any social relations. It is called *nominal* because it does not require a true group; it can be used by a collection of people who are brought together to make a decision.

When using this technique, the leader states the problem to the group. People write down their solutions to the problem in private. Then, each person publicly states his or her answer, and the answers are recorded so that everyone can see them. Group members can ask questions to clarify the positions of others, but they cannot criticize the ideas. The participants then use a rank-ordering procedure to rate the values of the solutions. This rank ordering is used to select the group's preferred solution.

The advantage of the nominal group technique is that it is relatively quick, discourages pressure to conform, and does not require the group members to get to know each other before the decision-making process (Delbecq, Van de Ven, & Gustafson, 1975). However, it requires a trained facilitator to conduct it and can address only one narrowly defined problem at a time.

| DELPHI TECHNIQUE

The *Delphi* technique uses a series of written surveys to make a decision (Dalkey, 1969). A group of experts is given a survey that contains several open-ended questions about the problem to be solved. The results of this survey are summarized and organized into a set of proposed solutions. This is sent back to the participants, who are then asked to comment on the solutions from the first survey. This process is repeated until the participants start to reach consensus on a solution to the problem.

The Delphi approach is useful when it is necessary to include a specific set of people in a decision but those people are distributed geographically and cannot meet in a group (Delbecq et al., 1975). The number of people involved makes no difference, so a large group of people could participate at the same time. This approach also is useful when there is a large amount of disagreement on an issue that requires subjective judgments to resolve. However, the process takes a lot of time (more than a month for a typical decision) and requires skills in developing and analyzing surveys.

| RINGI TECHNIQUE

The *Ringi* technique is a Japanese decision-making technique that is used for dealing with controversial topics (Rohlen, 1975). It allows a group to deal with conflict while avoiding a face-to-face confrontation. (Face-to-face confrontations are considered inappropriate in Japanese culture.) In this approach, a written document that presents the issue and its resolution is developed anonymously. This document is circulated among group members, who individually write comments, edit the document, and then send it to other group members. After completing a cycle, the comments are used to rewrite the document, and it is recirculated among the group again. This process continues until group members stop writing comments on the draft.

The Ringi approach can be a slow process, and there is no guarantee that the group will come to agreement in this way. However, anonymous comments allow everyone to state their true beliefs while avoiding embarrassing others in a confrontation.

| EVALUATION OF DECISION-MAKING TECHNIQUES

These techniques structure the group decision-making process to eliminate all but task-oriented communication among group members. The Delphi and Ringi techniques use only written communication. The nominal group technique requires each group member to generate ideas independently and then to interact only to choose among alternative ideas. This structuring of the decision-making process allows decisions to be made by larger groups of people who do not have to meet. Research on the effectiveness of these approaches shows that they can produce decisions that are as good as, or better than, decisions produced from group discussions and can do so with less productivity losses. In addition, people are satisfied with their levels of participation with these approaches (Van de Ven & Delbecq, 1974).

However, these techniques are based on the assumption that socializing, unequal participation, and other aspects of group discussions are problems. Not all group researchers agree on this point (McGrath, 1984). These other aspects of the group process may have significant benefits. The detached and impersonal atmosphere of these decision-making techniques reduces people's acceptance and commitment to a decision. In addition, the political acceptability of the solution might not be as sensitive to the organization as a solution produced by a group discussion, which typically is dominated by the higher status participants.

APPLICATION: CONSENSUS DECISION MAKING

Consensus decision making uses all of a team's resources fully, encourages support for implementation of decisions, and helps to build the skills of the team. Consensus decision making is a slow process because people typically are not good at doing it. A team should practice consensus decision making to improve its decision-making skills so that when important problems arise, the team has the ability to handle the problems effectively. This is a developmental process; learning to do consensus decision making increases the team's ability to use it.

Reaching consensus does not mean that every team member believes that the solution is best (Hackett & Martin, 1993). Consensus is achieved when each team member can say (or nod) yes to the following types of questions:

- Will you agree that this is what the team should do next?
- Can you go along with this position?
- Can you support this alternative?

In other words, a team can support the position or decision 100% even though not all members totally agree with the position. Consensus is the voluntary giving of consent.

A team leader or facilitator can help get consensus through a number of techniques. The team needs to be given adequate time to work through an issue. Conflict should be viewed as inevitable, so team members need to be encouraged not to give in just to avoid conflict. Flipping coins or voting when differences emerge is not an acceptable alternative. The team members also need to recognize that giving in on a point is not losing and that gaining is not winning. The goal is to negotiate a collaborative solution, not to beat the other side in a debate. Table 9.4 presents some guidelines that can be given to team members to help them reach consensus.

If a group gets stuck trying to reach consensus, there are several options that it can use to escape the impasse. The team can agree to not agree and then move on to a related issue. Changing topics and returning to an issue later can help by reducing the emotional tension created during a conflict. If a decision must be made quickly, then the team can decide that it must use an alternative such as voting. Or, it can decide to develop a compromise solution in which each side gives in on part of its demands. When time is available, the team might ask for outside guidance, input, or help.

SUMMARY

The largest benefit of group decision making is the ability to bring more resources to help solve a problem. It also helps to motivate team members and develop their skills. However, group decision making takes time and does not always succeed. Group decisions are better than individual decisions when the team has a diversity of perspectives, the discussion is open, and the problem is suitable for a group.

The main approaches to group decision making are the consultative, democratic, and consensus approaches. These approaches vary in the amounts of time required, the quality of the decisions, and the amounts of support for implementation. The best decision-making approach depends on the nature of the problem. The normative decision-making theory provides a way in which to analyze problems to help determine the best decision-making approach.

A team's ability to make a decision can be disrupted by too much or too little conflict, pressure to decide quickly, outside stress, and unequal status among the team members. Group decisions also tend to be more extreme than individual decisions because of the group polarization effect. The desire to maintain good relations within the group can disrupt the group

TABLE 9.4
Guidelines to Help Reach Consensus

1. Avoid arguing for your own position without listening to the positions of others.
2. Do not change your position just to avoid conflict.
3. Do not try to reach a quick agreement by using a conflict reduction approach such as voting or flipping a coin.
4. Try to get others to explain their positions so that you better understand the differences.
5. Do not assume that someone must win and someone must lose when there is a disagreement.
6. Discuss the underlying assumptions, listen carefully to others, and encourage the participation of all members.
7. Look for creative and collaborative solutions that allow both sides to win rather than compromises in which each side gets only some of what it wants.

SOURCE: D. W. Johnson & F. P. Johnson (1997), *Joining Together: Group Theory and Group Skills*, 6th ed., by Allyn & Bacon. Reprinted/adapted by permission.

decision-making process and cause groupthink. Groupthink leads to inadequate decisions that are strongly defended by the group members.

Several structured techniques for decision making have been developed to manage certain problem situations. The nominal group technique can be used in large groups with limited social interaction. The Delphi technique uses a series of surveys for decision making so that it can be used with large groups that never actually meet. The Ringi technique is a Japanese approach that helps to avoid confrontations in the decision-making process. These techniques gain efficiency by structuring the decision-making process, but they may reduce support for the decision due to a decreased sense of participation.

Consensus decision making is the approach that best uses the resources of a team. There are a number of techniques that can be learned to help improve the team's ability to make consensus decisions.

ACTIVITY: CONSENSUS DECISION MAKING

Objective. Consensus decision making requires discussing an issue until all agree to accept it. By acceptance, this does not mean that the decision is one's favorite alternative. It means that one is willing to accept and support the decision. Learning how to do consensus decision making is an important skill for a team.

Activity. Form a group and have it develop consensus answers to the following questions:

- What is the most important skill for a team member to possess?
- What is the most important characteristic of a good team leader?
- What is the largest benefit of using teamwork?
- What is the largest problem with using teamwork?

While the group is trying to reach consensus, have an observer use Activity Worksheet 9.1 to note whether the group follows the "Guidelines to Help Reach Consensus" presented in Table 9.4.

Analysis. Was the group successful at reaching consensus for its decisions? Did the group follow the guidelines for consensus decision making?

Discussion. What advice could you give a team to improve its ability to make consensus decisions?

ACTIVITY WORKSHEET 9.1
Observing the Guidelines to Help Reach Consensus

Did the Team Follow the Guidelines Presented Below?	*Yes*	*No*
1. Avoid arguing for your own position without listening to the positions of others.		
2. Do not change your position just to avoid conflict.		
3. Do not try to reach a quick agreement by using a conflict reduction approach such as voting or flipping a coin.		
4. Try to get others to explain their positions so that you better understand the differences.		
5. Do not assume that someone must win and someone must lose when there is a disagreement.		
6. Discuss the underlying assumptions, listen carefully to others, and encourage the participation of all members.		
7. Look for creative and collaborative solutions that allow both sides to win rather than compromises in which each side gets only some of what it wants.		

Chapter 10

LEADERSHIP

A team has many ways of selecting a leader and assigning leadership roles. The leader can be assigned by the organization, the team can be self-managing, or the leadership roles can be distributed among the team members. What is the best style of leadership? There is no definitive answer to this question, but many approaches have been suggested. Situational leadership theory is one approach to help the leader decide the best way in which to act depending on the readiness level of the team.

Organizations are experimenting with new forms of team leadership. In self-managing teams, many of the leadership functions are turned over to the teams. Self-managing teams provide a variety of benefits, but they require the development of group process skills and social relations to operate effectively. In addition, leadership of teams might require new skills and responsibilities compared to those of traditional leadership approaches.

▶▶ *LEARNING OBJECTIVES*

1. How do leaders vary by the roles they perform and the amount of power they possess?
2. What factors influence who becomes a team's leader?
3. What are the different types of leadership that a team can have?
4. What are the main approaches to studying leadership, and what are their implications?
5. What are some of the substitutes that reduce the importance of leadership?
6. What is situational leadership theory? How does a leader's behavior relate to the readiness level of the group?

7. What are the benefits of and problems with self-managing teams?
8. What are the functional roles and responsibilities of team leaders?

ALTERNATIVE DESIGNS OF LEADERSHIP FOR TEAMS

Leadership is a process in which an individual influences the progress of other group members toward the attainment of a goal. Teams can have a variety of types of leaders that vary by how they are selected and the roles they perform. The person who emerges as the leader of a team might not be the one best suited for the role. Although most teams have designated leaders, the use of self-managing teams provides an alternative to the traditional approach.

CHARACTERISTICS OF TEAM LEADERSHIP

Although we normally think of a single individual holding the position of a leader, this is not always the case. Rather than talking about leadership as a single person, we need to recognize that teams have a variety of leader roles that can be filled in different ways. Teams vary in their types of leaders, the distribution of leadership roles, and the amounts of power their leaders have.

Teams can have a variety of types of leaders. There are leaderless groups, teams with leaders assigned by their organizations, teams that select their own leaders, and self-managing teams. Most teams have one person assigned to the role of leader. A team leader can be selected in several ways. The leader can be selected by the organization and assigned to the team, the leader can be elected by the team, or the leadership position can be rotated among the team members. A team also can start out sharing and rotating the leadership functions until a leader emerges from the team's interactions.

Rather than centralizing the roles of leadership, a team's leadership roles can be divided based on the different tasks that the team performs. Many teams use the STAR (situation or task, action, result) structure for distributing leadership functions (Wellins, Byham, & Wilson, 1991). The team's task is divided into specific functions, and the responsibilities for each function are assigned to a team member to perform. Team members may be rotated through the different roles so as to develop the skills within the team. For example, a factory team may divide its task into quality, safety, maintenance, supplies, and administration. Rather than the team leader being responsible for all of these functions, one team member may be responsible for each function.

Leaders also vary in how much power or authority they possess. When a leader is assigned by an organization, the leader may have the responsibility and authority to make the team's decisions. It is then up to the leader to decide how decisions should be made. When the leader is elected or rotated, he or she typically has limited power and serves primarily as the facilitator of the group process. A designated leader with organizational power may be important when the task is very complex and structure is needed, when there is a lot of potential conflict among team members, and/or when someone is needed to manage the relationship between the team and other parts of the organization (Lumsden & Lumsden, 1997).

A team leader is not the same as a manager. A manager is given power and authority by the organization over subordinates, whereas a team leader typically does not have this type of power. A manager is responsible for the actions of his or her subordinates, whereas it is the team (and not the leader) that is responsible for the actions of its members. A manager has the authority to make decisions, whereas a team leader facilitates decisions rather than make them alone. Finally, a manager is responsible for handling personnel issues (e.g., employee hiring, evaluation, reward), whereas an organization typically does not give a team leader the authority to perform these personnel functions.

| LEADER EMERGENCE

When no leader is assigned to a group, a leader emerges from the group to help coordinate its actions (Hemphill, 1961). Research on who becomes the leader shows that becoming a leader is not necessarily related to being an effective leader. Stogdill (1974), in a meta-analysis of leadership research, shows that leaders tend to be taller and older than their followers, but these characteristics are not related to effectiveness. Men are five times more likely than women to be group leaders (Walker, Ilardi, McMahon, & Fennell, 1996). However, gender does not relate to leader effectiveness (Eagly, Karau, & Makhijani, 1995). Studies of military teams show that leaders have more physical ability and better task performance skills (Rice, Instone, & Adams, 1984). Although task skills relate somewhat to leader effectiveness, physical ability has little relationship to effectiveness.

The most important predictor of who a group selects as its leader is the participation rate (sometimes called the "babble effect"). Group members are more likely to select the most frequent communicator as the leader (Mullen, Salas, & Driskell, 1989). Unfortunately, the quantity of communication is more important than quality for leadership selection. It appears that people who communicate frequently demonstrate active involvement and interest in the group, and this implies a willingness to work with the group members.

Another way in which to explain the emergence of leaders with characteristics not related to effective leadership is with *leader prototype theory* (Lord, 1985). This theory examines the relationship between the leader and the perceptions of the group members. Members have certain implicit notions about what a good leader is like. To the extent that the leader meets these expectations, the leader is more influential. Although the specific traits of good leadership vary in the minds of followers, effective leaders usually are assumed to be intelligent, be dedicated, and have good communication skills.

Leadership prototype theory can be used to explain some of the problems with the ways in which team members select leaders. Members rely on their prototypes to decide who should be their leaders. Unfortunately, members' prototypes of good leaders are not necessarily accurate. For example, gender differences in leadership may be due to how gender stereotypes relate to prototypes about leaders. The typical female stereotype emphasizes expressive qualities such as emotion and warmth, whereas the typical male stereotype emphasizes instrumental qualities such as productivity and power (Williams & Best, 1990). Although both expressive and instrumental qualities are needed in leaders, members tend to emphasize the importance of instrumental qualities (Nye & Forsyth, 1991). This causes team members to view males as more likely candidates for being leaders and to see male behaviors as more important for leaders.

| LEADERSHIP OPTIONS FOR TEAMS

The most common form of leadership for a team is the designation of a leader by the organization. This designation gives the leader formal authority and power in the team. However, the leader is not always the most capable person in all areas, so some of the leadership roles may be taken over by other members. For example, a leader may be selected because of his or her technical skills, so other team members might be needed to handle the group process facilitation aspects of team leadership. In a traditional work group, the leader maintains control over most of the group's decisions. Because the leadership often is autocratic, the work group does not experience autonomy, so it often fails to improve productivity, quality, and morale (Stewart & Manz, 1995).

The main alternative to a designated leader is a self-managing team. In a self-managing team, there is no leader with organizational authority, and decisions are made by consensus. In this type of team, the leader is a facilitator who manages the team's decision-making process (and sometimes other administrative tasks) rather than serving as the manager of the group. The idea of self-managing teams became popular during the 1980s as a way in which to manage factory work teams, but the idea has spread to other types of teams.

Self-managing teams can have two types of leadership: power-building leadership and empowered leadership (Stewart & Manz, 1995). In *power-building* leadership, the leader is an active, democratic-oriented person who teaches the group team skills and guides team-building efforts. The leader provides structure, helps coordinate the team, and encourages and rewards good performance. Through the use of delegation and democratic decision making, the skills and abilities of the team grow. However, the leader retains control over team behaviors and long-term strategic direction. Under this type of leadership, self-managing teams develop skills and typically improve performance, quality, and morale.

Empowered leadership is a more passive form of democratic leadership. The leader operates as a facilitator but does not control the team's work processes or major decisions. The team is truly self-governing. Even in this situation, there are important leadership roles. The leader models appropriate behavior, helps to promote learning and skills development, and deals with issues outside the team. This type of leadership is the most effective for improving performance, quality, and morale. However, it requires a highly skilled and well-developed team. In many cases, organizations that want to create self-managing teams must go through the stage of power-building leadership before they can make the transition to empowered leadership.

APPROACHES TO LEADERSHIP

Leadership is a topic that most people believe is very important, and it has been the subject of an immense amount of research. However, we do not understand leadership very well. There are some difficult problems with doing research on leadership that cause this dilemma. The fact that people believe that leadership is important does not make it true (Meindl & Ehrlich, 1987).

Rather than there being one best type of leader, different types of leaders are useful in different situations, and leaders are more important in some situations than in others.

The research on leadership can be divided into four historical approaches that have different implications for organizations and teams (Table 10.1). The *trait* or *personality* approach is based on the belief that good leaders have certain characteristics. If this is true, then personality tests could be used to identify and select good leaders. An alternative is the *behavioral* approach that defines leadership by the ways in which leaders act. This approach attempts to determine what good leaders do so that people can be trained to be good leaders. The *situational* approach questions the necessity of leadership. It attempts to determine when leaders are needed and what factors can substitute for leadership. The final approach is the *contingency* approach, which attempts to combine personality or behavioral characteristics of leaders with situational characteristics. For example, it might be impossible to say what a good leader does, but it might be possible to define good leadership in an emergency situation.

| TRAIT OR PERSONALITY APPROACH

Historically, the trait approach is the oldest model of leadership, with hundreds of studies conducted during the 1930s and 1940s (Yukl, 1989). It assumes that good leaders have a certain set of characteristics. If one identifies and measures these characteristics, then one would know how to select good leaders.

Over the years, many traits have been examined, and most research has failed to confirm a strong relationship between traits and leadership (Kirkpatrick & Locke, 1991). Some of the more recent research suggests that sets of traits are associated with good leadership. For example, effective leaders have more drive, honesty, leadership motivation, self-confidence, intelligence, knowledge of business, creativity, and flexibility. No one trait can predict good leadership, but effective leaders do differ from typical followers in exhibiting higher levels of these characteristics overall. The basic problem is that people who are successful leaders in one situation (e.g., business) are not necessarily successful leaders in other situations (e.g., politics, religion).

A good example of the problem with the trait approach is the value of intelligence. Good leaders should be intelligent. This seems like an obvious

---

TABLE 10.1
Models of Leadership

Model	Implication
Trait or personality	Use tests to select good leaders
Behavioral	Train people to be good leaders
Situational	Understand substitutes for leadership
Contingency	Link traits or behaviors to situations

statement, but is it true? Are the most intelligent people the best leaders? Are the smartest U.S. presidents the most effective ones? Would most college professors make great business leaders? It is true that good leaders tend to be more intelligent than average people, but leaders are not necessarily the most intelligent people in their organizations. In addition, the importance of intelligence varies. In a dictatorship (e.g., the military), intelligence is an important characteristic of good leaders. In a democracy (e.g., local politics), good leaders need to be able to easily relate to others and have good communication skills. These communication skills are more important than intelligence.

Motivation is another example of the problem with the trait approach. Successful leaders are motivated, but what type of motivation is important? The difference between successful entrepreneurs of small businesses and managers of large companies is not a difference in the amount of motivation; rather, it is a difference in the type of motivation. Successful managers in large organizations have a strong need for power and a moderately strong need for achievement (McClelland & Boyatzis, 1982). The power motivation of these managers is focused on building their organizations and empowering their subordinates rather than on gaining personal power and control. By contrast, successful entrepreneurs have a high need for achievement and independence and a less strong need for power.

Flexibility, or the ability to adapt to the situation, is considered an important characteristic of good leaders. Obviously, not all situations require the same approach given that we also like consistency and leaders who stand for things. We malign politicians who are too influenced by the public opinion polls, but that is a flexible approach to leadership. Clearly, we do not want too much flexibility in our leaders.

| BEHAVIORAL APPROACH

The behavioral approach defines leadership as a set of appropriate behaviors. The goal of this approach is to define how good leaders act so that people can be trained to be good leaders. Rather than focusing on issues such as intelligence and creativity, most of the research on leader behavior focuses on two issues: decision-making style and task focus versus social focus of the leader.

The decision-making approach has primarily examined the benefits of authoritarian leadership compared to those of democratic leadership. During recent years, this research has included other forms such as consultative and consensus decision making. As was noted in Chapter 9, there is no one best way in which to make a decision. The best type of decision-making approach depends on the situation or problem (Vroom & Jago, 1988).

Research in this area has demonstrated some of the problems and benefits of different decision-making approaches. Democratic leaders tend to create followers with higher morale, job satisfaction, and commitment. However, democratic decision making can be slow, and leaders can be viewed as weak. Autocratic leaders tend to be more efficient decision makers, but this style can create dissatisfaction and implementation problems among the followers.

Behavioral research also examines whether leaders should focus on the tasks or the social relations among the group members (Likert, 1961). Is a leader's primary role to organize and manage the task, or should the leader help to ensure that social relations are good, group members feel satisfied and motivated, and the group can maintain itself? Research in this area has been contradictory and inconclusive except for the finding that group members like leaders who show social consideration (Yukl, 1989).

As with the decision-making style issue, the correct answer here depends on the situation. If a team is performing a routine task, then the leader should focus on social relations because the team does not need help with the task. If a project team is working on a difficult problem, then a good leader helps the team to better understand and make decisions about the task. If a team is capable of self-management, then the leader should ignore both task and social issues and focus on concerns outside the team.

One new example of the behavioral approach to leadership is the *leader-member exchange model*. This approach looks inside a work group to see how the leader and subordinates interact (Graen & Uhl-Bien, 1995). Leaders form different types of relationships with subordinates, and this creates in-groups and out-groups. In-group members get more attention from leaders and more resources to perform their jobs. Consequently, they are more productive and more satisfied than out-group members. This distinction is made by leaders early in the relationship and is based on little information about the subordinates. Sometimes, it also is influenced by irrelevant factors such as similarity, personality, and attraction rather than by actual performance. The importance of this perspective is the recognition that a team contains a variety of individuals. A leader does not treat everyone the same, and a leader may be performing effectively with some team members but ineffectively with others.

| SITUATIONAL APPROACH

Are leaders really important to the success of teams? When are leaders important? These questions are the basis for the situational approach to leadership. The value of this approach is in understanding the situational factors that affect leadership and the alternatives to leadership.

When historians study great leaders, they note the relationship between leaders and situations. Charismatic leaders require situations in which people have important needs and are searching for others to help resolve them (Bass, 1985). The same is true for many other historically important leaders; they were leaders during dramatic times.

The importance of leaders often is overrated, especially by business managers (Meindl & Ehrlich, 1987). Although leaders can have a strong impact on the success of organizations, in most day-to-day operations their impact is much smaller. However, leaders are cognitively important for followers. It is difficult to explain the success or failure of organizations, so leadership becomes a simplified explanation for what has happened and why.

One of the main values of the situational approach is in examining alternatives to leadership or the factors that can substitute for leadership. These factors relate to the characteristics of employees, jobs, and organizations (Yukl, 1994). Competent, well-trained, and responsible employees need leaders to a lesser degree. Routine jobs that are highly structured do not require the supervision of leaders. Organizing into teams and developing a cohesive team spirit can reduce the need for leaders.

| CONTINGENCY APPROACH

The contingency approach is the researcher's answer to the complaints made about leadership research. If one cannot define the traits or behaviors of good leaders separate from the situation, then leadership theories should combine these factors. However, a good theory may be difficult to use in practice. Contingency theories are complex and may be difficult to understand and apply.

Contingency theories start by focusing on some characteristic of a situation. Various theories examine the type of task, amount of structure, and favorableness of the situation for the leader. The theories then examine some aspect of the leader's personality or behavior such as interpersonal skills or task orientation. These two sets of factors are linked to show either how the leader should behave depending on the situation or what type of leader would be best given the situation. For example, some people tend to be autocratic leaders due to preference or training. Autocratic leaders work well in situations where they have a lot of power and followers are motivated to comply. This is why the military trains leaders to handle emergency situations forcefully and selects leaders who can act in this way.

Yukl's (1989) *multiple linkage model* is a contingency theory that relates to leading teams. The theory states that successful performance of a team depends on the following six intervening variables: member effort, member ability, organization of the task, teamwork and cooperativeness, availability of resources, and external coordination. Situational factors both directly influence these variables and determine which variables are most important. The role of the leader is to manage and improve these intervening variables so as improve the effectiveness of the team. In the short run, most leader actions are intended to correct problems in these six variables. In the long run, the leader tries to make the situation more favorable by implementing improvement programs, developing new goals and directions, improving relations with other parts of the organization, and improving the team's climate. These actions are designed to raise the intervening variables to higher levels.

SITUATIONAL LEADERSHIP THEORY

From a teamwork perspective, one of the most important leadership theories is *situational leadership theory* (Hersey & Blanchard, 1993). This theory links the leader's behavior to characteristics of the group. The value of this theory goes beyond just telling the leader how to behave. Situational leadership theory is a developmental theory that assumes that one of the goals of leadership is to develop the group. As such, it is the most team oriented of the leadership theories.

Situational leadership theory starts with the assumption that there are four basic styles of leadership based on a combination of task and people orientation. Leaders can be *directing* (high task oriented), *coaching* (high task and people oriented), *supporting* (high people oriented), or *delegating* (neither task nor people oriented). The appropriate use of these styles depends on the readiness level of the group. Group readiness is based on the skills of the group members, their experience with the task, their capacity to set goals, and their ability to take responsibility for their actions. The connection between the leader's behavior and the group's readiness level is shown in Figure 10.1.

To see how this theory works, imagine being the leader of a group of adolescents in a summer work program. On your first day as leader, your group has little experience with the task and little experience in working together. As the leader, you need to take control of the situation and get the group to start working together. A task-oriented (directing) approach is needed. As the group gains some experience, your leadership style should soften (coaching) so as to reward group members' accomplishments. Once the group learns how to perform the job and act responsibly, you need to further reward members by allowing them to participate in the decision-making process (supporting). This helps both to increase their commitment to the group and to develop their leadership skills. When the group can take full responsibility for performing its task, your job shifts to addressing issues outside of the team because, as the leader, you no longer are needed to help the team to function. As the leader, you delegate most of the internal leadership functions and let the group manage itself.

As can be seen from this example, situational leadership theory makes two important points. First, the leader needs to adjust his or her style of acting relative to the readiness of the group. Second, leadership is a developmental process, and the leader's behavior should promote group readiness.

SELF-MANAGING TEAMS

As organizations become more team oriented, they sometimes shift to the use of self-managing teams (Wellins & George, 1991). Self-managing teams provide a number of benefits beyond the use of standard work teams.

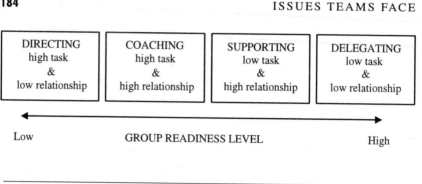

However, developing self-managing teams can be a difficult process, and this type of team is not suited for all situations.

Self-managing teams place their entire tasks under the control of team members (Hackman, 1986). This reduces the need for managers, allows organizations to reduce the levels in their organizational hierarchies, and allows the remaining managers to focus on other tasks such as long-range planning and external relations. Self-management shifts the responsibility for team success to the team members. This requires the team members to handle the internal social relations of their teams. When they are successful, self-managing teams encourage the empowerment of employees and further improve the team members' skills.

Although the idea of using self-managing teams at work has been around since the 1960s (as part of *sociotechnical systems theory*), the use of self-managing teams was not common until the 1980s when they were used primarily with factory and service workers (Manz, 1992). By the 1990s, more than 40% of large companies in the United States were using self-managing teams with at least some employees (Cohen, Ledford, & Spreitzer, 1996). The most important reasons for companies to introduce self-managing teams in manufacturing were to improve performance and improve quality (de Leede & Stoker, 1999). Rarely were improving working conditions, employee relations, or workplace democracy important goals.

All self-managing teams rotate at least some of their tasks among members (de Leede & Stoker, 1999). In manufacturing teams, employees are cross-trained so that they can work on different parts of the production process. They also receive training in teamwork skills so that they can manage work assignments and internal relations. In most cases, these production

TABLE 10.2
Team Empowerment Levels

Level of Responsibility	Team Tasks
Level 1: 20% of job responsibility	Maintenance Quality control Continuous improvement of process
Level 2: 40% of job responsibility	Managing supplies Customer contact Hiring new team members
Level 3: 60% of job responsibility	Choosing the team leader Equipment purchase Facility/work area design
Level 4: 80% of job responsibility	Budgeting Personnel (e.g., performance appraisal, compensation) Product modification and development

SOURCE: Adapted from Wellins, Byham, and Wilson (1991).

teams exist as part of organizational development programs that provide supportive environments for them.

The main impact of self-managing teams is to shift responsibilities from management to the team members. This is not an all-or-nothing process. Instead, there are many levels of self-management depending on how willing the organization is to give the team responsibility and authority. For example, Table 10.2 shows four different levels of responsibility that a factory team could possess. As the team is given more power or responsibility, it takes on more tasks that were handled by managers. When the team reaches the fourth level, 80% of the tasks that used to be performed by managers now are performed by the team.

One of the main problems with self-managing teams of factory and service workers is resistance from middle managers and professionals who fear that the increased use of teams might reduce the need for their jobs (de Leede & Stoker, 1999). This makes it a difficult challenge for self-managing teams to develop good working relationships with other parts of their organizations. Often, technical support functions, such as engineering, are more accustomed to dealing with supervisors than with workers. In addition, some leadership functions are difficult to replace with teamwork, especially those that deal with external relations and personnel issues.

The success of self-managing teams primarily depends on the organizational context (Cohen et al., 1996). Context plays a key role in the amount of support that teams obtain from their organizations, teams' access to relevant information, and teams' ability to act independently. The more power and autonomy that organizations give to self-managing teams, the greater impact the teams have on improving their performance and the success of their organizations (Cohen & Bailey, 1997).

The benefits of self-management for production and service teams do not necessarily apply to professional and managerial teams. Cohen and Bailey's (1997) review of the factors that relate to team success in different types of work teams found that self-management did not improve the performance of project teams. The highest performing project teams had leaders who helped to make team assignments and developed task procedures. This might be because members of project teams already have a substantial amount of autonomy, so they do not view self-management as a personal benefit. In addition, the projects they work on are nonroutine and difficult, so leaders who help to provide structure are viewed as a benefit rather than as unneeded supervisory control.

There are a number of other advantages that production teams have for self-management compared to professional or managerial teams. In production teams, the team members can be cross-trained. This allows them to understand the issues involved in each other's work. In professional teams, the team members have different types of expertise or represent different parts of their organizations, thereby limiting the members' understanding of each other's perspectives (Uhl-Bien & Graen, 1992). Production teams have clear performance measurements and can use quantitative feedback to evaluate and improve their performance. In most cases, it is difficult to analyze and measure the performance of professional teams (Orsburn, Moran, Musselwhite, Zenger, & Perrin, 1990). Finally, production workers place more importance on their social relations and are less competitive compared to professionals and managers (Lea & Brostrom, 1988).

In their study of professional teams, Levi and Slem (1996) found little evidence that self-managing teams performed better or that employees preferred to work on them. The idea of self-management is attractive to many employees in theory, but so is having a good leader to work under, learn from, and be rewarded by. The lack of a single best approach to leadership should not be too surprising. The tasks of teams and the characteristics of team members vary considerably. When the task is complex and the goals of the team are unclear, a strong leader often is needed to provide clear direction. When the task is relatively routine, the need for a leader is greatly diminished. The more experience that people have in performing the task and working as a team, the better able they are to become self-managing.

APPLICATION: THE FUNCTIONAL APPROACH TO LEADING TEAMS

The functional approach to leadership focuses on what the leader needs to do so as to help the team work effectively (Hackman & Walton, 1986; Zaccaro & Marks, 1999). The goal of this approach is to identify the factors on which the leader should focus so as to improve the team's performance. From this perspective, leadership is a form of social problem solving. The leader monitors the situation, diagnoses problems affecting the team, and implements solutions to these problems. Advocates of the functional approach have identified three main areas of focus for team leaders: direction, structure, and external relationships.

One of the primary roles of the team leader is to help set the direction for the team. The leader has the important internal role of motivating the members and helping them to achieve their own goals as well as the team's goals. Establishing a clear and engaging direction for the team is a crucial part of motivating team performance.

The leader needs to create a situation that enables successful performance. This includes a facilitative group structure, a supportive organizational context, and the availability of expert coaching. A facilitative group structure contains tasks that are engaging, a group whose members have the skills to complete the task, and group norms that encourage effective performance. A supportive context provides the team with necessary information and rewards team excellence. The team leader also is responsible for coaching and facilitating the team's internal group process.

The third team role is oriented toward the external relations of the team. The leader links the team to the organization and buffers the team from interference from the organization. The leader has a public relations job to perform, making sure that the team has the resources and support it needs from the organization.

This chapter concludes with a bit of advice for team leaders. Research shows that leaders who actively listen to team members and incorporate their ideas into the teams' recommendations help to improve both team members' evaluations of the teams and the quality of the teams' decisions (Cohen & Bailey, 1997). Problem leaders tend to micromanage their teams, engage in autocratic decision making, and be overconfident about their skills (McIntyre & Salas, 1995). This pattern of leadership reduces respect for such leaders and prevents constructive feedback from improving the leaders' behavior.

SUMMARY

Leadership is a process that can be centralized in one person or distributed among various roles. Teams vary in the types of leaders they have, how the leaders are selected, and how much power the leaders have. Teams rarely exist without leaders because leaders emerge through teams' interactions. Leaders can be designated by their organizations, or teams can select their own leaders and be self-managing.

There are four main approaches to studying leadership. The trait or personality approach defines the personality characteristics of successful leaders. The behavioral approach examines the value of different behavioral styles such as task orientation versus social orientation. The situational approach identifies the factors that make leaders important (change) and less important (mature teams). The contingency approach links traits and behaviors to the situations in which they best apply. Each of these approaches has different implications for the way in which leaders should be selected and trained.

One of the most important leadership theories for teams is situational leadership theory. This theory defines four styles of leadership: directing, coaching, supporting, and delegating. The leader should select which style to use depending on the readiness level of the group. In addition, the leader should use an appropriate style to promote group readiness.

Self-managing teams shift authority and responsibility for the teams from management to the team members. The main examples of self-managing teams at work occur among factory and service workers, where employees are cross-trained and taught teamwork skills. Developing self-managing teams among professionals and managers can be difficult because of the nature of their tasks and the relationships among the team members. Although self-managing teams can be very successful, implementing these teams in the workplace can be difficult.

The functional approach to leadership provides advice about what factors a leader should focus on to improve the team's functioning. The primary role of the team leader is to provide direction for the team. The leader also is responsible for establishing the structure to support the team's work. Finally, the leader manages the external relations of the team.

ACTIVITY: OBSERVING THE LEADER'S BEHAVIOR

Objective. Situational leadership theory defines four types of leader behavior: directing, coaching, supporting, and delegating. The most useful behavior depends on the readiness level of the group. Group readiness relates to the skills, experience, and responsibility level of the group.

Activity. Observe the leader's behavior in a team meeting (or, alternatively, review video segments of leaders interacting with teams). After observing the leader's behavior, classify the leader's behavior using the types from the situational leadership theory and use Activity Worksheet 10.1 to rate the readiness level of the team.

ACTIVITY WORKSHEET 10.1
Rating the Leader's Behavior

Which of the following styles best describes the leader's behavior?

_____ Directing (high task and low relationship)
_____ Coaching (high task and high relationship)
_____ Supporting (low task and high relationship)
_____ Delegating (low task and low relationship)

Overall, how would you rate the readiness level of the team?

_____ Low _____ Medium _____ High

Analysis. Compare your ratings of the leader to the impressions of the other team members and the leader. Is there agreement among team members about how the leader behaves? Does the leader view his or her behavior in the same way as the members view it?

Discussion. According to situational leadership theory, does the style of behavior used by the leader match the readiness level of the team? How should the leader change his or her behavior to improve group functioning given the group's readiness level?

Chapter 11

PROBLEM SOLVING

Group problem solving has been studied by looking at three different approaches: how groups actually go about solving their problems, what types of behavior contribute to effective problem solving, and what techniques can be used to improve group problem solving. Teams should base their problem-solving approaches on a rational model of the process including six stages: problem definition, evaluation of the problem, generating alternatives, selecting a solution, implementation, and evaluation of the results. In practice, however, this rational approach rarely is followed, and teams often find themselves developing solutions before they understand the problems.

At each stage of the problem-solving process, teams can use a number of techniques to improve their problem-solving abilities. These techniques are described so as to help teams be more effective problem solvers.

➤ **LEARNING OBJECTIVES**

1. What perspectives can be used to describe how groups typically solve problems?
2. What factors help to improve a group's ability to solve problems?
3. What factors disrupt a group's ability to solve problems?
4. What are the main steps in the rational approach to problem solving?
5. How do the characteristics of the problem, group, and environment affect the way in which a group analyzes a problem?
6. What is the value of using a structured approach to generating and evaluating alternatives?

7. What factors affect the implementation of a solution?
8. Understand some of the techniques that teams can use to help in their problem-solving efforts.
9. How does force field analysis help a team to implement solutions to a problem?

APPROACHES TO PROBLEM SOLVING

A problem is a dilemma with no apparent way out, an undesirable situation without a solution, a question that cannot currently be answered, the difference between the current situation and a desired state, or a situation to which group members must respond so as to function effectively (Pokras, 1995). The problem can come from the environment or arise from within a group. Problems often first surface for a group as symptoms that cause undesirable effects. Problems can be caused by incomplete, inaccurate, or unknown information; confusion because people involved are stressed or overwhelmed by information; or conflicting viewpoints about solutions.

In a work environment, a problem for many teams is simply how to complete their tasks. Most team tasks or assignments are complex problems. These team projects contain two primary problems: (a) determining the nature of the assignments and how to complete them and (b) managing the problems and obstacles encountered when performing the projects. These obstacles can be technical issues, conflicting viewpoints, or personality clashes.

Problem solving differs from decision making in that it includes more actions (Beebe & Masterson, 1994). Decision making is concerned with the selection of alternatives to solve a problem. Problem solving also must address problem definition, generation of alternatives, implementation, and evaluation issues.

The perfect way in which to solve a problem is to define the problem and then decide how to solve it. This might seem obvious, but the biggest problem that a team often has is that it starts by generating a solution without understanding the problem. Defining and evaluating the problem is the most difficult step to perform.

The first step in problem solving is to discuss and document individual views and information until everyone agrees on the nature of the problem

(Pokras, 1995). Teams often are given ill-defined problems and undeveloped criteria for evaluating them. Teams need to challenge the definitions of the problems, searching for their root causes. They also need to define what successful resolutions would look like so as to evaluate alternative solutions. The result should be agreement on the issues that need resolution and clear statements of the problems.

Many times, teams rush through the problem definition stage only to find that they have to return to it during the solution or implementation stage. This is a very time-consuming approach to problem solving. Understanding as much as possible about a problem at the beginning can reduce the overall time spent on a project.

Another common problem is ignoring the final stage—evaluating the project. Often, teams are created to solve problems but are not responsible for implementation or evaluation. Evaluation also is ignored because no one wants to present negative information to his or her superiors in an organization. Rather than learning from one's mistakes, the mistakes are hidden from the team and organization, so they often are repeated due to a lack of feedback.

There are three approaches to group problem solving: *descriptive* (which examines how groups actually solve problems), *functional* (which identifies the behaviors that relate to effective problem solving), and *prescriptive* (which recommends techniques and approaches to improve group problem solving) (Beebe & Masterson, 1994).

DESCRIPTIVE APPROACH: HOW GROUPS SOLVE PROBLEMS

The descriptive approach attempts to examine how groups actually solve problems. Researchers focus on different aspects of the group process so as to understand the problem-solving process. These different perspectives give alternative ways of understanding the process.

One perspective using the descriptive approach is to identify the stages that a group actually goes through when trying to solve a problem (Beebe & Masterson, 1994). This approach is very similar to the stages of group development discussed in Chapter 3. The four stages that a group uses when solving a problem are forming, storming, norming, and performing.

In the *forming* stage, the group examines the problem and tries to better understand the issues related to it. The *storming* stage is a time of conflict, where different definitions of the problem and preliminary solutions are discussed. Often, the group jumps ahead to arguing about solutions before it has reached agreement on the problem, so it must return to the problem definition stage to resolve this conflict. In the *norming* stage, the group develops methods for analyzing the problem, generating alternatives, and selecting a solution. The establishment of these methods and other norms about how to operate helps the group to work together effectively. In the *performing* stage, these methods are used to solve the problem and develop plans to implement the solution.

An alternative to this stage model is an approach that examines the types of activities that a group performs when problem solving (Poole, 1983). There are three types of activities: task process activities, relational activities, and topical focus activities. *Task process activities* are focused on defining the problem, generating solutions, and making a decision. *Relational activities* are focused on the social relations among group members and the emotional aspects of the group. *Topical focus* deals with the general themes or major issues and concerns of the group. While a group is solving a problem, it examines the specific problem in the context of the group's overall goals and mission.

Groups do not focus on one of these three types of activities in any particular order. Often, they focus on one aspect until they reach a break point that causes a shift. For example, a group may be very task oriented but get stuck in a conflict. This may cause the group to shift its focus to the emotional aspects of the conflict so as to make sure that the group is not being damaged by the conflict. Or, it may shift to a discussion of the larger goals of the group so that the conflict is put in better perspective. Changes in the agenda, conflicts, or disruptions in the group process can cause break points that shift the group away from task-processing activities. Eventually, the group is able to spend sufficient time in task-processing activities to solve the problem.

A third perspective examines the group discussion process to understand how a group generates alternatives and selects a solution. A group can use one of the following strategies: selecting a solution at random, voting for the best solution, taking turns suggesting each member's favorite solution, trying to demonstrate that a solution is correct, or inventing new and novel solutions (Laughlin & Hollingshead, 1995). Once a solution becomes the focus, the group analyzes it to determine whether it is correct (or at least better than the proposed alternatives). If the majority of members believe that it is, then the solution is accepted. If they do not, then a new solution is generated by one of the preceding techniques.

FUNCTIONAL APPROACH: ADVICE ON IMPROVING GROUP PROBLEM SOLVING

The functional approach tries to improve a group's ability to solve problems by understanding the factors that relate to effective problem solving and the factors that disrupt group problem solving.

| FACTORS THAT IMPROVE GROUP PROBLEM SOLVING

An effective group should include intelligent problem solvers (or vigilant critical thinkers). The group should analyze the problem, develop alternatives, and select the best solution. The problem-solving process should be relatively free of social, emotional, and political factors that disrupt a rational approach to problem solving. Researchers have identified a number of characteristics of effective group problem solvers (Beebe & Masterson, 1994; Janis & Mann, 1977). The following is some of their advice:

- Skilled problem solvers view problems from a variety of viewpoints to better understand the problem.
- Rather than relying on its own opinions, an effective group gathers data and research a problem before making a decision.
- A successful group considers a variety of options or alternatives before selecting a particular solution.
- An effective group manages both the task and relational aspects of problem solving. It does not let a problem damage the group's ability to function effectively in other areas.
- A successful group's discussion is focused on the problem. Too often, groups have difficulty in staying focused on the issues, especially when there are conflicts.
- An effective group listens to minority opinions. Often, the solution to a problem lies within the knowledge of a group member but is ignored because the group focuses on the opinions and ideas of the majority.
- Skilled problem solvers test alternative solutions relative to established criteria. The group defines what criteria a good solution must meet and uses those criteria when examining alternatives.

| FACTORS THAT HURT GROUP PROBLEM SOLVING

Project teams often jump quickly to the solution stage without doing an adequate job of defining the problems (Hackman & Morris, 1975). The teams do not discuss their problem-solving strategies or develop plans to follow. Typically, they try to apply solutions that have worked in the past. When teams spend time developing and following a structured approach to problem solving, their decisions are better and members are more satisfied with the problem-solving process.

There are many reasons why groups do not follow a logical structured approach to problem solving. There may be constraints on the problem-solving process such as limited time, money, and information. Because of these constraints, groups often seek "satisficing" solutions rather than optimal solutions (Simon, 1979). Perfection is expensive and time-consuming. Collecting all of the relevant information to solve problems may take longer than the time or resources available to groups. In most cases, groups try to find acceptable solutions (which meet their basic needs) given the time and information constraints of the situations.

In addition, it often is difficult to determine what is the best solution. There are trade-offs such as cost versus effectiveness of the solution. Solutions differ according to their probabilities of success, the availability of resources to implement them, and the politics of actually implementing them. These trade-offs do not have correct answers; they rely on the judgments of the group members. This limits a group's ability to objectively select the best solution.

As discussed in Chapters 6 and 9, communication problems may interfere with a group's ability to analyze and solve problems. During a group discussion, more time is spent on reviewing shared information than on discussing specialized information that might be important for a solution (Stasser, 1992). Although the group's discussion should be focused on the problem, group discussions can get sidetracked and disrupted in many ways (DiSalvo, Nikkel, & Monroe, 1989). Ideally, a group would spend more of its time on sharing information, planning, critically evaluating ideas, and monitoring tasks than on discussing non-task-related issues. This would increase the group's ability solve problems, but groups often fail to do this (Jehn & Shaw, 1997).

A group's problem-solving process also can be disrupted by a number of non-task-related factors. Group members may support a position because of their desire to reduce uncertainty or avoid social conflict. Politics may encourage members to support alternative solutions due to loyalty to the creators of the ideas or payback for past political support. Power and competition can disrupt a group's ability to solve problems (Johnson & Johnson, 1997). Competition in the group may encourage political advocacy rather than searching for the best alternative. Groups are better able to solve problems when power is relatively equal among group members. This encourages more open communication and critical evaluation. Groups are better at problem solving when power is based on competence or knowledge rather than on formal authority or control of resources (reward and coercion power).

PRESCRIPTIVE APPROACH: RATIONAL PROBLEM-SOLVING MODEL

The functional approach illustrated what can go right (and wrong) with the group problem-solving process. The prescriptive approach presents a strategy that encourages groups to solve problems more effectively. This approach is based on the assumptions that (a) group members should use rational problem-solving strategies and (b) using a structured approach will lead to a better solution. The value of formal structured approaches to problem solving depends on the type of problem. The more unstructured and complex the problem, the more helpful using specific procedures or guidelines will be to the group process (Van Gundy, 1981).

An outline of the prescriptive approach is presented in Figure 11.1, which shows the main steps in a formal, rational problem-solving approach.

PROBLEM RECOGNITION, DEFINITION, AND ANALYSIS

Problem recognition, definition, and analysis are key processes in effective problem solving. However, groups often rush through these stages of the problem-solving process. In their desire to develop solutions quickly, groups often focus on the symptoms of the problems rather than trying to understand the real causes of the problems (Pokras, 1995).

Unfortunately, even when a group takes the time to identify and analyze a problem, the group may misinterpret the problem and its causes. There are many things that can go wrong in the problem analysis process. The ability to successfully identify and analyze a problem depends on characteristics of the problem, the group, and the environment (Moreland & Levine, 1992).

Problems vary in their levels of severity, familiarity, and complexity. The more severe a problem is, the more likely it is to be identified as a problem. Acute problems with identifiable onsets and impacts often are recognized and addressed, whereas chronic problems that are less visible and more on-

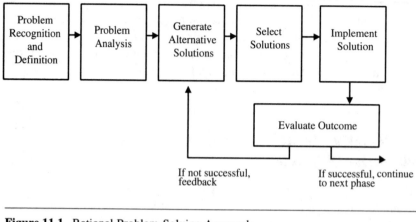

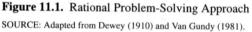

Figure 11.1. Rational Problem-Solving Approach

SOURCE: Adapted from Dewey (1910) and Van Gundy (1981).

going often are ignored. Problems that are familiar are more likely to be recognized by groups. Novel problems are more difficult to interpret, and groups might assume that they are unique one-time events that will go away by themselves. Complex problems are difficult to analyze and interpret. It is common for a group to select just part of a complex problem to analyze and solve so as to simplify the situation (although this might not be an effective way in which to actually resolve the problem).

Groups vary in their levels of desire and ability to identify problems. Group norms can have a strong effect on problem identification. Groups with norms supporting communication and positive attitudes toward conflict are more likely to identify and discuss problems. Groups vary in how open they are to the environment. Closed groups that are internally focused are less likely to be aware of problems in the environment. Open groups monitor what is happening in the environment, so they are better able to prepare for problems in the future because they have identified the issues beforehand.

Group performance also affects the problem identification process. Groups that are performing successfully sometimes will ignore problems. From the perspective of successful groups, the problems cannot be very important because the groups currently are successful. Unsuccessful groups also have a tendency to ignore problems. These groups must focus on their main performance problems, so they are less likely to see other problems that are affecting the group. The notion of *continuous improvement* is a teamwork concept designed to help deal with this issue. In continuous improvement, teams assume that part of their function is to improve their operations. In essence, successful and unsuccessful teams are required to identify problems and work to solve them on an ongoing basis.

Characteristics of the environment also affect groups' ability to identify and analyze problems. Many modern environments (e.g., political, business, technological) have substantial amounts of change and uncertainty. The high amount of change creates the need to stay alert and prepare for future problems, whereas the amount of uncertainty makes this more difficult to do. Groups vary in their relations to the outside environment. For example, work teams typically exist within an organizational context, so they often are forced to accept the definitions of problems from above them in their organizational hierarchies. Other types of groups may be more open to information about potential problems from outside sources (e.g., customers, suppliers, the public, and the media).

Once a group identifies a problem, it might not decide to solve it (Moreland & Levine, 1992). There are a number of other alternatives. The group could decide to deny and distort the problem so that it has a good justification to ignore it. The group may decide to hide from the problem given that problems sometimes go away by themselves. If the problem is difficult for the group to understand (due to novelty or complexity), then it may decide to just monitor the problem for the time being. Working collaboratively to solve a problem, or obtaining outside help to solve a problem, requires identification, belief that the problem is solvable, and motivation to solve the problem. These are the necessary conditions for the first two stages of the rational problem-solving process.

| GENERATION OF ALTERNATIVES AND SELECTION OF A SOLUTION

Finding an effective solution depends on developing high-quality alternatives (Zander, 1994). The ability of a group to do this relates to the knowledge, skills, and intelligence of the group members. However, it also depends on the group's climate and processes. An effective group has a climate that encourages open discussion of ideas, where minority ideas are listened to and taken seriously by the majority.

Groups sometimes use creativity and other structured techniques to help generate alternative solutions to problems. Techniques such as brainstorming and the *nominal group technique* (discussed in Chapter 12) are used to generate alternatives. One of the important values of these techniques is the participation of people who would not normally participate in the group discussions. There are a variety of other approaches that facilitators can use to enhance participation. But again, these are useful only if the group process is structured so that divergent ideas are given fair evaluations. Too often, conformity pressure leads groups to adopt solutions used in the past because of majority support.

The goal is to develop alternatives that use the resources available in a group. Providing a structure so that ideas are encouraged and appropriately considered is important. In addition, group members are able to pool their ideas together more effectively if they limit the number of ideas they present. When presenting alternatives, members should make the group aware of how their backgrounds relate to the problem and help the group to understand the information they have available that might be used to solve the problem (Stasser, 1992).

Researchers have examined the value of using structured problem-solving and decision-making approaches. This research suggests that structured approaches help groups to make better decisions, increase members' satisfaction with the solutions, and increase commitment to implementing the decisions. Structured problem solving also helps to promote more equitable participation in the decisions, reduces the negative impact of unequal status, and increases the likelihood that low-status people's ideas will be considered (Pavit, 1993).

The selection process of groups must consider a variety of issues to determine the best solutions. Groups should consider the positive and negative effects of each alternative on the groups and the external environment. The ability to implement the solutions also must be considered. This involves the ability of groups to enact the solutions and the ways in which outside groups and organizations will respond to the solutions.

Sometimes, none of the alternative solutions available is appealing. In this case, a group selects the least objectionable proposal. This often leads to rationalizing among group members to bolster their belief that the decision is acceptable. This process can lead to an overemphasis of the positive attributes of the selected solution and an overemphasis of the negative attributes of the other alternatives. Also, denying the adverse reactions that may occur from a decision and exaggerating the need for immediate action help the group to justify its choice (Janis & Mann, 1977).

Any good solution should meet the criteria that (a) it is a prudent agreement that balances the needs of various group members, (b) it is an efficient

problem-solving approach that does not consume too much time and resources, and (c) it is a process that fosters group harmony (Fisher, Ury, &
Patton, 1991). Once a set of alternatives has been developed, the group
should not argue about the merits of each solution because this encourages a
conflict based on positions. Instead, the group should develop ways of evaluating the benefits and costs of the alternatives. The focus should be on analyzing the alternatives to help selection rather than on the politics of getting
one's position adopted. This often will lead to a final solution that contains
elements from multiple alternatives.

After the group has made its decision, it may want to hold a "second
chance" meeting to review the decision. Even when the group decides by
consensus, it often is useful to have a second chance meeting to air concerns
about the decision. This meeting helps to prevent factors such as groupthink
and conformity pressure from having inappropriate influences on the decision.

| IMPLEMENTATION AND EVALUATION

A solution is not a good one unless it is implemented. This requires commitment from a group to support and enact its solution. As mentioned in
Chapters 8 and 9, one of the benefits of group decision making is that participation in the decision helps to create a sense of commitment to it.

One of the obligations of a problem-solving group is to think about implementation issues when making a decision (Zander, 1994). It is not useful
to agree on a solution that the group cannot implement. This means that the
group should plan how the solution will be implemented. Planning includes
consideration of the people, time, and resources needed to implement the
solution. The group also needs to develop instructions on implementation
and a rationale justifying its solution if the group will not be the implement-
ers. It also may be useful to bring the people who will be affected by the decision into the decision-making process so as to encourage their acceptance
of the solution.

Evaluation requires examining how the solution was implemented and
what the effects were (sometimes called process evaluation versus outcome
evaluation). This often requires that the group provide a definition of a successful outcome, something that it should have done during the problem
identification stage.

Sometimes, even when the solution resolves the problem, the undesirable situation does not change significantly. This happens when a group

solves only part of a larger problem, so the rest of the problem comes to the foreground because a part of it has been solved. By taking a larger perspective on the problem, the group might be able to determine the more critical parts of the problem that should be solved. The evaluation stage can help to provide information for future problem identification and solving.

APPLICATION: PROBLEM-SOLVING TECHNIQUES FOR TEAMS

There are useful techniques to help a team at each stage of the problem-solving process. These techniques help to structure the group process so that the group is better able to focus on the problem. Four of these problem-solving techniques are presented in Figure 11.2. *Symptom identification* is a technique to help in the problem analysis stage. The *criteria matrix* is used to assist in the selection of a solution. *Action plans* help to improve the implementation of the solution. *Force field analysis* can be used in many stages of the problem-solving process. The following subsections examine these and other techniques in more detail.

| SYMPTOM IDENTIFICATION

Problem solving must begin by recognizing that a problem exists and that most of the real problem lies hidden. Typically, the first encounter with a problem is only with the symptoms. The team must then find and agree on the most fundamental source of the problem. It should try to separate the symptoms (which are effects) from the causes. Before using the tools in this approach, the team members investigate the problem by gathering more information about it. With this new information, the team can analyze the cause of the problem.

There are several tools that can be useful at this stage (Pokras, 1995). Symptom identification is a technique that uses a simple form to tabulate all aspects of a problem. Force field analysis has the team analyze the driving and restraining forces that affect a problem. Charting unknowns has the team members discuss what they do not know about the problem. This helps to generate hidden facts, questions, and new places to look for information. In *repetitive why analysis,* the team leader states the problem and then asks, "Which was caused by . . .?" This question is repeated several times to help examine the underlying causes of a problem.

Problem Analysis Stage:
  Symptom Identification Technique

Symptoms	Facts	Opinions

Selection of a Solution Stage:
  Criteria Matrix

Alternative Solutions	Evaluation Criteria			

Implementation Stage:
  Action Plan

Action	Responsible Person	Expected Result	Completion Date

Multiple Problem-Solving Stages:
  Force Field Analysis

Driving Forces: What Do You Want?	Restraining Forces: What Prevents You From Getting It?

Figure 11.2. Problem-Solving Techniques

SOURCE: Adapted from Pokras (1995); used by permission.

The symptom identification technique uses a chart to display what is known about a problem (Figure 11.2). The chart is a simple form used to tabulate all aspects of a problem. There are two types of facts. *Hard facts* are based on data and information, whereas *soft facts* are based on impressions, opinions, and feelings. Team members list all aspects of the problem they expect to encounter when trying to solve it and then note whether there are hard or soft facts that support their beliefs about that part of the problem.

| CRITERIA MATRIX

Techniques to generate alternatives are presented in Chapter 12. Once the alternative solutions have been generated, a selection process is needed to review and evaluate them. If the group has done a good job of generating alternatives, then there should be a number of options from which to choose. If creativity techniques such as brainstorming have been used, then there might be many unworkable ideas. Because some approaches obviously are not going to work, they should be eliminated from further analysis. Then, the team should review the options and look for ways of combining solutions into categories. After this, a criteria matrix should be developed to evaluate the alternatives objectively.

A criteria matrix is a system used to rate the alternatives (Pokras, 1995). The first step is to decide what criteria are to be used to rate the alternatives (or what standards are to be used to evaluate them). These criteria are used to create a chart to evaluate the alternatives (Figure 11.2).

What evaluation criteria should be used? Many options exist including ease of implementation, effectiveness, expense, and quality. A team may want to use a rating scale for its analysis (e.g., 0 = *not acceptable,* 1 = *somewhat acceptable,* 2 = *acceptable,* 3 = *very acceptable*). It is important to not merely select the alternative with the highest score because not all evaluation criteria are equally important. The criteria matrix allows the team to analyze and discuss the relative merits of the alternatives in a structured manner.

| ACTION PLANS

The implementation stage focuses on generating action plans, considering contingency plans, and managing the project based on these plans. An action plan is a practical guide to translate the solution into reality—a step-by-step road map, if possible (Pokras, 1995). It emphasizes the timing of various parts and assigning responsibility for actions. The plan also should establish standards to evaluate successful performance (Figure 11.2).

Things rarely go as planned. A monitoring and feedback system should be established so that team members are informed and aware of the progress that has been made. Larger action items should be broken down into components or stages and monitored. Feedback to the team on progress with individual assignments should be a regular part of team meetings.

| FORCE FIELD ANALYSIS

Force field analysis is an approach to understanding the factors that affect any change program (Lewin, 1951). It examines the relation between the driving and restraining forces for change. This approach can be used at many stages of the problem-solving process, but it is especially valuable for examining implementation issues.

When implementing a solution to a problem, teams want to increase the driving forces that encourage the change and reduce the restraining forces that prevent the change from occurring. Teams often focus on the driving forces that are promoting the change. However, most unsuccessful change efforts are due to the restraining forces (Levi & Lawn, 1993). Reducing the power of the restraining forces is a necessary precondition for change.

Force field analysis provides a method for teams to study and guide their problem-solving activities. Using Lewin's action research model, group discussions and surveys are used to identify the driving and restraining forces affecting any proposed change. The team uses this information to decide on strategies to support the change effort. A cycle of generation, survey, and application of results may be repeated during the stages of the problem-solving process.

Levi and Lawn (1993) used this approach to analyze the driving and restraining forces that affected project teams developing new products. The project teams were driven by interest in new technology and an organizational culture that encouraged innovation. However, the success of producing and marketing new products was restrained by technical problems in manufacturing and financial issues. Understanding these forces encouraged the project teams to include members from manufacturing and marketing in the teams so as to address these problems during the design process.

In force field analysis, the team analyzes the driving and restraining forces that affect a problem (Figure 11.2). The driving forces are what the team wants to achieve and the factors that minimize the problem. The restraining forces are the obstacles that prevent success and the factors that contribute to the problem.

SUMMARY

Problem solving requires a team to analyze the nature of the problem and then develop and implement a solution. Unfortunately, many things can go wrong during these two steps. The study of group problem solving uses descriptive, functional, and prescriptive approaches to understand and improve the problem-solving process.

The descriptive approach looks at how a group solves a problem. The problem-solving process goes through developmental stages similar to overall stages of group development. A group shifts among focusing on the task, its social relations, and larger context issues while working on a problem. Solutions often are generated in a rather haphazard fashion that seems more political than logical.

The functional approach provides advice on how to improve the group problem-solving process. An effective group views problems from multiple perspectives, analyzes a variety of alternatives using established criteria, and manages the group process so that all members can participate. The group's ability to solve problems can be hurt by rushing to the solution stage, constraints that limit the amount of analysis, confusion about evaluation criteria, and social factors that disrupt the group process.

The prescriptive approach to problem solving goes through a series of structured stages. The problem identification and analysis stage is affected by the severity and complexity of the problem, group norms about discussing problems, and the amount of uncertainty in the environment. The process of developing and selecting alternative solutions is improved by creativity techniques to generate alternatives and by analysis techniques to examine alternatives in a systematic manner. Implementing solutions requires planning and an evaluation system to provide feedback on the process.

There are a variety of techniques that a team can use to help improve its problem-solving skills. Symptom identification techniques help to clarify what is known about a problem. A criteria matrix is used to evaluate alternative solutions. Action plans create a map to guide implementation. Force field analysis can be used at several stages to evaluate alternatives and implementation programs.

ACTIVITY: USING PROBLEM-SOLVING TECHNIQUES

Objective. Problem solving is improved when a team follows a structured approach. The team should analyze the problem thoroughly before developing alternatives. It should develop a set of alternatives and then use evaluation criteria to help select a solution. Force field analysis can be used to understand the issues related to implementing a solution.

Activity. Have the team follow a structured approach to problem solving. The team can be given either an organizational problem or a social problem to solve. For example, develop a program to reduce cigarette smoking, increase the use of seat belts, or encourage the use of condoms. After a problem has been selected, the team should use the symptom identification chart (Activity Worksheet 11.1) to understand the problem, develop several alternative solutions, use the criteria matrix to analyze the alternatives, select an alternative solution, and use force field analysis to understand the issues that will affect implementation of the solution.

ACTIVITY WORKSHEET 11.1
Symptom Identification Chart

Symptoms	*Facts and Data*	*Opinions and Feelings*

SOURCE: Adapted from Pokras (1995); used with permission.

Step 1: Analyze the symptoms of the problem using the symptom identification chart. This symptom analysis should help you understand the different causes of the problem.
Step 2: Generate alternative solutions to the problem.

Step 3: Develop criteria that can be used to evaluate the alternative solutions. Criteria may relate to issues such as quality, cost, and acceptability.

Step 4: Use the criteria matrix (Activity Worksheet 11.2) to analyze the alternative solutions. Rate each solution on the criteria that your team has developed. Then, select a preferred solution.

Step 5: Evaluate the implementation of your solution using force field analysis (Activity Worksheet 11.3).

ACTIVITY WORKSHEET 11.2
Criteria Matrix

Alternative Solutions	Evaluation Criteria			

SOURCE: Adapted from Pokras (1995); used with permission.

ACTIVITY WORKSHEET 11.3
Force Field Analysis

Driving Forces: What Factors Will Encourage Successful Implementation?	Restraining Forces: What Factors Will Prevent Successful Implementation?

Analysis. Did the team members find the use of the structured problem-solving approach helpful? What aspects of it did they like or dislike? Did it help to improve the quality of the solution?

Discussion. What are the benefits of and problems with using a structured approach to problem solving?

Chapter 12

CREATIVITY

Developing creative solutions is an important concern for groups, and a number of techniques can be used to stimulate creativity within teams. However, the dynamics of groups tend to limit creativity because members are concerned about behaving appropriately in front of others. The solution to promoting creativity for teams may require a variety of approaches that combine the benefits of individual and group creativity. Organizations also can help to encourage creativity by providing supportive organizational climates.

➤➤ *LEARNING OBJECTIVES*

1. What are the different ways in which to define creativity?
2. What are the psychological factors that hurt individual creativity?
3. Why do groups have problems in developing creative ideas?
4. What factors improve groups' ability to be creative?
5. Why do organizations have mixed views of the value of creativity?
6. What are some of the organizational factors that affect creativity?
7. How can brainstorming, the nominal group technique, and brainwriting be used to improve group creativity?
8. What are the advantages of using multiple group sessions to encourage creativity?

CREATIVITY AND ITS CHARACTERISTICS

Creativity can be defined by focusing on the person, the process, or the product (Amabile, 1996). From this perspective, creativity is something that creative people do, some things or ideas are creative, and it is a process that produces creative things or ideas.

Most research examines creativity from the person perspective, trying to find out who is creative using personality tests, product analysis, or subjective judgments. However, there are several problems with the person-oriented approach. Creativity varies in degrees; it is not simply a personality trait that some people have and others do not. Creativity skills can be enhanced through training in both individuals and groups. Creativity implies a match between the person and the application. In other words, most people are not creative in all areas. Talent, learned skills, and situational factors also affect creativity. Creative talent alone is not sufficient.

From a teamwork perspective, it is more useful to define creativity in terms of its products and processes than in terms of personality because this shifts the focus from the individual to the group. What is a creative product or idea? How should a group act to be creative? The answers to both of these questions show the dual nature of creativity (Table 12.1). It is the search for both novel and useful ideas as well as the balancing of divergent and convergent thinking. In the generation stage, people or teams use divergent thinking to develop novel ideas. In the application stage, they use convergent thinking to make those ideas useful.

Something is creative if it is novel and appropriate, acceptable, useful, or correct. A creative solution is something that is nonroutine; the path to the solution is not straightforward, and the solution is not defined by the situation. However, novelty is not enough; a creative solution also must be effective.

Creativity requires both creative and analytic thinking; it is a combination of divergent and convergent thinking processes (Van Gundy, 1987). Divergent thinking generates potential ideas, whereas convergent thinking analyzes and focuses solutions. These two types of thinking relate to the novelty and usefulness aspects of the definition of creativity.

To encourage divergent thinking, people need to suspend judgment of ideas. Participants should try to generate as many ideas as possible and be receptive to new ideas. Creativity also requires time for incubation because creative solutions often occur to people when they are not thinking about the

TABLE 12.1
Aspects of Creativity

	Generation	*Application*
Product	Novel	Useful
Process	Divergent	Convergent

problem. Ideas need to be combined, modified, and played with to encourage creative alternatives.

Taking a systematic approach to the problem encourages convergent thinking. Evaluation criteria are developed and then used to sort out ideas. All of the alternatives need to be analyzed so as to avoid premature acceptance. People need to be realistic about what can be accomplished and not too critical about the ideas of others. The overall goals of the issue should help guide the analysis and selection process.

Researchers examining the social aspects of creativity view it as an interaction of personal and situational factors (Amabile, 1996). Their model of creativity has three components: domain-relevant skills, creativity-relevant skills, and task motivation.

Domain-relevant skills are the skills, knowledge, and talent that people have in a particular application area. People are creative in the areas that they understand. For example, artists are not creative bridge designers and vice versa.

Creativity-relevant skills are the appropriate cognitive styles and knowledge about creativity techniques. Cognitive style includes the ability to break out of established cognitive and perceptual sets, the ability to understand complexity, suspending judgment, and using broad categories to view issues.

Task motivation includes intrinsic motivation, attitude toward the task, and the presence of environmental factors that encourage or discourage creativity. Intrinsic motivation is motivation that comes from personal interest or desire rather than from an external reward. Motivation is needed to encourage people to apply their creative skills. In addition, the concept of motivation can be used as a link between the characteristics of the situation and the response of the individual.

IMPORTANCE OF CREATIVITY FOR ORGANIZATIONS

Organizations benefit from creativity. For example, businesses want to be innovative so as to create new products and services to expand their operations. Companies get stuck in old patterns of behavior and look for new ideas to help them break out. The world is a more dynamic and turbulent place with a faster rate of change, so organizations need to change creatively to survive.

For organizations to be more creative, they need to hire creative people, use group creativity effectively, and create organizational climates that promote creativity. It is fairly obvious that organizations need creative people so as to be creative, but there are important reasons why just having creative people in organizations is insufficient.

The reason why organizations must rely on group creativity is that the problems they face are too complex for an individual. Often, creative solutions for problems require a multidisciplinary perspective. The development of the first Macintosh computer is a good example. How can one recreate the computer considering electronic, manufacturing, artistic, psychological, and human factor issues? It is not a job for an individual; it is a job for a design team. To combine the talents of a variety of fields and specializations, organizations need group creativity.

Organizations also have to develop creative solutions for problems that cut across organizational boundaries. This, too, requires a group perspective rather than an individual perspective to fully understand and integrate the issues involved. In addition, the use of a group to develop creative solutions for cross-department problems helps to encourage support for the implementation of the solutions.

INDIVIDUAL VERSUS GROUP CREATIVITY

Creativity is a problem for both individuals and groups. Individual creativity can be disrupted by several psychological factors. Groups have been criticized as being less creative than individuals. Brainstorming, the best-known technique for encouraging group creativity, has been criticized as being ineffective. However, there are examples of creative groups that are capable of overcoming these problems.

| INDIVIDUAL BARRIERS TO CREATIVITY

There are a variety of psychological factors that negatively affect creativity. Many of these operate by shifting one's focus away from the task to issues external to the task.

Intrinsic Versus Extrinsic Motivation

In general, intrinsic motivation encourages creativity, whereas extrinsic motivation is a detriment to creativity (Amabile, 1996). Intrinsic motivation relates to the qualities of the task itself. When people are intrinsically motivated, they engage in an activity for its own sake, not to achieve a reward for performing the task. Extrinsic motivation is motivation that is not related to the task such as a reward or incentive for performance. Extrinsic motivators can hurt creativity by shifting attention away from the task to receiving the reward.

Extrinsic motivators can hurt productivity in several ways. Being rewarded to perform a task sometimes can reduce one's intrinsic motivation for the task (Deci, 1975). A person may enjoy the creativity of painting, but being paid to paint all day for a commission may reduce the personal reward he or she feels when painting. Also, the use of rewards focuses one on satisfying the person or organization providing the rewards. Rather than trying to be creative, a person is trying to satisfy someone else. This can cause the person to be more conservative in what he or she produces.

However, rewards do not always reduce creativity. Rewards may foster creativity if they signify competence or enable the person to perform more interesting activities. For example, Hewlett-Packard gives out rewards to employees who go against management by working on creative ideas even after being told to stop. The rewards acknowledge creativity and give positive feedback to the employees. In addition to recognition, the employees are given more freedom to work on their own projects. This type of reward encourages others to pursue their own creative ideas.

Evaluation Apprehension

The negative effects of evaluation on group creativity have been researched extensively (Amabile, 1996). When someone talks in a group, the listeners often are thinking about what is wrong about what the person is saying rather than listening to the person's ideas. People in a group often are evaluating each other, and this evaluation process discourages creativity. The likelihood of negative evaluation makes group members concerned about appearing stupid, outrageous, or inappropriate. This anxiety limits creativity.

Evaluation hurts creativity, especially the ability to generate novel ideas or solutions. Evaluation has a more detrimental impact on people with low skills than on people with high skills. There is an exception to this negative impact. In work environments where the evaluation focuses on providing information or feedback about the task, or where the evaluation is part of a climate that uses positive recognition to reward competence, evaluation may have a positive impact on creativity.

Freedom

Choice and freedom affect creativity. People are more creative when they can choose the type of task to work on and how to work on the task. As was noted in Chapter 8, groups encourage conformity. This type of social pressure can be unspoken and implied in the group process. Conformity pressure causes people to not state their true opinions so as to avoid controversy. This process makes groups conservative. Creativity techniques must address this bias.

Paradigms

Our internal mental sets and paradigms limit creativity. It is difficult to view a situation from a different perspective. Many famous creative ideas come from looking at something fairly commonplace from a different perspective. For example, Post-It notes come from wondering about the value of glue that does not stick very well. Many creative ideas in science come from younger scientists who are not fully indoctrinated into the existing paradigm or from interdisciplinary scientists who are changing fields. We become locked in an old way of thinking and stuck in our paradigm or routine way of working, so we might not see creative alternatives to our situations.

THE PROBLEMS WITH GROUP CREATIVITY

When it comes to analyzing creativity, groups face many of the same problems as do individuals. When people try to creatively solve a problem as a group, they typically will produce fewer ideas than will the sum of individuals working alone (Amabile, 1996). There is little evidence that the quality of ideas improves because of working together as a group. Even when individuals are working alone in the presence of others, individual creativity is reduced. This is especially true if the others observe and evaluate what individuals are doing.

There are several group dynamic factors that limit creativity (Van Gundy, 1987). Groups can develop negative or critical communication climates that discourage creativity. Interpersonal conflicts within groups can discourage creativity. Groups consume more time, so it is not faster or more efficient to use groups. Finally, the group process can hurt creativity due to conformity pressure and domineering members.

The most well-known and widely used group creativity technique is brainstorming (Osborn, 1957). It was designed to deal with the problem of using group discussions for creativity. In group discussions, groups spend too much time evaluating and criticizing ideas and not enough time generating ideas and solutions. The four basic rules of brainstorming are that (a) criticisms are strictly forbidden, (b) free thinking and wild notions are encouraged, (c) numerous ideas are sought, and (d) combining and building on the ideas of others is good. (How to conduct a brainstorming session is presented at the end of this chapter.)

Research on brainstorming shows that it improves creativity more than do unstructured group discussions (Stein, 1975). It can be improved by having the participants think of ideas alone before the brainstorming session, facilitating the process so that participation is equalized, and making sure that people do not criticize others' ideas in the generation stage. The primary benefit of brainstorming is separating the generation of ideas from the evaluation of ideas. This reduces criticisms during the discussion of new ideas and encourages the participation of some people who otherwise would remain silent.

However, research on the effectiveness of brainstorming generally shows that it is not superior to individuals working alone (Mullen, Johnson, & Salas, 1991). Brainstorming does not increase the number or quality of creative ideas compared to the sum of individuals working separately. It does not lead to more creative decisions. The main explanation for the problem with brainstorming is that group discussions make people wait (Diehl & Stroebe, 1987). People in a brainstorming session must attend to the other participants in the discussion and take turns rather than stating their ideas when they first appear. While people are waiting for their turns, they are not using their time effectively by trying to develop other creative ideas.

Despite the negative reviews of brainstorming in the research literature, it remains a very popular technique, especially in business organizations. There seem to be several reasons for this (Parks & Sanna, 1999). First, people in business believe that group interaction stimulates others. This is such a compelling idea that people are unwilling to reject it based on research. Second, people involved in brainstorming sessions believe that they work. Their personal experiences support the benefits of brainstorming. In addition, participating in a brainstorming session may help to encourage commitment to the final solution.

Some of the recent research on electronic brainstorming (discussed in Chapter 15) suggests that computer-based forms of brainstorming are more effective than traditional brainstorming in improving group creativity. Using electronic communication helps to minimize the problems of production blocking and evaluation apprehension. In computerized brainstorming, people can review the ideas of others and develop and modify their own ideas at their leisure. A number of research studies have shown that computerized brainstorming is very effective (Dennis & Valacich, 1993).

Research on computerized brainstorming shows a number of interesting effects. In computer groups, group size increases the number of creative ideas rather than reducing creativity. The number of ideas increases when group members receive feedback about their performance rather than being discouraged by evaluations. The anonymity of the medium seems to encourage people to make more comments on others' ideas.

| STRENGTHS OF GROUP CREATIVITY

There also are benefits of using groups to develop creative solutions to problems. Groups are able to develop more ideas than are individuals. The social interaction of working in groups can be rewarding. Groups can create supportive environments that encourage creativity. Groups that have diverse sets of backgrounds and viewpoints are more likely to reach creative solutions than are homogeneous groups or individuals.

The key to encouraging group creativity is dissent (Nemeth, 1997). A group that is in creative conflict produces more creative ideas. When the group is exposed to contradictory ideas from a few of its members, the thinking of the majority is stimulated and more creative ideas are produced. How does dissent improve creativity in a group? It encourages a search for more information to test conflicting ideas. It stimulates divergent thinking and encourages the group to view the issue from multiple perspectives. Dissent also encourages more original, and less conventional, thoughts about the issue. These effects occur even when the group does not accept the minority's opinion as correct.

As is discussed in the next chapter, diversity of background, training, and perspective increase group creativity (Jackson, 1992). Diversity increases cognitive conflict on issues. Diverse groups generate more ideas, try out more novel ideas, and view issues from multiple perspectives. This effect is one reason why organizations use cross-functional teams that include members with different areas of expertise or from different parts of their organizations.

The ways in which groups operate also can have a positive effect on group creativity. Brainstorming is better for creativity than is unstructured group discussion. There are ways in which to improve the brainstorming process to make it better at promoting creativity. When trained facilitators run brainstorming sessions, groups generate more creative ideas (Offner, Kramer, & Winter, 1996). This creativity improvement continues to affect the group later after the facilitator leaves because the group learns how to do brainstorming better.

The research on brainstorming often examines the effects of a single brainstorming session. However, this is not the most effective way in which to conduct brainstorming. Many variants of brainstorming include a mixture of individual and group activities. For example, one could use a two-step process in which individuals write down their ideas, they present their ideas to the group, and then the group brainstorms additional ideas. This approach incorporates the benefits of both individual and group creativity (Paulus, 1998).

Group creativity relates to three factors: the individual, the group, and the organization or environment. Although group and organizational factors may discourage individual creativity, there are potential benefits of group creativity that come from having a diversity of perspectives. Are groups more or less creative? It depends on how the process is managed. However, the question is really not relevant in many organizational situations. Important problems often require group creativity and the use of the creativity of all members at the same time. Problems are too complex to rely on individual creativity.

ORGANIZATIONAL ENVIRONMENT AND CREATIVITY

Individual and group creativity can survive only in organizational environments that support it. Although organizations often say that they want to encourage creativity, their actions might not support creativity. Organizations want both stability and change, and this contradiction creates problems. There are many things that organizations could do to promote creativity, but there probably are just as many obstacles that prevent it from happening.

Organizational leaders say that creativity is important and that there are many famous examples of innovations that have led to organizational renewal and growth. But is this really true? Creative people are deviants whose ideas are likely to be rejected by organizations. In most circumstances, organizations really value consistent and predictable performance rather than creativity.

Creativity implies risk. Organizations are focused on providing consistency, minimizing error, and reducing risk. This is the inherent conflict with organizational creativity. The problem that organizations have with creativity is not that individuals and groups are not creative but rather that creativity is not recognized or rewarded by the organizations.

To foster creativity, organizations need to develop climates that support creative people and teams. Organizational climates can promote both the task and social aspects of creativity (Van Gundy, 1987). Climates that support the task aspects of creativity provide the freedom to do things differently, empower people to act on their ideas, encourage active participation, and provide support to the people involved in creative tasks. Climates that support the social aspects of creativity allow the open expression of ideas, encourage risk taking, promote the acceptance of unusual and novel ideas, and show their belief and confidence in their employees.

Work environments can either stimulate creativity or provide barriers to creativity. Table 12.2 presents a list of environmental factors that research has shown to affect creativity in the workplace (Amabile, 1996).

In their research on visionary companies such as Hewlett-Packard, IBM, General Electric, 3M, and Disney, Collins and Porras (1994) found that these innovative companies have strong core values and socialization programs to instill these values in new employees. These core values strengthen commitment to the companies and increase cohesiveness. This loyalty to the organizations helps employees to implement new ideas, but it does not encourage them to be creative. Creativity requires new perspectives, questioning the ways in which the organizations operate, and deviating from the norms.

These visionary companies have acknowledged the problem and have developed a number of mechanisms to promote creativity within their organizations (Nemeth, 1997). They have organizational norms that tolerate

TABLE 12.2
Environmental Stimulants and Obstacles to Creativity

Factor	Stimulant to Creativity	Obstacle to Creativity
Freedom	Employees need the freedom to decide what tasks to perform, the freedom to decide how to perform them, and control over their work process.	A lack of freedom in how employees select projects and perform tasks discourages creativity.
Management	Managers need to be good role models, have good technical and communication skills, provide clear directions but use limited controls, and protect teams from negative organizational influences.	A management style that hurts creativity includes unclear direction, poor technical and communication skills, and too much control.
Encouragement	New ideas need to be encouraged, and there should be an absence of the threat of evaluation.	A lack of support or apathy toward new approaches reduces the motivation to be creative.
Recognition	Employees should believe that creativity will receive appropriate feedback, recognition, and reward from the organization.	Inappropriate, unfair, and critical evaluations and the use of unrealistic goals limit creativity.
Cooperation	The organizational climate should support cooperation and collaboration, acceptance of new ideas, rewards for innovation, and the allowance for risk taking.	Interpersonal and intergroup competition within an organization or work group disrupts the creative process.
Time	Creativity requires time to explore new ideas rather than rigid schedules.	Too great a workload, or day-to-day crises that take one's focus away from long-term projects, reduce creativity.
Challenge	Tasks that are interesting, important, and not routine encourage creativity.	Organizations that emphasize consistency and do not support risk taking discourage creativity.
Motivation	There should be a sense of urgency from oneself to complete the task because of competition from outside the organization or the desire to do something important.	Organizational factors such as bad reward systems, excessive bureaucracy, and a lack of regard for innovation reduce creativity.

SOURCE: *Creativity in Context* by Teresa M. Amabile. Copyright © 1996 by Westview Press, a member of the Perseus Books Group. Reprinted by permission of Westview Press, a member of Perseus Books, L.L.C.

and encourage diversity of opinions and ideas. They provide support for mavericks and people with creative ideas while limiting the fear of failure and providing rewards for risk taking. In addition, these companies have developed a number of specific programs to encourage creativity. Hewlett-Packard has a program to reward creative defiance of the organization. 3M rewards creative employees with "free time" to work on any project they want. Dupont provides funds to work on ideas that are not supported by management. Pfizer moved its research and development facilities away from the corporate center to reduce the influence of management on the research staff. Motorola, Chrysler, and many other companies use teams made of members from different parts of the organizations to encourage creative interactions.

APPLICATION: GROUP CREATIVITY TECHNIQUES

Coming up with creative ideas is an important part of a team's work. The tools used by the team to promote creativity can be used to address a variety of team issues. For example, creativity techniques are useful in all of the stages of problem solving (Van Gundy, 1987). The techniques can help to clarify objectives, define and analyze the problem, generate alternative solutions, and prepare for implementation.

The biggest problem limiting team creativity is premature evaluation. Team members might want to try out new ideas, but critical comments from other team members prevent this. Team members often are not good at supporting each other's ideas, so designating times when they are not being critical is important for creativity. A team should develop rules for openness and safety in presenting ideas, and members need to practice the technique of supporting or building on an idea rather than criticizing it. If they do not like an idea, team members should try going with it by suggesting other related ideas that do not have their objection. Learning this skill is very helpful.

A team often does not have to decide on an outcome right at that moment. Sometimes, it is better to run a brainstorming session, eliminate some of the options, and then wait until the next meeting before selecting an alternative. Waiting can allow members to come up with fresh ideas on their own. This approach to team creativity captures both individual creativity (which often is done alone) and synergistic creativity (which comes from group interaction).

Developing creative ideas is a process that includes more than just a group session (Figure 12.1). It starts with developing an open climate to encourage participation in the process. Team members are more likely to de-

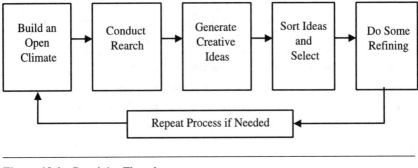

Figure 12.1. Creativity Flowchart

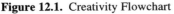

velop creative ideas if they have time to prepare and research the topic. After the generation of creative ideas, the best ideas are selected and refined. Finally, it might take multiple sessions to fully develop creative ideas that are useful.

| BRAINSTORMING

Brainstorming includes a variety of methods for structuring group creativity sessions. Besides classic brainstorming, alternatives include the use of procedures that force group members to combine the ideas of others, the use of pictures to "comment" on ideas, and the taking of new perspectives such as cartoon characters. Group facilitators who use brainstorming often add procedures to equalize the amounts of participation from group members.

To start a brainstorming session, the team leader clearly states the purpose or issues to be discussed and reviews the guidelines for brainstorming (Table 12.3). A distinct period of time (perhaps 10 to 20 minutes) should be set aside for the brainstorming session. During the actual brainstorming, the leader acts primarily as the facilitator and recorder. After the ideas have been generated, the leader helps the group to prioritize the list into a manageable size for further consideration.

During the brainstorming session, all team members should try to suggest as many ideas as possible. Every idea is accepted by the team and written down on the blackboard or recorder's sheet. The leader's job is to keep the team members on track by refocusing them on the issue or problem that needs to be solved. No one is allowed to criticize others' ideas; instead, people are encouraged to build on the suggestions made by others. It is up

TABLE 12.3
Guidelines for Brainstorming

Question	Announce the question or issue to be addressed.
Toss out	All team members toss out as many ideas as they can.
Accept	All ideas are accepted regardless of how practical they are.
Record	All ideas are listed for everyone to see.
Prompt	The facilitator re-asks the main question to help keep people on track.
No editing	The facilitator reminds the team that no one is allowed to criticize or evaluate until the process is done.
Build	Everyone should build on each other's ideas, using the ideas to go off in new directions.

SOURCE: Adapted from Pokras (1995); used with permission.

to the leader to make sure that no criticisms occur during the brainstorming session.

NOMINAL GROUP TECHNIQUE AND BRAINWRITING

The nominal group technique and brainwriting are similar approaches that try to combine the benefits of individual and group creativity. Like brainstorming, they separate the idea generation stage from evaluation. However, these approaches have individuals generate their ideas in writing rather than in a group discussion.

Both the nominal group technique and brainwriting start with the same general approach as does brainstorming. A group is brought together, and the facilitator announces the question. In the nominal group technique, each participant spends 10 to 20 minutes writing down his or her ideas. After this stage has been completed, the ideas are listed for all participants to see, and the group is able to ask clarifying questions about the ideas.

There are several variations of brainwriting. One approach is to have a person write down an idea on a sheet of paper and then pass the paper to the person on the right. The next person is required to write a new idea that builds on the previous idea(s). This cycle repeats until the time is up or the group is exhausted. An alternative is for each group member to write down several ideas on a sheet of paper, throw the papers into a central pool, and then pull out someone else's paper for each member to write on. Again, the group members are to build on the ideas presented in the papers they receive. When the group is done generating ideas, all of the lists are combined for the group to review.

These approaches are effective alternatives to brainstorming. Because individuals are writing out their ideas, there are no problems with having to wait for one's turn to contribute. The techniques are structured to encourage participation from all group members. Typically, they include group discussions at the end so that members have the opportunity to build on each other's ideas.

| SELECTING A SOLUTION

One of the problems with creativity activities such as brainstorming is that they generate many possible options and no clear or easy way in which to select the best one. However, after a brainstorming session, it often is easy to prioritize most of the suggestions and focus on a limited number of options.

One approach to this is multiple voting (Scholtes, 1994). A team reviews the alternatives generated by the brainstorming session and combines items that seem similar. Then, each team member selects two to five alternatives that he or she would like to support. After all team members have completed their selections, the votes are tallied and items that received no votes or only one vote are removed. The alternatives that have been selected are discussed, and ways of combining or synthesizing alternatives are considered. These steps are repeated until only a few options remain from which the team can select. At this stage, the group can use consensus to select the final alternative.

| MULTIPLE-STAGE CREATIVITY APPROACHES

To get the benefits of group and individual creativity, teams can use a multiple-stage process. This approach uses time as a buffer between group creativity activities. People often are creative at odd moments when they are not thinking about the problem such as while walking or taking a shower. It is difficult to be creative on command, especially in front of others. Creativity is something that is hard to rush given that stress and time pressure tend to make individuals and groups more conservative.

One of the problems with group creativity research is that it assumes that groups have to be creative immediately. In most organizational contexts, a group works on problems over time. There is a meeting in which the problem is discussed, sometime later the group tries to be creative, and sometime later the group reconvenes to make its selection process. By separating activities in time and allowing group members to enter new ideas over time, the benefits of both individual and group creativity are realized. Problem solving in organizations typically occurs over time, and the challenge is to use this flow of time to enhance creative problem solving.

SUMMARY

From a group dynamics perspective, creativity typically is defined as a product or process. Creativity leads to the development of something that is both novel and useful. The creative process uses divergent and convergent thinking to develop creative ideas. Creativity requires skills in the topic area, creativity skills, and motivation.

Both individuals and groups have problems with being creative on demand. Extrinsic motivators and rewards, evaluation apprehension, a lack of freedom, and paradigms or mental sets reduce individual creativity. In many cases, groups are not more creative than individuals working alone. The presence of others and poor group processes limit creativity. Brainstorming, the most widely used technique to help group creativity, is better than just using unstructured discussions but has a limited effect on improving group creativity. However, under certain conditions, groups can encourage creativity. Groups that acknowledge the value of constructive conflict and diverse membership can use these forces to stimulate thinking and encourage creativity.

Although organizational leaders say that they want to encourage creativity, their actions often do not match their words. Creativity is needed to help organizations adapt to the changing environment. However, many factors inside organizations encourage consistency and stability rather than innovation. Organizations can either encourage or discourage creativity through a variety of factors such as management orientation, availability of resources, recognition for risk taking, cooperative climate, and challenging assignments.

Several techniques have been developed to improve group creativity. Brainstorming helps structure group discussions to reduce the negative effects of evaluation. The nominal group technique and brainwriting combine individual and group creativity techniques. Selection techniques can be used to reduce the number of alternatives from which to select. It is important for groups to use creativity techniques, but it also is important to use multiple group sessions so that creative ideas have time to incubate. When these techniques are used, group creativity is improved.

ACTIVITY: COMPARING DIFFERENT CREATIVITY TECHNIQUES

Objective. Creativity can be improved by using one of the creativity techniques presented toward the end of this chapter. Teams can try out these techniques to see how well they work.

Activity. Divide into two teams and have each team use a different creativity technique—either brainstorming or brainwriting. Each of these techniques is useful for generating alternative solutions. Spend about 20 minutes using the creativity technique. Then, use the multiple voting technique to select the preferred alternative. For a creative challenge, try to develop a new advertising slogan for your organization.

Brainstorming: To start a brainstorming session, the team leader must clearly state the issues to be discussed and must review the guidelines for brainstorming. During the brainstorming session, all team members should try to suggest as many ideas as possible. Every idea is accepted by the team and written down on the recorder's sheet. The leader's job is to keep the team members on track by refocusing them on the issue. No one is allowed to criticize others' ideas; instead, people are encouraged to build on the suggestions made by others. It is up to the leader to make sure that no criticisms occur during the brainstorming session.

Brainwriting: Brainwriting starts with the same general approach as does brainstorming. Teams are brought together, the leader announces the issue, and team members are told to be open and build on each other's ideas. The difference is that the team's interaction is in writing. Have each person write down several alternative ideas, throw their papers into a central pool, and then pull out someone else's paper for each person to write on. Team members are to build on the ideas presented in the lists they receive. When the team is done generating ideas, all of the lists are combined for the team to review.

Selecting a solution using multiple voting: The team reviews the alternatives generated by the creativity session and should combine items that seem similar. Then, each team member selects two to five alternatives that he or she would like to support. After all team members have completed their selections, tally the votes and remove items that received no votes or only one vote. Discuss the alternatives that have been selected, and look for ways in which to combine or synthesize them. Repeat these steps until only a few options remain from which the team can select.

Analysis. Which technique generated the most creative solution? What did the team members like and dislike about the creativity technique they used? Would they want to use the technique in the future?

Discussion. What are the advantages of and problems with using these two creativity techniques? How can you encourage a team to be more creative?

Chapter 13

DIVERSITY

Diversity in a group stems from differences in psychological, demographic, and organizational characteristics. Research shows various effects of this diversity, with results depending on how the research is conducted, the type of diversity examined, and the type of tasks performed. In most cases, diversity is a benefit once a team learns how to manage diversity issues. A group with diverse members performs better on production, problem-solving, and creativity tasks.

Diversity in a group also can lead to problems caused by misperceptions about others and competition among groups. These problems disrupt communication within the group and reduce the ability of the group to fully use its resources. Research shows that diversity problems are unlikely to go away by themselves, but there are a number of actions that organizations can take to help teams improve the relations among their members.

➤➤ *LEARNING OBJECTIVES*

1. Why is the importance of managing diversity increasing for organizations?
2. What are the different types of diversity?
3. What is the difference between the trait approach and the expectation approach to explaining diversity?
4. How do cognitive processes, leader behavior, and competition explain the cause of diversity problems?
5. What are the main problems that diversity causes for groups?
6. What are the differences between the performance of homogeneous groups and that of heterogeneous groups?

7. What are the challenges of using cross-functional teams?
8. What are some of the approaches that organizations can use to manage diversity problems?

THE NATURE OF DIVERSITY

From sociological and organizational perspectives, the topic of diversity is increasing in importance. Diversity has many meanings, and the various types of diversity have different impacts on how groups function. This section of the chapter examines these issues, and later sections examine the psychological and sociological causes of diversity problems, the impact of diversity on team functioning, and how organizations can better manage diversity issues.

| WHY DIVERSITY IS IMPORTANT NOW

The importance of understanding diversity in work teams has increased substantially during the past two decades. This is due partly to the increasing numbers of women and ethnic minorities that have been entering the workforce. However, there also are other changes that are making these demographic changes more important today (Jackson & Ruderman, 1995).

Not only are more women and ethnic minorities in the workforce, but they now are in all areas of the organizational hierarchy. It no longer is the case that women and ethnic minorities primarily work in only certain types of jobs (Jackson, 1992). In the new organizational environment, diversity occurs in jobs in all parts of organizations.

Age diversity also is increasing in organizations. People are living longer, retirement ages are increasing, and the baby boomers are getting older (Carnevale & Stone, 1995). The relationship between younger and older workers also is changing. Younger and older workers are more likely to work together because organizational hierarchies are flatter. The addition of new technology also has reversed some of the differences between younger and older workers in that younger workers may be more knowledgeable and skilled in new technology and may serve as mentors for older workers.

Diversity also is increasing by design. Organizations are recruiting a more diverse workforce so as to improve relationships with customers. A design team does not create a car for only male buyers; products must be sensitive to all of the potential customers. Increasing the diversity of the workforce helps organizations be more sensitive to the diverse markets in society. In addition, globalization is increasing diversity. As organizations become more global, the people in them must be able to interact in culturally diverse teams.

In addition to these changes in the character of the workforce, organizations are making other changes that affect diversity. The increased use of teams increases the importance of diversity issues because representatives of the diverse workforce must interact with each other to perform their jobs. Teams also must deal with the diversity that comes from differences in occupations, departments, and organizational statuses. The widespread restructuring of larger organizations has reduced the number of organizational levels. In these flatter organizations, more people interact as peers rather than in more structured hierarchical relations. Work is more interdependent, so the ability to communicate with different types of people in new ways is a necessity.

| TYPES OF DIVERSITY

Although we often think of diversity in terms of gender or ethnic issues, there are three different types of diversity that affect groups in organizations: demographic diversity (e.g., gender, ethnicity, age), psychological diversity (e.g., values, personality, knowledge), and organizational diversity (e.g., tenure, occupation, status). Table 13.1 presents an overview of these types of diversity. *Demographic diversity* relates to the social categories that people use to classify others (McGrath, Berdahl, & Arrow, 1995). In our society, gender, race, ethnicity, nationality, age, and religion are considered important in many situations. However, these distinctions vary in importance depending on the society and era. For example, religion is a more important demographic variable in the Middle East than in the United States. Differences among European immigrants were considered very important in the United States during the early 1900s, but these are not viewed as culturally important differences today.

Psychological diversity relates to differences in people's cognitions and behavior. There are three types of psychological diversity. People vary in their values, beliefs, and attitudes; they may be conservative or liberal, religious or not religious, risk oriented or risk averse. There are differences in personality and cognitive and behavioral styles. As discussed in earlier chapters, people may be competitive or cooperative, and they may be asser-

TABLE 13.1
Types of Diversity

Demographic	Psychological	Organizational
Gender	Values, beliefs, and attitudes	Status
Race and ethnicity	Personality, cognitive, and	Occupation
Nationality	behavioral styles	Department/division
Age	Knowledge, skills, and	Tenure
Religion	abilities	

SOURCE: Adapted from McGrath, Berdahl, and Arrow (1995).

tive or aggressive. Finally, people differ in task-related knowledge, skills, and abilities. Team members may be technical experts, have artistic skills, and/or be good communicators.

Organizational diversity is caused by differences in people's relationship to an organization. Factors such as organizational rank, occupational specialty, department affiliation, and tenure are examples of organizational variables. These variables primarily affect an individual's status in the organization.

In organizational settings, the different types of diversity cannot easily be isolated from each other. Teams often have diversity based on all three types. There also is confusion in the ways in which people categorize the types of diversity (Cox, 1995). On the one hand, it makes sense to view demographic factors (e.g., gender) as different from organizational factors (e.g., status). On the other hand, one of the main impacts of demographic differences is that we give more power and status to certain group members than to others. Demographic and organizational factors interact through the flow of power and status.

The types of diversity vary in how easily they can be observed and changed. Knowledge, values, and personality are not easily observed. However, these often are inferred from the demographic and organizational characteristics of individuals. For example, stereotypes exist about age, gender, and job category that influence people's beliefs about individuals' attitudes, personalities, and knowledge. We often assume that our classifications of people are unchangeable, but both the psychological and organizational characteristics are subject to change.

The effects of different types of diversity have both similarities and differences (Nkomo, 1995). On the one hand, diversity arises due to differences in personality, ability, culture, age, race, and organizational position. These all are types of diversity, and these factors share similar properties. On the other hand, different types of diversity have different effects. The effects of gender diversity in a team are not the same as differences in values or knowledge among team members.

| HOW DIVERSITY AFFECTS A GROUP

There are two different ways in which to view how diversity affects a group (McGrath et al., 1995). The *trait* approach assumes that diversity affects the ways in which people act. In other words, people with different backgrounds have different values, skills, and personalities, and these differences affect the ways in which they interact in a group. The *expectations* approach focuses on the beliefs that people have about what other people are like. These expectations or beliefs change the ways in which they interact with people from different backgrounds.

As people work together in a group, they develop a sense of identity with the group. This sense of identity becomes stronger as the group becomes more cohesive and people establish working relationships with each other. Over time, members develop emotional bonds, create a common language for communicating, and have a number of shared experiences. This leads to a convergence of attitudes, beliefs, and values that reduces the importance of background differences among team members.

Although continued interaction affects some types of diversity, it does not affect all types. Interaction does not change people's personalities, their specialized skills, their races, or their ages. However, it does not have to change these characteristics to reduce the impacts of diversity. People identify with a group to the extent that membership is emotionally important to them and they care about the collective goals of the group (Brewer, 1995). One implication of team formation is that team members shift their social categories and create a new social identity. As people work together in a team, they develop the category of *teammate,* and this category can become emotionally more important than other ways in which to categorize the people in the team.

CAUSES OF DIVERSITY PROBLEMS

There are several ways in which to view the causes of diversity problems. One view sees diversity as arising from our cognitive processes; it is an arti-

TABLE 13.2
Perceptual Biases: Common Ways in Which People Misperceive Others

Fundamental attribution error	This is the tendency to explain why someone is acting the way he or she is by using personal explanations rather than situational ones. We tend to explain other people's behavior using personality traits and demographic variables rather than looking at situational causes.
First impression error	This is the tendency to base our judgments on our first impression of someone and to ignore later information that contradicts it. Once we form a positive first impression, we create the circumstances to justify it.
Halo effect	Once we have an overall positive or negative impression of someone, we assume that he or she is good or bad at everything. For example, if we like someone, then we often assume that he or she is competent and dependable.
Similar-to-me effect	This is the tendency to view people who are similar to us in a positive light.
Selective perception	This is the tendency to focus on and remember only information that confirms our beliefs and to ignore information that contradicts them.

SOURCE: Adapted from Greenberg and Baron (1997).

fact of our need for social classification. This misperception creates interpersonal problems in the group. A special case of this is misperceptions by the team leader. An alternative view sees diversity as due to power conflicts arising from intergroup competition. Rather than being caused by psychological issues, diversity problems reflect competition and power struggles between groups.

DIVERSITY AS A COGNITIVE PROCESS

Diversity is a social construction based on our cognitive processes. People categorize their social world into groups and treat the members of those groups differently based on their categories (Wilder, 1986). These categories are relatively arbitrary. For example, we are more likely to categorize people in ways that are easily observable (e.g., race rather than religion). Once these categories are formed, they have important implications for how people perceive and interact with others.

Social perception is the process of combining and interpreting information about others. The primary reason why people categorize others is to simplify the world (Srull & Wyer, 1988). By dividing people into categories or groups, people are able to predict what others are like. It is a simplification. It often is not very accurate, but it is an unavoidable component of human cognition. The problem with social perception is that it leads people into making premature judgments about what others are really like.

Stereotypes are cognitive categorizations of groups that describe what people in the groups are like. Stereotypes can be positive, negative, or both. People might believe that engineers are very analytic, and this may be a good or bad attribute depending on the context. Stereotypes cause the people in a category to seem similar to each other yet different from us (Wilder, 1986).

This social perception and categorization process, by itself, is not bad. It helps people interact with others. The problem is that the process creates a number of inaccuracies and biases that lead to misperceptions of others. Table 13.2 contains a set of common perceptual biases that negatively affect the ways in which we perceive others. From these biases, it is easy to see how our social perceptions can go wrong.

The problem of diversity is more than just categorization and perceptual biases. When people classify others, they divide their social worlds into in-groups and out-groups. This cognitive distinction has an emotional component (Tajfel, 1982). The group one belongs to is viewed more positively, and we like, trust, and act friendlier toward in-group members. In addition, similarity in demographics often is assumed to relate to similarity in other areas such as values, beliefs, and attitudes. Consequently, people are more likely to believe that in-group members are better than out-group members.

The addition of an emotional component to our categories shows how stereotypes become prejudices and discrimination. Prejudice is an unjustified negative attitude toward a group and its members. Prejudices typically are based on stereotypes. Prejudices may lead to discrimination depending on whether there is organizational and social support for the discrimination.

From this cognitive perspective, diversity is a cognitive categorization process that has an emotional component. The problem of diversity is that we misperceive people. People prejudge what others are like based on their categories rather than on how others actually are behaving. This causes people to treat them inappropriately, to have poorer communication because of their misconceptions, and to dislike and distrust people without getting to know them.

TEAM LEADER

One way in which the effects of diversity affect a team is through the relationship between a team member and a team leader (Tsui, Xin, & Egan, 1995). As was noted in Chapter 10, leader-member exchange theory describes the dynamics of this relationship. According to this model, the team leader decides early in the relationship whether the team member is part of the in-group or out-group. If part of the in-group, the team member will receive more resources, mentoring, and assistance; have higher performance evaluations; and be more satisfied with being part of the team than will members of the out-group.

There are two important issues to note in this description of the leader-member exchange. First, the evaluation of whether a team member is part of the in-group or out-group occurs very early in the relationship, before the leader actually knows much about the performance of the team member. Second, the impact of this early impression has long-lasting effects on the relationship.

A leader's quick decision that a team member belongs to the in-group or out-group often is due to the perceptual biases listed in Table 13.2. During the initial interaction with the leader, the team member is categorized (*first impression error*). The leader is more likely to rate favorably a team member who is similar to the leader (*similar-to-me effect*). The leader is more likely to rate a team member more favorably on many issues if the member's overall stereotype is positive (*halo effect*). Subsequent interactions rarely change from this first impression because information that supports the impression is remembered, whereas conflicting information is ignored (*selective perception*).

DIVERSITY AS A SOCIAL PROCESS

Rather than diversity arising from an individual's cognitive processes, an alternative view is that diversity arises from social competition and conflict. Why are gender and ethnicity important ways in which to classify people? To a sociologist, it is because women and minorities are challenging the power position of white males in our organizations and society. Women and minorities are competing for scarce resources (e.g., jobs, office space, project resources) that the majority group wants to control.

Research on competition shows that when groups compete, their members form prejudices against each other. As was noted in Chapter 5, when competing groups are united by common goals, these prejudices are reduced. A person can classify his or her social world in a variety of ways, but prejudices arise when the out-group is perceived as a threat to one's resources or power.

One of the primary impacts of diversity is on power in a group (McGrath et al., 1995). Diversity affects group interaction primarily by creating power differentials within the group. Many of the negative effects of diversity can be viewed as impacts of unequal power within a group. As was discussed in Chapter 8, unequal power in a group disrupts its communication process. In groups with unequal power, the amount of communication is reduced and the powerful members control the communication process. Power differences also affect group cohesion because individuals with similar status are more likely to interact with each other and to form friendships (Tolbert, Andrews, & Simons, 1995).

PROBLEM OF DIVERSITY

Diversity among group members can lead to misperceptions that reduce communication from minority members. It also may increase emotional tension and conflict within a group. These impacts may discourage participation by minority members, thereby preventing the group from using its resources.

| MISPERCEPTION

The false stereotypes and prejudices of team members cause diversity problems. People from different backgrounds hold different values and respond to situations differently. These differences in values and behavior can be threatening to people's sense of what is appropriate. To deal with this psychological anxiety, people often either ignore or misinterpret the actions of people with diverse backgrounds.

These perceptual biases may cause people to discount the contributions of minority members. (Minority in this case means people with different demographic or organizational backgrounds from those of most of the group members.) Over time, the minority members respond to this by contributing less to group communication. The lack of power that these members experience also may cause them to have less impact on the group's decisions (Tolbert et al., 1995).

One of the potential benefits of diversity is to increase the amount of information and the number of perspectives that can be used to analyze and solve problems in a group. This benefit is lost if the group ignores the input of minority members or if the minority members do not provide input. The problem of diversity in teams occurs when the team overlooks the right answer because of who came up with it.

| EMOTIONAL DISTRUST

Diversity may create emotional problems among team members. The dividing of a group into in-group and out-group members creates social friction. Power conflicts within the group create a climate of distrust and defensive communication. Rather than the group forming a social unit, it may become divided into cliques.

These emotional issues create several group process problems. Diversity can lead to an increase in conflict because people are more distrustful. Not only are there more conflicts, but the conflicts are more difficult to resolve. The emotional distrust also may prevent the group from forming the social bonds necessary to form a cohesive group. Group cohesion has many benefits to a group, and diversity can prevent these benefits from being realized.

| FAILURE TO USE GROUP RESOURCES

Poor adaptation to diversity can cause a group to ignore and silence the views from the minority. This means that the group is not fully using its resources. Diversity has other effects that limit the resources of the group. It may limit the careers of minority members. If minorities are not recognized and rewarded for their actual contributions, then they might not become motivated team members.

The way in which the group treats minority members not only reduces their input to the group but also may reduce their desire to contribute. Over time, minority members become less committed to the team's goals and less motivated to perform for the team (Ancona & Caldwell, 1992). This, in turn, is used to justify not rewarding them or providing them with the opportunity and support to achieve more.

Diversity has been shown to affect turnover and socialization in work teams (McGrath et al., 1995). Minority members are more likely to have higher turnover in a team. It is easier for a team to socialize new members into the team if their characteristics are similar to those of the majority.

However, a team that starts with a high level of diversity has less of these effects; it is more likely to have low minority turnover and to have a less difficult time socializing diverse new members.

EFFECTS OF DIVERSITY

The results of research on the effects of diversity on groups depend on how the research is conducted, the type of diversity examined, and the tasks that the groups are performing. Cross-functional teams are an example of diversity by occupation or department. An organization uses this type of diverse team to deal with complex issues that require a variety of skills and participation from several parts of the organization.

| RESEARCH ON THE IMPACTS OF DIVERSITY ON GROUPS

The research on the impacts of diversity on groups is contradictory. Part of the problem is the difference between short-term laboratory research on groups and the study of actual working groups. Homogeneous groups do better in the short run. However, many of the problems with diversity are related to miscommunication that goes away over time (Northcraft, Polzer, Neale, & Kramer, 1995). Another issue relates to the criteria used to evaluate success. Diversity is a benefit for some types of tasks but is a problem for other types of tasks and criteria. There also is confusion about the type of diversity that is used in these studies. Is diversity in demographic variables (e.g., gender, ethnicity) the same as diversity in personal variables (e.g., values, personality, skills)? Does it make sense to mix all types of diversity studies together?

Finally, one has to ask whether this even is the right question. Does it make sense to study the effects of diversity separate from an organizational context? The impact of diversity on a work team depends on the organizational climate and how the team manages diversity (Adler, 1986). Diversity is a fact of life for most organizations. The important question is not whether diverse groups are better or worse than nondiverse groups but rather how to make diverse groups operate more effectively.

There is a growing collection of research from work groups on the effects of diversity. This research typically compares homogeneous and heterogeneous (diverse) work groups. Jackson (1992) conducted a meta-analysis of this research that can be used to understand the impact of diversity on work groups. Her analysis categorizes the research along two dimensions: the type of diversity and the type of task.

Not all types of diversity are the same. One of the most basic divisions of types of diversity is into two types: personal attributes and functional attributes (Table 13.3). *Personal* attributes include differences in personality, values, attitudes, and various demographic variables (e.g., age, gender, race). *Functional* attributes concern people's knowledge, abilities, and skills that relate to the work environment.

The impact of these types of diversity interacts with the type of task being performed and the group process. Tasks can be performance, intellective, or creative/judgmental. *Performance* tasks require perceptual and motor skills, which typically are evaluated using objective standards of quality and productivity. *Intellective* tasks are problem-solving tasks for which there are correct answers. These are the types of tasks that knowledge workers (e.g., engineers, teachers, accountants) perform. *Creative/judgmental* tasks typically are decision-making tasks that do not have correct answers. Besides studying the outcome of a group's task performance, researchers also examine the impact of diversity on the group process. Group cohesion and conflict are typical measures of the group process used in diversity research. Cohesion and conflict do not refer to the outcome of a group's work; rather, they refer to the group process itself. The relationship between these types of diversity and tasks is shown in Table 13.3.

The results presented in Table 13.3 lead to a number of conclusions about the effects of diversity. When a group's outcome is examined, diversity has either a neutral or positive impact on the group for all types of tasks. It is only when the group process is examined that diversity has a negative impact. Although diverse groups may have more problems managing the group process, this does not seem to prevent these diverse groups from performing better than homogeneous groups.

Diversity in personal and demographic attributes has mixed effects on the group, whereas diversity in functional attributes is either positive or neutral effects. Diversity in skills and knowledge helps a group improve problem solving (McGrath et al., 1995). Diversity in values often hurts a group by increasing the amount of conflict when it is trying to reach consensus.

For example, Baugh and Graen (1997) examined the effects of gender and racial composition on perceptions of team performance in cross-functional teams. Members of teams that were heterogeneous with regard to race or gender rated their teams as less effective than homogeneous teams. This lower rating was due to lower ratings given the teams by their white male members. However, outside evaluations of team performance found no dif-

TABLE 13.3
Impact of Diversity on Work Groups

	Type of Diversity	
	Personal Attribute(s)	*Functional Attribute*
Type of task		
Performance	Mixed effects	Diversity is beneficial
Intellective	Limited research evidence Diversity may be a benefit	Limited research evidence
Creativity and judgment	Diversity is beneficial	Diversity is beneficial
Group process		
Cohesion and conflict	Diversity is a problem	Limited research evidence

SOURCE: Adapted from Jackson (1992).

ference between heterogeneous and homogeneous teams. This may imply that heterogeneity leads to less pleasant working relationships but does not affect actual team performance.

The clearest situation in which diversity is a benefit is for creative and judgmental tasks. Although diversity can create conflict in judgmental tasks and make a group less efficient, diversity and conflict also can help to improve the quality of the judgments. Many different types of diversity can improve the creative performance of a team (Amabile, 1983). Diversity in cognition, age, organizational tenure, and education all have been shown to be relevant to creativity. The value of this diversity increases for "identity-relevant" tasks such as designing a marketing program that attempts to reach different groups in society.

| CROSS-FUNCTIONAL TEAMS

In most cases, diversity is something that happens to a group. The group members who come together to complete a task may or may not be a diverse set of individuals. However, there are cases in which diversity is created for a purpose. Cross-functional teams are a good example of diversity by design.

The complexity of modern organizations and the tasks they perform often requires cross-functional teams (Northcraft et al., 1995). For example, when an organization designs a new product, the design team often includes members with different technical skills (e.g., electronics, materials, programming) because of the complexity of the product. The design team also may include members from different departments (e.g., marketing, engineering, manufacturing) so as to ensure that the innovation gets adopted by the entire organization. Cross-functional teams are an example of diversity created by differences in knowledge and skills as well as differences in organizational position, occupation, and subculture. These two types of diversity (functional and organizational) create both benefits and problems for the team.

Teamwork can be evaluated by looking at effectiveness and efficiency. Effectiveness relates to a team's ability to complete its task, whereas efficiency relates to performing the task with the least amount of time, labor, and resources. The diversity in a cross-functional team increases its effectiveness. The team is more creative and better able to support the implementation of decisions. However, diversity has mixed effects on efficiency. Diversity is a benefit to efficiency because of specialization of labor. Having a diverse group means that experts can be assigned to perform tasks that they are well qualified to perform. However, diversity can increase the amount of conflict in decision making and the amount of group process time that must be spent in coordinating and performing tasks.

A cross-functional team has unique characteristics that make team development and leadership different (Uhl-Bien & Graen, 1992). Because of the multidisciplinary team structure, team members typically have dual assignments to both their departments in the organization and the team. The team leader might not be able to provide technical guidance to the team due to the multiple areas of expertise. The role of the leader becomes one of coordination and facilitation within the team and coordination outside the team. Because of the separate backgrounds of team members, communication and conflict problems are more likely to occur. Resolving these issues requires more management of the group process and an increased commitment to the goals of the team.

Although there is a need for organizations to use cross-functional teams, these types of teams can be difficult to establish and operate. The diversity that makes a team so valuable to an organization might make it difficult for the team to operate successfully. The positive conflict that makes the team valuable might prevent it from being functional. A successful cross-functional team is like a successful negotiation; the participants retain their individual values and differences while forming an agreement that uses these differences in a synergistic way.

One of the challenges of cross-functional teams is to manage conflict. Some of these conflicts arise from legitimate organizational or professional differences. The resolution of these conflicts is part of the value of cross-functional teams. However, other conflicts are related to stereotyping, distrust, and biases that limit communication among the team members. These biases can prevent teams from negotiating agreements even when the agreements are in everyone's best interest.

APPLICATION: MANAGING DIVERSITY

Because the implications of diversity are multifaceted, organizations use a variety of approaches to manage diversity. Diversity problems are caused by misperceptions and prejudices, which create communication and group process problems. However, diversity also is about competition and power conflicts. Both of these views of diversity are important and need to be addressed in diversity management programs. Programs to manage diversity focus on increasing awareness to deal with misperceptions and biases, improving communication and group skills, and dealing with group and organizational conflict issues. The success of diversity management programs depends on whether the practices are supported by the organizations.

| INCREASING AWARENESS

Many organizations try to deal with diversity issues through training programs to increase awareness. Awareness programs are designed to increase understanding of diversity issues and to make people more aware of the assumptions and biases they have about other groups. Their goal is to increase knowledge and awareness of the issues, challenge existing assumptions about minority groups, and eliminate stereotypes (Battaglia, 1992).

In some cases, diversity training can backfire (Gardenswartz & Rowe, 1994). Diversity training can heighten emotional tension because it makes people feel uneasy, it can lead to a polarization of attitudes about minorities, and blaming and personal attacks that can occur during training may leave lingering emotional conflicts.

Awareness training programs need to go beyond just teaching about cultural differences (Triandis, 1994). This increased understanding should lead to the development of social contacts and friendships that cut across demographic boundaries. It is these informal social contacts that develop into relationships that can reduce misperceptions, lead to improved understanding of differences, and promote trust.

IMPROVING SKILLS

Many of the conflicts within diverse groups are due to miscommunication caused by stereotypes and distrust. To deal with these problems, team members can be trained to communicate better with each other and to appreciate the unique contributions that other members can make (Northcraft et al., 1995). Skill-based diversity programs help to improve the skills that people have to manage diversity issues. These skills include improved communication and facilitation skills that can be used to resolve misunderstandings as well as increased flexibility and adaptability when dealing with others (Battaglia, 1992).

There are a variety of techniques that a team leader can use to help improve diversity relations within the team (Armstrong & Cole, 1995). Developing agreement on the team's purpose, norms, roles, and procedures helps to improve communication among members. The team leader needs to support communication from all members and to obtain the commitment of all members to the team's goals. Miscommunication needs to be clarified during team interactions. When problems occur, the leader should focus more on the task and the procedures. If the team is having trouble with open discussions, then procedures should be used to structure the communication. Finally, face-to-face interactions should be encouraged to develop social relations.

IMPROVING ORGANIZATIONAL ISSUES

One approach to managing diversity is to help break down the social boundaries created by categorization. It is clear that just having people interact in a team will not necessarily accomplish this. There must be approaches that equalize power within the team and organization for communication to break boundaries (Nkomo, 1995). One way in which to do this is to increase the amount of structure within a team. The leader should use his or her power to equalize power among the other team members. Increasing the structure can help to equalize participation.

Another approach is to use common or superordinate goals. Diverse groups within an organization should be encouraged to develop common group and organizational goals. It is useful to create a team identity and goal that unites the members and minimizes the differences. In addition, the team's work can be structured to require high levels of interdependence so that coordination and interaction are needed to complete the project.

It is important to separate diversity from task assignments (McGrath et al., 1995). A team should not assign Asian members the technical issues, women members the communication functions, and younger members the computer tasks. When tasks and stereotypes are linked, stereotypes and prejudices become a rational way in which to explain what happens in the team.

In many cases, the problems created by diversity in a team are related to the performance evaluation and reward system. When people in a team are not working cooperatively with each other, the evaluation and reward system is one of the first places to look for a cause. Often, what is called a diversity problem is not one at all (Northcraft et al., 1995). Members of the leader's in-group are more likely to get better performance appraisals and rewards. In a cross-functional team, members often are evaluated and rewarded by the departments they represent rather than by the team. Given this situation, they have limited commitment to the team's goals. These conflicts are primarily about the organization's reward system, not about diversity.

SUMMARY

Diversity is increasing in importance for organizations because of the increased numbers of women and minorities in the workplace, the desire to have a workforce that reflects the diversity in society, and changes in the ways in which people work together. Although we often think of diversity in terms of demographic differences (e.g., gender, ethnicity, age), diversity also includes psychological (e.g., personality, values, skills) and organizational (e.g., department, status) differences among people. The impact of diversity on groups can be caused by differences among types of people or expectations about differences that cause people to treat others differently.

The problems created by diversity have several causes. People categorize others and use stereotypes to explain the differences between groups. This categorization process can lead to misperceptions and cognitive biases. Team leaders are affected by these biases and may treat team members differently because of their backgrounds. Diversity also can be viewed as due to competition and conflict between groups. The problems of diversity are related to attempts by majority groups to maintain power and status in organizations and society.

The biases created by diversity can cause members of a group to misperceive and discount the contributions of minority members. This reduces minority members' ability to contribute to the group's efforts. Emotional distrust can lead to defensive communication and power conflicts within the group. These factors disrupt the operation of the group and reduce the motivation of minority members to participate.

Research on the effects of diversity in groups often is confusing. Analyses of the differences between homogeneous and heterogeneous groups show that the results of research depend on the types of diversity and tasks that are studied. For personality and demographic diversity, the effects of diversity are mixed for tasks but are negative for group cohesion and conflict. For functional diversity (which relates to differences in skills), the effects of diversity are positive for most types of tasks. Cross-functional teams are an example of diversity created on purpose by organizations. Diversity in these teams comes from differences in skills and organizational departments. These teams can be very effective but also can be difficult to establish and operate.

Organizations can develop programs to help groups better manage diversity issues. Diversity programs may be designed to increase awareness of the differences among types of people, to improve groups' ability to communicate and resolve conflicts, and to create goals and organizational reward systems that encourage working together.

ACTIVITY: UNDERSTANDING GENDER AND STATUS DIFFERENCES IN A TEAM

Objective. Diversity can be caused by demographic (e.g., gender) or organizational (e.g., status) differences. The more powerful group is more likely to communicate, to speak more forcefully, and to contradict others. It sometimes is assumed that women's communication will be more polite and deferential than men's communication. However, this difference might have more to do with status than with gender. This activity will help to explore this question.

Activity. Use the observation form (Activity Worksheet 13.1) to record the various communication styles in a team meeting.

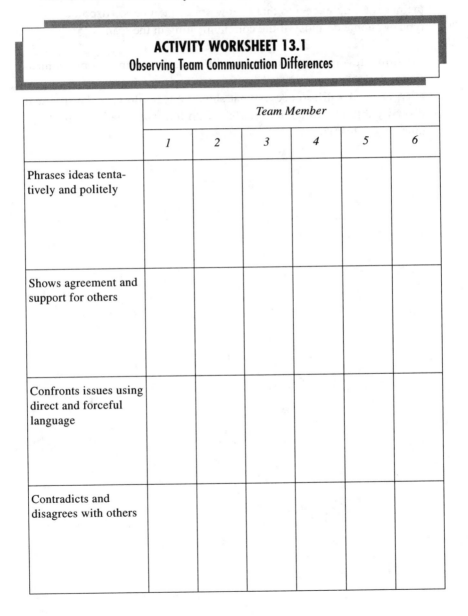

ACTIVITY WORKSHEET 13.1
Observing Team Communication Differences

	Team Member					
	1	*2*	*3*	*4*	*5*	*6*
Phrases ideas tentatively and politely						
Shows agreement and support for others						
Confronts issues using direct and forceful language						
Contradicts and disagrees with others						

Analysis. The first two communication styles are used more often by women and low-status team members, whereas the last two communication styles are used more often by men and high-status team members. Compare the various communication styles of women to that of men in the team, and compare the various communication styles of high-status members (e.g., leader) to that of low-status members. Also note which type of people do most of the communicating in the team.

Discussion. How can you explain the differences among the communication styles of team members? Are these differences due to status, personality, or gender differences? What should a team do to make sure that diversity differences do not interfere with full participation and acceptance in the team?

PART IV

TEAMS AT WORK

Chapter 14

ORGANIZATIONAL CULTURE

The shared values, beliefs, and norms of an organization are known as its organizational culture. Organizational cultures vary regarding the ways in which individuality, status, and uncertainty are accepted and used. These cultural differences affect group norms and processes.

The success of work teams depends on the amount of support they receive from the organization, which in turn depends on the organization's culture. Successful organizational cultures create good environments for teams. At the same time, the use of teams also can change an organization's culture. Teams need to be sensitive so that they do not violate the existing organization's culture, but they also should help encourage changes to support teamwork.

▶ LEARNING OBJECTIVES

1. What is organizational culture and how does it affect people in organizations?
2. How do cultures vary by levels and networks of subcultures?
3. What are the main dimensions of organizational culture?
4. How do the different dimensions of culture affect teamwork?
5. How are U.S. and Japanese teams different?
6. What are the two main types of organizational cultures that affect the use of teams?
7. What are the characteristics of successful and innovative organizational cultures?
8. How can organizational cultures be changed to support teamwork?

DEFINING ORGANIZATIONAL CULTURE

The concept of organizational culture arose during the 1980s, partly as a result of the many comparisons between U.S. and Japanese organizations. Peters and Waterman (1982) used the concept of organizational culture as a way of describing the practices of the best U.S. companies. Schein (1992) was influential in arguing that the principles for examining national cultures could be used to describe organizational cultures.

Organizational culture refers to the shared values, beliefs, and norms of an organization. Researchers studying organizational culture emphasize various aspects as key to understanding how organizations operate. To Deal and Kennedy (1982), an organization's customs, rituals, and traditions help one to understand the underlying values that guide organizational decision making. Davis (1984) focuses on the shared meanings and beliefs of organizations because they affect an organization's strategies and operating procedures. Kilmann and Saxton (1983) view culture as determining the group norms and behavioral patterns of employees.

Regardless of which characteristic of organizational culture one selects to study, there are features common to all perspectives (Schein, 1992). All members of an organization share its organizational culture. Culture provides structural stability to the organization because its influence is pervasive and slow to change. The various aspects of culture are integrated and form a consistent pattern. Culture reflects the shared learning by members of the organization that contains cognitive, behavioral, and emotional elements. Finally, organizational culture affects both the internal operations of the organization and how it relates and adapts to its external environment.

The concept of culture also can be used at the team level (Aranda, Aranda, & Conlon, 1998). A team's culture is defined through its values and rituals; it determines how things get done in a team. The main cultural values of a team are related to commitment, accountability, and trust. *Commitment* relates both to the task and to the other people on the team. Commitment concerns the willingness to participate and become involved in the task and to support the other people on the team. *Accountability* relates to who is responsible for the team's success. Accountability could reside with the individual, the team, or the organization's hierarchy. An important part of accountability is empowerment. The team cannot be held accountable if it does not have the authority and power to act on its own. The third aspect is *trust*. Without a culture of trust, the team cannot have free and open communication.

A team and an organizational culture have a mutually influencing relationship. Teamwork occurs more easily in some types of organizational cultures than in others. For example, cultural norms about power and control affect the way in which communication flows among levels in an organization (Zuboff, 1988). New, team-based work practices such as *total quality management* may be unsuccessful because they contradict cultural norms about communication and power (Bushe, 1988). The use of teams changes the ways in which people work and relate to each other, and this changes the organizational culture. Over time, an organization's work systems tend to become congruent with its organizational culture.

Organizational culture researchers show that culture affects organizational performance, leadership style, role conflicts, cooperation, and styles of decision making. However, some researchers have criticized the concept of organizational culture for being poorly defined (Parks & Sanna, 1999). Culture, at the international level, refers to deeply held values that are reflected in patterns of behavior in a society. These behavioral patterns are very difficult to change. Hence, equating national culture with organizational culture may be misleading because organizational cultures vary in strength and are more open to change.

Does an organization have a single organizational culture? How should the different aspects of culture be analyzed? Many different models of organizational culture have been proposed to examine how organizations operate. In the following subsections, organizational culture is discussed as levels or depths and networks with subcultures.

| LEVELS OF CULTURE

Organizational culture is primarily about the deeply held beliefs and assumptions of an organization (Schein, 1992). These can be viewed as three levels of depth, from surface rituals to underlying values.

On the surface, there are the symbols, rituals, artifacts, and stories that display the culture to members and outsiders. Culture is visibly symbolized in things such as what employees wear, office layouts, and parking spaces. Rituals also are used to demonstrate an organization's culture and values. Teams often develop rituals for handling important situations such as socializing new members with orientation activities, day-to-day activities such as ground rules for meetings, and celebrations for team success.

The middle level is the strategic culture. This is about the distinctive styles and approaches that the people in an organization use to perform their functions. It concerns the shared ideas and actions that define appropriate behavior in a variety of situations. For example, organizational culture tells employees when it is okay to be competitive and tells managers how they should communicate with subordinates. The strategic level shows the ideals and standards of the organization that often are stated in the corporate mission statement.

The final underlying core level of culture consists of the ideologies, values, and underlying beliefs of an organization. These are fundamental beliefs about human nature, the world, and the purpose of the organization. The core level defines what is important at work. For example, basic assumptions about the nature of employees, such as McGregor's (1960) Theories X and Y, are defined here. This theory proposes that the two types of assumptions that organizations can make about their employees are that either (a) employees are lazy and need to be coerced (Theory X) or (b) employees are responsible and need to be encouraged (Theory Y).

| CULTURES AS NETWORKS

Organizations are not uniform, and they do not necessarily have uniform cultures. Rather than viewing organizations as having single cultures, organizations also can be viewed as containing networks of groups that develop their own styles of operating and interacting. These are organizational subcultures. These subcultures can arise due to mergers and acquisitions, geographic differences among facilities, or positions in the organizations.

Organizations can be characterized by how integrated these separate subcultures are. In strong organizational cultures, the networks are strong and the organizations have dominant cultures; in weak organizational cultures, the subcultures are relatively independent (Van Maanen & Barley, 1985). When the shared beliefs and assumptions held by working groups are similar across organizations, the organizations have strong cultures. For example, Hewlett-Packard has a strong organizational culture that defines how managers should treat employees—open-door policy, fostering independence, and promoting equal-status relations. These practices operate throughout all divisions of the company.

One important cause of subcultures relates to an employee's occupational community. An occupational community refers to the shared knowledge, language, training, and identity formed by working in a particular area of specialization (Schein, 1992). For example, engineers and sales representatives have different occupational communities and, therefore, occupy different subcultures within an organization. Even within strong organizational cultures such as Hewlett-Packard, people from engineering and sales use different professional languages and have different styles of interacting with others.

The importance of studying organizational subcultures arises in situations where teams cross boundaries between subcultures. For example, new product development teams typically are composed of professionals from different functional areas within an organization. These cross-functional teams have problems due to the competitiveness between divisions in the organization (Adler, 1991). In addition, the teams often have communication and coordination problems because the members come from different subcultures. Representatives from sales, manufacturing, and research and development often use different languages, have different criteria for evaluating success, and operate using different attitudes toward time and deadlines.

DIMENSIONS OF ORGANIZATIONAL CULTURE

A number of approaches are used to determine the dimensions of national and organizational cultures. Dimensions allow one to establish frameworks that can be used to compare different cultures. Triandis (1994) reviewed several approaches used by anthropologists. Hofstede (1980) studied the employees in international companies to develop ways in which to compare national differences. Aranda and colleagues (1998) examined work teams in different organizations. Each of these approaches has identified a similar set of key dimensions.

Organizational cultures can be compared on three dimensions: individualism versus collectivism, power, and uncertainty (Table 14.1). The following subsections examine these three dimensions and then show how they can be used to compare teams in the United States and Japan.

| INDIVIDUALISM VERSUS COLLECTIVISM

In an *individualist* culture, people have loose ties with each other and expect to be responsible for themselves and their immediate families. People seek individual achievement and recognition and might have trouble committing to team goals. *Collectivists* value the ties between people. People

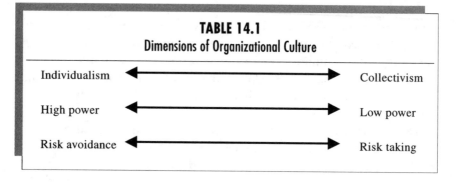

TABLE 14.1
Dimensions of Organizational Culture

Individualism	⟷	Collectivism
High power	⟷	Low power
Risk avoidance	⟷	Risk taking

are expected to look after each other. Self-interest is subordinate to the interest of the social group or team.

This distinction also relates to how people respond to conflict and conformity pressure. Collectivists often value compliance because the harmony of the team is important. Conformity is expected, and open conflict is discouraged. Individualists often enjoy conflict, competition, and open controversy. They seek arguments for their own sake. A successful team finds ways in which to encourage the participation of the compliance-oriented members, who might be shut out of the team's decision-making process by the conflict-oriented members.

This dimension has a mixed affect on the use of teams. Collectivists are easier to organize into teams because they value cooperation. However, a team can run into problems because the conformity pressure prevents it from achieving the open communication and constructive conflict that is one of the benefits of teamwork.

Although collectivists value cooperation, this does not mean that they cannot be competitive when appropriate. Japanese business organizations are collectivist. Cooperation among employees is highly valued and rewarded. However, they are very competitive toward outside organizations.

POWER AND STATUS

The *power* dimension refers to the degree to which unequal power is accepted or rejected by people in a culture. In high-power cultures, large power and status differences are acceptable to people. In these cultures, people show great respect and deference to higher status people and feel uncomfortable in challenging authority. Within a team, they are more willing to accept the leader's decisions.

In low-power cultures, people are less willing to accept others' authority just because of the positions others hold in the organizations. People take a more egalitarian view. Team members take initiative and do not automatically accept management directives.

A high-power culture can be a problem for a team. It makes team members more willing to accept management's or the team leader's view. This lack of independence reduces team creativity. Participation is not easy for people in high-power cultures because they believe that communication from above is more important than their own ideas. Equal-power status has benefits to teams in communication. In an unequal-status situation, the higher status person does most of the communicating, and most communication is directed at the highest status person.

However, a team in a low-power culture can be difficult to manage. Members' more open communication style can create more conflicts. Their sense of independence from the organization's authority can lead the team into making decisions that are not sensitive to the politics of the organization. Egalitarian communication in the team's decision-making process may improve the quality of the decisions but also may reduce the team's ability to implement the decision because of this lack of deference to the surrounding organization.

| UNCERTAINTY AND RISK AVOIDANCE

Cultures vary in how much people are willing to accept uncertainty and in their desire to avoid taking risks. Uncertainty is the degree to which people feel threatened by and try to avoid ambiguous situations or change. In risk-avoiding cultures, people value social harmony and stability. They want to have rules and norms that define appropriate behavior, and they prefer things to stay the same so that they know what is expected of them.

Risk-avoiding cultures value social harmony more than they do change. Open conflict is considered inappropriate, so they avoid controversies or become compliant during controversies. People in risk-avoiding cultures try to maintain the security of the status quo, partly because they fear the potential for failure during changes.

Risk-taking cultures value change. They tend to be action oriented rather than planning changes in advance. People in these cultures are open to and willing to try out new ideas. Conflict is more likely to be viewed as positive because it encourages new ideas and change.

| COMPARING THE UNITED STATES TO JAPAN

The United States and Japan make an interesting comparison of the effects of culture. These two countries have different national cultures, and their organizations and teams operate within different organizational cultures. Using the dimensions already described, U.S. organizations tend to display individualism, low power, and risk taking, whereas Japanese organizations tend to display collectivism, high power, and risk avoidance. These differences have significant impacts on the use of teams and on how teams operate.

The focus of U.S. management practices is on trying to control, motivate, and reward individual performance. The individual remains independent of the organization and is expected to stay committed to the organization only so long as it is in his or her best interest. The use of teamwork in the United States is less than that in other industrialized countries (Cole, 1989). In addition, the focus on competition and individualism in U.S. culture limits teamwork among the professional and managerial staff.

In the Japanese approach to management, the individual does not have a job but, rather, becomes part of the organization (Ouchi, 1981). Japanese organizations stress the interdependence of all employees. They have a participative style marked by mutual respect and common interest (Pascale & Athos, 1981). Consensus decision making is practiced at all levels of organizations.

Teamwork programs such as quality circles and production teams are more common in Japanese companies. Management creates these teams to serve as mechanisms for employee participation. However, the focus of teamwork is on improving the productivity of the work system. Participation allows employees to make suggestions, but management retains control over all decisions (Cole, 1989). Unlike teamwork programs in the United States, participation does not imply power sharing with the workers in hierarchical Japanese corporations.

The Japanese have a more cautious view of change because their culture is more attuned to the value of promoting social harmony. Japanese companies tend to implement incremental changes because of their concern about social relations and job security (Prochaska, 1980). Within teams, there is less conflict and more conformity because of this. Consequently, Japanese teams often are viewed as less creative and less willing to take risks than U.S. teams.

Japanese teams use consensus decision making. Consensus is easier to reach in Japanese teams because people are less independent and try to avoid conflict. They are confident that compromise solutions can be found, so they do not rush to decide. This makes Japanese decision making slower, but the implementation of decisions is faster. Once a Japanese team has made a consensus decision, it knows that everyone will support the implementation of the decision.

This comparison between U.S. and Japanese cultures demonstrates several points about organizational culture. First, cultures affect the ways in which teams operate. Second, national cultures affect organizational cultures. Third, cultures do not prevent the use of teams, but they do create an environment for teams that affects how teams operate.

ORGANIZATIONAL CULTURE AND TEAMWORK

An organizational culture that encourages employee involvement and participation is a necessary support for teamwork and self-managing teams. In a supportive organizational culture, managers are less likely to resist using teams, and there are better relations between teams and other parts of the organization. Self-managing teams are much more likely to be successful in organizations where the organizational cultures and value systems support empowerment and teamwork. Overall, organizational culture is one of the largest predictors of the successful use of teams by companies (Levi & Slem, 1995).

Organizational culture defines the norms that regulate the acceptable behaviors in an organization. When these cultural norms conflict with the use of teams, organizations will have a difficult time using teams successfully. For example, norms about communication that are embodied in an organization's culture may limit the organization's ability to use teams. Many corporations do not have open communication from workers to managers, across departments, or from top management to the rest of the organizations. This limits the types of communication that occur within a team and limits the team's ability to relate to other parts of the organization.

Thomsett (1980) identifies several features of a supportive culture for a team. First, there should be a belief in the organization that people are an asset to be developed. People should be grouped together so that they can use their skills and expertise to perform a task rather than having their jobs broken down so that only individuals can perform them. The organization should have a participative management structure that has few organizational levels. The control system should emphasize self-regulation and be focused on commitment rather than on control. Finally, the environment should be nonhostile. Fear and anxiety, which result in employees being defensive and distrustful, drive hostile organizational cultures.

Walton and Hackman (1986) identify two distinct types of organizational cultures that affect the use of teams: control cultures and commitment cultures. (This distinction is similar to McGregor's [1960] Theories X and Y management.) Status and power drive the *control* strategy; it is hierarchical and tightly controlling. The relations among people are adversarial and nontrusting. Teams are difficult to form and operate in this context. The *commitment* strategy reduces the number of organizational levels of authority and control, commits to quality, and adopts methods to encourage open communication and participation. It uses teams to operate and gives teams the autonomy and authority to operate successfully. This type of culture empowers both individuals and teams so as to increase commitment to their organizations' goals.

Obviously, most organizations fall somewhere in between these two approaches. Although managers often want to shift to a commitment strategy, the existing culture is control oriented and difficult to change. Developing teams is a struggle because their use is not compatible with the existing cultural practices. Teams operate better within a commitment-oriented culture because they are given the resources, training, and power needed to operate.

It is critical that the organizational culture support collaborative work for teams to operate successfully (Dyer, 1995). It is very difficult for a traditional control-oriented culture to change so as to promote teamwork. Announcements by management or simple attempts to create teams will be viewed cynically by the people of the organization if the culture does not support the use of teams.

Many organizations want to change; they want to promote teamwork; and they want commitment-oriented organizational cultures. However, they do not want to change the existing systems of power, authority, performance evaluations, and rewards. When these organizational system processes are divergent from the announced cultural changes, employees are rightfully skeptical. Incongruence between the cultures and the work systems creates confusion. Organizations cannot announce that people are their most important assets, enact layoffs to improve profitability, and then expect employees to believe their announcements.

CULTURES OF SUCCESS AND INNOVATION

Although the notion that successful companies have had certain styles of behaving was common throughout the 20th century, the focus on organizational culture as an explanation for this is relatively recent (Hayes, 1997).

Studies of high-performing companies in the United States show that they have certain distinctive organizational cultures. Probably the most famous example of this approach is from Peters and Waterman's (1982) *In Search of Excellence,* which presents their analysis of the organizational cultures of successful companies. Their results are presented in Table 14.2.

Many of the principles of successful organizational cultures listed in Table 14.2 also encourage the development and use of teams. Successful companies encourage teams to act rather than be controlled by a centralized bureaucracy. Teams are used to scan the environment and form relationships with customers. Teams are given power and authority so that they can act independently. People are valued, so team members are given the training and resources to operate successfully. Managers are encouraged to work with employees and to act as team leaders rather than distant authority figures. Hierarchical levels are reduced, and teams are used to replace outdated power structures. Finally, teams are given the freedom to act independently while the organizations monitor and provide feedback on their performance. In excellent companies, the cultures provide the contexts for teams to operate successfully.

Research on innovative organizations suggests that their organizational cultures are more supportive of teamwork. Organizational cultures are an important concern for highly innovative organizations because they must rely on informal mechanisms to provide stability to the organizations while they are changing. Project teams and task forces are used by innovative organizations to set the direction of changes while a shift to team-based organizational structures is used to increase the flexibility of the organizations to adapt to change (Mohrman, Cohen, & Mohrman, 1995).

There are a number of core values that often are held by highly innovative organizations (Lawler, 1986). One value is the recognition that employees are valuable corporate assets that need to be invested in and developed. Employees can be trusted to make important decisions, and the power and authority for decision making should be made at the level of the issue. Organizational values also often emphasize a commitment to customer service and the importance of quality. Finally, there is a belief that change is necessary and that the organizations will support and promote changes initiated by their employees.

The norms of innovative organizations stress informality, high work standards, flexibility in decision making, and informal connections (Tushman & Nadler, 1986). Open communication, strong and informal communication networks, and employee participation in decision making are common practices. Organizations view task-oriented conflict as appro-

TABLE 14.2
Principles of Excellent Companies

1. Bias for action
2. Close to the customer
3. Autonomy and entrepreneurship
4. Productivity through people
5. Hands on, value driven
6. Simple form, lean staff
7. Simultaneous loose-tight properties

SOURCE: *In Search of Excellence*, by T. Peters and R. Waterman. Copyright © 1982, HarperCollins Publishers.

priate and provide constructive ways in which to resolve conflicts. There is acceptance of risk taking and protection of those employees who take reasonable risks for the organizations. Successes are rewarded, but there is no punishment for failures when innovating.

Organizations with values and norms that support independence in decision making, open communication, acceptance of risk taking, and the need for change tend to be more innovative. These commitment-oriented organizational cultures use teams to manage the innovation process.

CHANGING ORGANIZATIONAL CULTURE TO SUPPORT TEAMWORK

Teams require supportive organizational cultures to operate effectively. This creates the dilemma of how to implement teamwork in difficult organizational cultures.

TEAMS AND CULTURAL CHANGE

The importance of organizational culture as a primary support for teamwork is both a problem and a benefit (Levi & Slem, 1995). An organization's culture is not easy to change. Developing an organizational culture that supports teamwork is a long-term process; it is not something that can be dictated by top management or announced as a new organizational program. Changing an organization's culture requires a consistent effort on the part of management to show that employee involvement and teamwork are valued and rewarded by the organization. This needs to be done through both communication and action.

In organizations without uniform cultures, cultural change can occur within subcultures (Dyer, 1995). However, even when these subcultures are successful, they will not necessarily spread to other parts of the organizations. For example, General Motors created a new organizational culture at its Saturn facility to support teamwork. Although this team-based approach to manufacturing has been successful, this approach was not easy for other General Motors facilities to adopt.

Congruence between the espoused organizational culture and the actual culture in practice is important. The espoused culture (which is written in the corporation's mission statement) must be translated into action. If there is incongruence between what an organization says it believes in and its actual behavior, then a cynicism gap is created and trust between the organization and its members drops.

There is a benefit to this important relationship between organizational culture and teamwork. Once an organization begins to create an organizational culture that supports teamwork, the culture will support a wide variety of teams and, eventually, the transition to self-managing teams. Organizational culture provides the foundation, and from it the organization has the ability to experiment with the development of the types of teams it needs to successfully fulfill its mission.

IMPLEMENTING TEAMS IN DIFFICULT ORGANIZATIONAL CULTURES

Changing organizational culture is a slow and difficult task that may be especially difficult in traditional work environments. It is a relatively easy task to identify the aspects of organizational culture that limit the use of teamwork. Once these problems are identified, there are many solutions that can be used to mitigate them. The problem is how to get these solutions implemented if they are incompatible with an organization's culture. One approach to dealing with this problem is to examine the organization's culture and use it to help select organizational change strategies (Davis, 1984).

Davis (1984) recommends using surveys on organizational culture to identify and analyze proposed organizational changes so as to determine their acceptability. The relationship between organizational culture and the potential to adopt organizational changes is shown in Figure 14.1. To have the most impact, one should select actions that are both important (they will

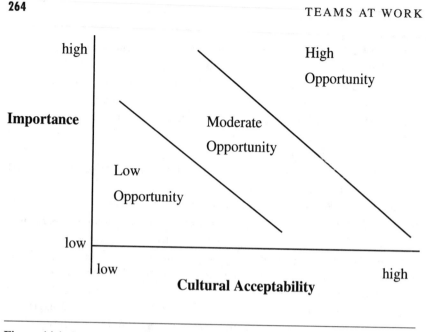

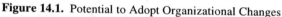

Figure 14.1. Potential to Adopt Organizational Changes

have a large impact) and relatively acceptable to the existing culture. When these organizational changes are implemented, they cause the organizational culture to change. Eventually, other important changes become more acceptable to the new culture.

A study using this approach examined the organizational changes needed to support using teams at manufacturing facilities (Levi, 1988). In some companies, a wide variety of organizational changes that supported teamwork were culturally acceptable. This allowed the change agents to make substantial changes to support the use of teams such as changing work processes and reward systems. However, in other companies, most of these important organizational changes were unacceptable to the organizational cultures. Managers were reluctant to relinquish power and authority to the teams, so many changes needed to support teams were not implemented.

For many of the problems created by the introduction of teams, training may be viewed as the most culturally acceptable alternative, but training alone is not sufficient to support the use of teams. Even though training usually is not high in importance, training might be the only approach that is acceptable in traditional organizational cultures. This makes training a good first step to developing teams in traditional cultures.

This cultural approach can be used to analyze the types of team decision making that organizations use. Organizations rarely shift from traditional management to self-managing teams because the amount of power sharing in self-managing teams is not culturally acceptable. Instead, traditional organizations start by using teams with supervisors who use consultative decision making. Once the organizational culture accepts this approach, democratic decision making becomes more culturally acceptable. Eventually, the use of self-managing teams might be acceptable to the organizational culture.

One value of this incremental approach to organizational culture is that it helps select the programs that have the highest opportunity for success. These successes may help to change the organizational culture. However, there is a danger to this incremental approach of trying to accommodate the existing organizational culture even though it is the path of least resistance. There is not a direct link between teamwork and organizational culture. Teams can be adopted in a control-oriented culture, and the teams might have some success. However, the organizational culture might not change, and the organization might discourage the wider use of teams because of the cultural threat caused by the use of teams.

From a broader perspective, this incremental approach to organizational culture change describes the evolution of teamwork in the United States. Teamwork programs during the early 1980s, such as quality circles, were experiments in using teams at work (Cole, 1989). As the use of these temporary teams became more acceptable, companies began to expand the use of teams by creating permanent work teams. Rather than just providing advice about quality issues, these permanent work teams were used to perform the day-to-day operations of companies. When companies learned to accept this new way of work, they began empowering the teams and shifting to self-managing teams.

SUMMARY

Organizational culture relates to the shared values, beliefs, and norms of an organization. It helps to provide a sense of identity to people in an organization and to define what is acceptable behavior. Cultures vary in depth, from surface rituals to underlying values. Organizations may have unified cultures or may be composed of networks of subcultures based on occupation, background, or other issues.

Organizational culture can be viewed as varying along three dimensions: individualism, power, and uncertainty. The individualist-collectivist dimension refers to how group oriented and cooperative people are. The power dimension examines whether people accept power differences or strive for egalitarian relations. The risk dimension concerns whether people value rules and stability or are willing to take risks to change how they operate. U.S. and Japanese companies differ on these three dimensions of teamwork.

The use of teams in an organization is dependent on its organizational culture. Cultural norms can either support teamwork or limit a team's ability to operate effectively. Two distinct types of organizational cultures are (a) cultures based on power and control and (b) cultures based on participation and commitment. These two types of organizational cultures provide very different contexts for teamwork.

Successful and innovative organizations have distinctive types of organizational cultures. Many of the cultural characteristics of successful organizations support the use of teamwork. Innovative organizations rely on teams to help direct and implement organizational changes. The cultures of innovative organizations support teamwork because they value the ability to change rapidly.

The importance of organizational culture for teamwork is both a benefit and a drawback. Once an organizational culture supports teamwork, it usually is able to support a wide variety of types of teams. However, organizational cultures that do not support teamwork are difficult to change. Although organizational cultures can be encouraged to change incrementally to support teamwork, there is no guarantee that this approach will lead to environments that support the use of teams.

ACTIVITY: EVALUATING A TEAM'S CULTURE

Objective. Teams have cultures that are similar to and different from the cultures of their surrounding organizations. It is important to know both types of cultures because teams have difficulties when their cultures become too discrepant from the organizations' cultures. Cultures vary on four dimensions. In individualist cultures, people seek individual achievement and recognition, whereas collectivist cultures value the ties between people, and self-interest is subordinate to the interest of the group. In high-power cultures, people show great respect to higher status people and feel uncomfortable in challenging authority, whereas low-power cultures take a more egalitarian view and are less willing to accept others' authority. In risk-avoiding cultures, people value stability and group harmony, whereas people in risk-taking cultures are action oriented and willing to take risks. In control-oriented cultures, leaders attempt to monitor and control the behavior of subordinates, whereas leaders in commitment-oriented cultures are facilitators who guide and motivate subordinates.

Activity. Discuss with members of an existing team their team's culture and the culture of the organization surrounding the team. Use the rating form (Activity Worksheet 14.1) to note the team's and its organization's cultures on four dimensions.

ACTIVITY WORKSHEET 14.1
Evaluating a Team's and an Organization's Culture

Rate the *team* by placing a "T" on the scale. Rate the *organization* by placing an "O" on the scale.

Individualism - Collectivism

High power - Low power

Risk avoidance - Risk taking

Control oriented - Commitment oriented

Analysis. How similar are the team's and the organization's cultures? On which dimensions do the team and organization have culture gaps? What problems can occur when there are differences between the team's and the organization's cultures?

Discussion. Why is it important for a team's culture to be compatible with its organization's culture? If the organization's culture has difficulty supporting teamwork, then what should a team do?

Chapter 15

ELECTRONIC TEAMS

Most of our experience with teams is through face-to-face meetings. However, the past two decades have seen the creation of new forms of teams that interact through computer-based communication. The use of these new communication systems by groups changes the ways in which people interact and the dynamics of the group process. In addition, communication technologies are having widespread impacts on communication not only in teams but also throughout organizations. The impacts of these communication systems are both positive and negative. The technologies still are evolving, and groups still are learning how to use the technologies and adapt them to meet the groups' needs.

➤➤ *LEARNING OBJECTIVES*	1. What is the difference between the direct effects and secondary effects of a technology?
	2. How do communication technologies support teamwork?
	3. What are the main characteristics used to analyze communication technologies?
	4. How do communication technologies affect status, deindividuation, conformity, and communication norms?
	5. How are task performance and decision making affected by using communication technologies?
	6. What is the impact of communication technologies on involvement in organizations?
	7. How is the structure and functioning of organizations changed by the use of communication technologies?

8. What factors need to be considered when selecting
   the right communication technology to use?

USE OF COMMUNICATION TECHNOLOGIES

During the past two decades, people and organizations have adopted a variety of new communication technologies. These technologies include new forms of organizational communication such as electronic mail (e-mail), voice mail, fax machines, videoconferencing, and electronic bulletin boards. The characteristics of this new electronic media are similar to existing forms of organizational communication, but they add new dimensions to it.

The use of new communication technologies has widespread effects on organizations (Axley, 1996). Communication technologies have direct effects on work design, organizational design, and communication patterns as well as secondary social effects caused by the reduced social and organizational cues in the messages (Sproull & Kiesler, 1991). The primary goals of using electronic communication for groups have been to improve task performance, overcome the constraints of time and space on collaboration, and increase the range and speed of access to information (McGrath & Hollingshead, 1994). These goals are related to the direct effects of the technologies.

As with other types of technology, the largest impacts often are the secondary effects including unanticipated social and organizational effects. Because organizational communication plays an important role in maintaining social relations and organizational culture, the lack of social information in a type of communication might prevent the development of new social relations and might not build a sense of community or improve morale in the same way as traditional communication did (Taha & Caldwell, 1993). It is difficult to predict these secondary effects. Although the new electronic communication systems structure the ways in which the people and groups communicate, people do not passively accept the systems' constraints. Instead, they adapt and modify the technologies to suit their needs (McGrath & Hollingshead, 1994).

The use of communication technologies has both positive and negative effects (Harris, 1993). Positive effects include improved speed and dispersal of communication, increased access to information, increased amount of communication, easier connections to others, and improved planning and decision making. Negative effects include information overload, inconsistent access, decreased face-to-face communication, disrupted organizational relations, and increased isolation.

| COMMUNICATION TECHNOLOGIES AND TEAMS

Communication and information technologies can be used to support teamwork in four different ways (McGrath & Hollingshead, 1994; Mittleman & Briggs, 1999). First, there are technologies for gathering and presenting information such as collaborative document management systems and electronic whiteboards. Second, technologies help team members to communicate both internally and with outside organizations. Third, information technologies help teams to process information by providing systems to structure brainstorming, problem-solving, and decision-making activities. Fourth, technologies can be used to help structure the group process through meeting agendas, assignment charts, and project management tools.

Electronic communication technologies free teams from the constraints of time and place (Mittleman & Briggs, 1999). Their use creates new ways for teams to meet and interact. The options created by the use of information technology are presented in Table 15.1.

Same time, same place (STSP) meetings are the traditional face-to-face team meetings. Even when a team primarily communicates electronically, there is a value to face-to-face meetings. These are especially important when the team is formed to help establish social relations. Face-to-face interaction also is important to celebrate major team milestones or to deal with major changes in the team's focus or task.

Technology does have an impact on team meetings. High-technology meeting rooms provide computers to all participants so that they can interact directly with presentation materials. Computer decision support systems also can help to structure meetings, especially for activities such as brainstorming and voting.

Same time, different place (STDP) meetings are distributed meetings in which team members interact through a combination of telephone, video, and/or text. Although videoconferencing is the most popular image of STDP technology, it is not necessarily the most useful technology. Video images of participants may be less useful than audio with shared data. Participants often prefer to be able to manipulate data and images that relate to the task rather than focusing on images of the other participants.

TABLE 15.1
Types of Meetings Created by Information Technology

Type of Meeting	Example
STSP (same time, same place)	Face-to-face meeting
STDP (same time, different place)	Videoconferencing
DTSP (different time, same place)	Computer database
DTDP (different time, different place)	Intranet bulletin board

SOURCE: Adapted from Mittleman and Briggs (1999).

Different time, same place (DTSP) meetings occur for work teams that exist across different shifts or for teams whose members travel frequently or telecommute. The information technology serves as a storage system so that members can pass on information as needed. Project management and other software systems can help to create a framework to note the status of a project or an agenda.

Different time, different place (DTDP) meetings refer to team members sharing the same virtual space on an intranet (i.e., internal communication network). Technologies such as online bulletin boards, chat rooms, and databases can help support a team's operations. This allows team members to participate in the team process whenever and wherever they have the opportunity.

CHARACTERISTICS OF COMMUNICATION TECHNOLOGIES

Communication researchers have identified the characteristics of communication methods and used these characteristics to analyze new communication technologies (Table 15.2). Axley (1996) uses the following four criteria for evaluating different communication methods: speed, reach (number of employees receiving the communication), interactivity, and cue variety (or richness). Reichwald and Goecke (1994) believe that social presence and media richness are the main variables for analyzing communication technologies. Richness relates to the speed of feedback, the number and type of sensory channels, and the perceived personalness of the source. Social presence refers to how much using the technologies is like the experience of communicating with another person. This factor often relates to the

TABLE 15.2
Analysis of Communication Methods

Method	Speed	Interactive	Richness	Social Presence	Document Message
Face-to-face	Slow	High	High	High	No
Group meeting	Slow	Moderate	High	High	No
E-mail	Fast	Moderate	Low	Low	Yes
Web page	Moderate	Low	Low	Low	Yes
Print	Moderate	Low	Low	Low	Yes
Video broadcast	Fast	Moderate	High	Low	No
Videotape	Moderate	Low	Low	Low	No
Teleconference	Fast	Moderate	High	Moderate	No

SOURCE: Adapted from Levi and Rinzel (1998).

richness of the communication media. Harris (1993) asserts that richness is important because people are more satisfied with communication technologies that are richer.

Another characteristic of many communication technologies is the ability to document the message or communication. These electronic records can have important task and social impacts (Sproull & Kiesler, 1991). For example, the capability of communication technologies to document a message may inhibit managers from using them for fear of recording errors (Byrne, 1984). It also makes e-mail messages sent to team members valuable task reminders because the members can print out or store the messages.

One of the most important factors for analyzing the effectiveness of group communication is the richness of the communication. Richness of information media primarily relates to how much emotional information is transmitted (Daft & Lengel, 1986). The effectiveness of a communication technology will depend on the fit between the task requirements and the richness of the technology. A task requiring the group to generate ideas requires only the transmission of the ideas, whereas negotiating a task or resolving a conflict might require providing the emotional contexts of the messages. The messages need to include the facts as well as the emotions, values, attitudes, and expectations of the participants.

The impact of information richness can go in either direction. One of the reasons why face-to-face groups are not as good as computer groups for brainstorming is that the richness of media gets in the way. In brainstorming, the presence of others and the social information they provide is a distraction from the task. It is inefficient to use a medium that is too rich. However, to use a medium that is not rich enough for the task is ineffective or lowers quality. The more uncertainty in the communication, the more important the information richness. As we will see, this is why technologies such as e-mail are not good for tasks such as negotiation.

COMMUNICATION IMPACTS

When people communicate with each other using electronic media, their communication is changed. Communication technologies change the ways in which status is perceived, the amount of anonymity of the communicators, and the conformity pressure of others. However, some of these changes are simply due to a lack of norms to manage the communication process rather than to the characteristics of the technologies.

| STATUS DIFFERENCES

One of the main differences between face-to-face groups and computer-based groups relates to status differences (Parks & Sanna, 1999). Early research showed that status differences were reduced in computer-based groups. These reduced-status differences had the effect of equalizing participation in computer group discussions. In a face-to-face group discussion, a few dominant people who have higher status in the organization talk the most. Many group members add only limited amounts to the discussion and primarily support the main positions that emerge. In computer-based decision making, the interaction is more democratic. Social cues are reduced, and people communicate based on their knowledge or opinions rather than on their social status.

Not all of the research on computer groups has found this equalization effect. In actual organizational settings, group members may be aware of the status of the other communicators regardless of the media used. Status also may be conveyed by the subtle cues in the messages. The style and content of messages may be analyzed to form impressions of the communicators. Status may be given to the first person to introduce an idea or the person who communicates the most on a topic.

| DEINDIVIDUATION

The members of computer-based groups are more anonymous. This leads to what psychologists call *deindividuation*. Deindividuation is the loss of self-awareness and evaluation apprehension caused by feeling anonymous. It can have a number of negative social effects (Parks & Sanna, 1999). When not being evaluated, people are more likely to engage in social loafing in groups and are more likely to perform negative acts.

One of the impacts of deindividuation on computer-based groups is that people are more willing to say things that they would not say in face-to-face interactions. This is why the phenomenon of *flaming,* or the making of uninhibited negative remarks, occurs in e-mail systems. This increase in uninhibited communication can be both positive and negative. When the group members are anonymous, the communication becomes both more critical and more supportive. Basically, people feel freer to express emotions of all types.

Although deindividuation effects occur in e-mail and larger electronic conferences, they typically do not occur in computer-based work groups. In these smaller groups, the level of anonymity is not as great.

| CONFORMITY

Conformity pressure is decreased in computer-based groups. This is due partly to the anonymity of these groups. The lack of conformity pressure affects the ways in which groups manage conflict.

Computer-based groups have higher levels of conflict. Although conflict in any group can have both positive and negative effects, it often has negative effects on computer-based groups. This is because the increased conflict often is due to increased misunderstanding of the emotional aspects of communication. In addition, computer groups are less able to resolve conflicts and reach consensus in a variety of decision-making situations. These effects may be due to the lack of conformity pressure that normally would increase people's willingness to agree and to seek compromises during disagreements.

| COMMUNICATION NORMS

The use of e-mail provides a good example of how new communication technologies require new communication norms or social interaction rules. E-mail has features that make it different from other types of organizational communication. Unlike either the telephone or the written message, e-mail is asynchronous (i.e., the sender and receiver are not directly interacting) yet potentially interactive, it is private but capable of being distributed, and it can be used informally or with technical precision (Culnan & Markus, 1987). The benefits of e-mail come from these properties that are unique to the new communication medium, but so do some of its problems (Kiesler, 1986).

Compared to other organizational communication media, e-mail lies somewhere between the paper-based mail system and the telephone communication system. Like the paper system, it uses "printed" words that can be modified, stored, and distributed. Like the telephone, it is an instantaneous communication that links people across time zones and distance with ease. However, an e-mail is more formal than a telephone call because the former provides written documentation of the communication. In practice, an e-mail is less formal than a written communication because the former tends to be a shorter and more spontaneous communication that is less regulated by an organization's formal communication practices.

These differences between e-mail and other forms of communication have led to a number of "netiquette" errors because of the lack of established communication norms. Senders of e-mail messages often treat them like telephone calls (e.g., informal, private, no record), whereas receivers may treat them as letters (e.g., formal, public, copyable, sendable). Senders often are shocked, and sometimes are embarrassed, when their private e-mail messages get distributed to others. New users often show bad form by distributing "junk" news to people who do not care, writing messages that are too long, or trying to be funny. Emotions can be difficult for many people to communicate in writing. In e-mail messages, emotions seem to get easily out of control, and interpersonal conflicts can arise that are primarily due to miscommunication. The solution to these problems is the development of communication norms for the new technologies (Sproull & Kiesler, 1991). For example, a team might have a rule that limits the size of e-mail messages or does not allow using distribution lists for sending jokes.

TEAM IMPACTS

The use of electronic communication changes the ways in which teams perform. These changes in performance depend on the type of task. Decision making also is affected, both directly and indirectly, by the use of electronic communication systems. Many of these performance effects may change as people become more experienced in using the technologies.

TASK PERFORMANCE IN COMPUTER GROUPS

Overall, the performance aspects of face-to-face and computer-based groups are fairly similar (Parks & Sanna, 1999). This is especially true if one is studying experienced users. Although there are few overall differences in performance, some tasks may be better suited to computer groups. Computer groups are successful on idea generation tasks and on intellective or problem-solving tasks where the groups need to organize information to find the correct answers. However, computer groups perform poorly on decision making and negotiation tasks where the goal is to reach consensus on issues.

Again, brainstorming is the main example of improved performance from computer groups. Computer-based brainstorming gets better ratings on all criteria. There are more ideas generated, the ideas tend to be of higher quality, and people prefer doing brainstorming on computers. Unlike face-to-face groups, the brainstorming process is not disrupted by larger group size on computers. The anonymity of computer groups is a benefit in brainstorming because people are less concerned about criticism of their ideas by others. The only problem with electronic brainstorming is social loafing in large groups, but this occurs in large face-to-face groups as well.

When a computer support system is used to structure the task that a group is performing, this helps to improve the operation of the group (McGrath & Hollingshead, 1994). However, this is useful only for some types of tasks. These support systems help to better organize the information and to structure the analysis and decision-making process. This is useful in many problem-solving situations, but it does not help with the more emotionally charged issues such as conflict negotiation.

DECISION MAKING

Research on the effects of computer-based groups shows that use of the technologies can have dramatic effects on decision making (Kiesler, Siegel, & McGuire, 1984). On the surface, computer-based decisions might appear to be superior because of the reduced-status cues that limit participation. However, the research does not show that computer-based groups are superior to face-to-face groups. Although more people participate in the discussions, there is mixed evidence that the quality of the decisions is superior (Watson, DeSanctis, & Poole, 1988). People might feel less committed to computer-based decisions, and higher status employees might resent not being able to control the decision-making process. These factors may reduce the ability of groups to implement decisions. Finally, when issues are complex or when many people are participating in the decision-making process, computer-based discussions can get so confusing that nothing gets resolved. Leadership, and perhaps limited participation, helps organize and manage the face-to-face decision-making process.

Realistically, in most organizations, computer-based communication plays an important but limited role in decision making (Levi & Slem, 1990). E-mail is used for routine decisions in which employees want to check with others to make sure that the decisions are acceptable to them. For more complex and organizationally important decisions, most managers require face-to-face decision making.

Electronic communication does serve as a valuable resource in decision making, even when it is not directly used to make decisions. Organizations with e-mail send more information to employees, so participants are better prepared when faced with making important decisions. The ease of using distribution lists often means that employees not directly involved in a decision-making process are at least aware of it. Because of this increased awareness, they can provide input to the decision makers or request to be part of the decision-making process. Overall, many employees believe that e-mail improves the quality of organizational decisions because of increased information and opportunities for participation.

| CHANGE AND DEVELOPMENT

People are less likely to be satisfied working in a computer-based group compared to face-to-face group (Parks & Sanna, 1999). People may feel a lack of social support in computer groups; there may be increased stress because the task is presented in an unfamiliar environment; or it may be that current groupware software is not very user friendly. Some of these negative effects are likely to disappear over time (McGrath & Hollingshead, 1994). Any new communication technology takes time to learn how to use effectively. Computer-based work groups improve over time as they become more accustomed to using the technology, develop group norms for working with it, and develop social relations that improve communication.

Groups that already have developed good social relations may be more effective using communication technology for group work. The social relations among group members might have to be supported by occasional face-to-face meetings. When group members never have met personally, they might never be effective in using communication technology for difficult problems. This is because they have not developed the ability to "read" the emotional meanings of each other's communication. In addition, they have not developed the types of relations that allow group members to provide social support for each other through the media.

ORGANIZATIONAL IMPACTS

The primary use of computer-based communication systems is to augment traditional organizational communication (Strassmann, 1985). The use of technology tends to expand the amount of communication that takes place within an organization. The impact of these new communication systems goes beyond just improving the efficiency of the organization's communication (Sproull & Kiesler, 1991). Over time, the use of technology will change the ways in which organizations operate. Employees in companies already are discovering new ways of interrelating and becoming involved in their organizations. The creation of computer-based teams and networks is changing how organizations are structured and how they function.

| INVOLVEMENT

The use of computer-based communication systems creates a variety of new opportunities for communication, participation, and involvement in organizations. The ease of using distribution lists encourages employees to share their e-mail messages with others. Many e-mail systems have forwarding options that allow the receivers of messages to distribute them with the receivers' comments attached. Distribution lists connecting employees interested in certain topics often emerge in organizations with e-mail. These specialized lists create a form of electronic involvement.

An electronic bulletin board allows any employee to electronically participate in a "discussion" of an organizational issue with others (Zuboff, 1988). It is an interactive communication system in which one interacts not with specific individuals but rather with anyone who decides to participate. These bulletin boards allow employees to share their ideas on activities within their organizations. In some cases, bulletin boards serve as "electronic suggestion boxes" that are monitored by managers who may electronically respond to employees' suggestions. For example, in one organization, a new manager established a bulletin board to identify and respond to complaints from employees about the operation of the company's internal support functions (Levi & Slem, 1990).

The use of computer-based communication systems can create social changes within an organization. The electronically networked organization communicates across organizational levels and boundaries easily and quickly (Strassmann, 1985). Electronic groups can be formed where e-mail provides the only means of interaction. These groups can be organized around specific topics (e.g., introduction of a new technology, bowling club), connect employees with similar professional backgrounds (e.g., all of the accountants in the corporation), or develop as professional support groups for employees with common concerns (e.g., women professionals). This helps to keep employees aware of changes in the organization that may affect them and gives employees an easy means of commenting on proposed changes.

| VIRTUAL TEAMS AND COMPUTER-BASED ORGANIZATIONS

The use of computer-based communication systems allows for the creation of teams that do not directly interact and whose members might never meet. These are called *virtual teams*. These teams work together to produce or provide services, make decisions, or provide support and assistance to their members. Communication technologies create linkages among team members that are not limited by geography, time zones, or work hours. Virtual teams link employees with common concerns and provide information and support to them. Technicians can share their problems with co-workers in other facilities to help solve the problems. Supervisors on different shifts and in different plants can work together as a team to coordinate production. Engineers at different research facilities can work together on the design of new technologies. Managers can keep track of changes around the world regardless of whether they are in their offices.

Although employees' roles are changing due to the impact of new communication systems, organizational structures generally have not evolved sufficiently to completely accommodate these changes (Savage, 1990). However, over time, these new communication systems should lead to a reduction in organizational levels and a reduction in the importance of departments and divisions within organizations. Networks may reduce the importance of hierarchies and other structures. Organizational structures designed to control the flow of information will be supplemented by database management systems. Teams, which have been limited by the number of people that managers can effectively coordinate, will be able to expand and interconnect as part of the networks.

SELECTING THE RIGHT TECHNOLOGY

Acceptance of communication technologies by organizations remains below most expectations (Reichwald & Goecke, 1994). Even during the early years, studies on the implementation of office technologies showed high failure rates, but few of these failures were purely technical in nature (Bikson & Gutek, 1984). One of the reasons for this lack of success is that organizations fail to consider the match between the features of the technologies and organizational issues (Caldwell & Uang, 1994). Selecting the right technologies relates to both organizational issues and team issues.

| ORGANIZATIONAL COMMUNICATION

Research has not determined which communication technologies are best for use in organizations (Reichwald & Goecke, 1994). The selection of an appropriate technology depends on the task and user attitudes toward the communication and communicators. Too often, communication specialists focus on the technological capabilities rather than on understanding the users' information needs and the effects that the medium will have on the users (Gallaway, 1996).

The more powerful (or rich) multimedia communication technologies might not be the best for the tasks (Dertouzos, 1997). For example, because contracts require specific wording and the ability to store and study the documents, print always may be the preferred communication medium. Multimedia communication also might be distracting to the users. In some cases, professionals turn off the pictures during videoconferences so as to concentrate on the messages.

The effectiveness of a communication technology depends on the user attitudes toward the communication. Axley (1996) believes that the amount of uncertainty of a message and the level of impact on the receivers affect which communication technology is most appropriate. The greater the uncertainty and impact, the more the message needs to be interactive, faster, broader in reach, and higher in richness.

Levi and Rinzel (1998) show that preferences for using various communication technologies relate to attitudes toward the communicators. When people trust the source of the communication, nearly any communication medium is acceptable. However, when people do not trust the source of the communication, they prefer face-to-face communication or other information-rich communication so as to evaluate the truthfulness of the message.

DIFFERENCES AMONG TYPES OF TEAMS

Different types of teams have different communication needs, so the right information technology to use depends on the type of team and its tasks (Bikson, Cohen, & Mankin, 1999; Mittleman & Briggs, 1999). Production teams use information technology to coordinate activities, track work progress, communicate with other parts of the organization, monitor processes, and analyze production information. Information systems provide critical data to the teams and help team members analyze and use the information.

Members of service teams can be widely distributed across space, so they depend on communication technologies and shared databases. Because providing services often is time dependent, information technology helps service team members to coordinate their activities. Coordination is improved through better communication and the ability to share databases that contain information about customers and team members.

Electronic communication allows project teams to form without regard to place. This allows teams to include members with crucial skills or information who would not otherwise be able to part of the teams because of work location. Dispersed project teams depend not only on communication technologies but also on shared databases that all members can contribute to and access. In addition, project teams are more likely to use computer support systems to help them perform their work and manage the team process.

Oddly, management teams often are one of the least accepting of new information technology. The exception to this is that management teams tend to make heavier use of videoconferencing than do other types of users. This reflects their preference for face-to-face communication rather than written communication. They prefer technologies that are easy to learn to use and that have intuitive user interfaces.

| TEAM COMMUNICATION

There is disagreement about whether computer-based groups create their own new social contexts or whether they simply transfer their existing social contexts into the new situations (Parks & Sanna, 1999). Most researchers assume that existing social factors that affect groups will be modified by or adapted to the new communication media. The existing research does show a number of similarities in the ways in which face-to-face and computer-based groups operate. There are differences, but the basic group processes appear to be the same.

Teams adapt and modify the communication technologies to fit their needs. In addition, teams select different technologies to use for different types of team tasks. E-mail is used to keep team members informed and share information, but it rarely is used for negotiation and decision making. Videoconferencing is useful for discussing issues and listening to presentations, but when teams need to work on technical issues, they often prefer teleconferencing with shared computers. This allows them to focus on the tasks without the distraction of video images of people's faces. Project management software is modified and shared so that team members can monitor each other's performance and manage projects as teams.

There may be limits to the ability of teams to fully adapt to computer-based communication systems. Virtual teams are highly task focused. This is useful in the short run, but the teams do not develop social relations. This lack of social development creates communication problems. People do not learn how to "read" the emotions in each other's communication. In addition, teams do not develop a sense of trust in the communication. In many organizations, these problems are managed by having teams meet face-to-face for initial meetings and for periodic review meetings. These face-to-face meetings might not be necessary for task purposes, but they are necessary for the social development of the teams. Without this social development, teams can become mired in conflicts and failed negotiations due to miscommunication.

SUMMARY

The use of computer-based communication technologies has expanded rapidly and is changing the ways in which groups operate. These new technologies increase access to information for groups, support internal and external communication, and help groups to manage their task and group processes. Though the use of technology, team meetings no longer are constrained by time or place. Differences among the communication technologies are related to their speed, interactivity, richness, social presence, and ability to provide documentation of the communication.

Communicating through the use of technologies has a number of interpersonal effects. Status differences are reduced, so interactions are spread more evenly among the participants. People are more anonymous in computer-based groups, and this also can increase the amount of negative or emotional messages. Conformity pressure is reduced, and this makes it more difficult for groups to manage their conflicts. Many of these effects are due to the lack of communication norms to regulate behavior.

Computer-based groups are different from face-to-face groups. The former perform better on idea generation and problem-solving tasks but worse on decision-making and negotiation tasks. Decision making is improved in computer-based groups by more equal-status communication. However, groups may be less likely to develop support for implementing computer-based decisions, and these groups have a more difficult time in managing conflict in decisions. However, people are better prepared to make decisions because of the increased availability of information. One of the largest problems for computer-based teams is in developing the social relations aspects of the teams.

The use of communication technologies affects not only teams but also the functioning of entire organizations. These new communication systems provide new ways for people to become involved in the operations of organizations. Employees become networked in a variety of ways. Computer-based teams and networks cut across organizational boundaries, and this is changing the ways in which organizations structure themselves.

Selecting the right communication technology to use depends on the characteristics of the technology, people, and task. The most advanced technology might not be the best given that rich technologies sometimes can be distracting. Over time, teams adapt to communication technologies through modification of the technologies and the development of new communication norms and procedures.

ACTIVITY: DEVELOPING NETIQUETTE FOR VIRTUAL TEAMS

Objective: Virtual teams communicate via computer-based communication rather than meeting face-to-face. These teams need to develop different types of norms to regulate the team's interactions. Norms for virtual teams are sometimes called netiquette rules.

Activity. Develop a set of norms for a virtual team to use (Activity Worksheet 15.1). These norms should cover communication, participation, and decision making. What other types of norms are needed to help a virtual team to operate effectively?

ACTIVITY WORKSHEET 15.1
Norms for Virtual Teams

Communication norms:
Participation norms:
Decision-making norms:
Other team norms:

Analysis. Compare the norms you have developed with those of other members of the group. Through discussion, develop a common set of norms for virtual teams.

Discussion. What are the advantages and disadvantages of virtual teams? Can the development of new types of norms help to improve the ways in which virtual teams operate? What other actions should be taken to help support the use of virtual teams?

Chapter 16

WORK TEAMS

The recent emphasis on the use of teams at work has led to major changes in the ways in which organizations operate. This shift to teamwork occurs in a variety of ways within organizations. The effectiveness of teams depends on the characteristics of the organizations, the types of teams, and the nature of the workers. Examples from production, professional, and managerial teams illustrate the different advantages and disadvantages of teamwork. Regardless of the types of teams, there are supportive actions that organizations need to provide to deal with the common problems that make implementing teams challenging.

▶▶ LEARNING OBJECTIVES

1. What are the main benefits of using work teams?
2. What problems do organizations encounter when using teams?
3. What are the risks and opportunities in using different types of teams at work?
4. What are the main features of the new U.S. model of factory work teams?
5. What characteristics make professional teams unique?
6. What are the advantages and disadvantages of using research and development teams?
7. Why is forming top management teams difficult?
8. What types of supports do organizations need to provide for work teams?
9. What are the common problems that organizations encounter when using teams?

USING TEAMS IN THE WORKPLACE

Work teams are viewed as an important way in which to improve organizational effectiveness. The transition to using work teams in factories and offices is viewed as a necessity to help corporations remain competitive (Gwynne, 1990). In fact, the implementation of work teams is one of the most common organizational interventions in manufacturing firms (Sundstrom, DeMeuse, & Futrell, 1990). Research shows that it is one of the most effective interventions for improving organizational performance (Guzzo & Dickson, 1996). In addition to improving factors such as the financial success of companies, the introduction of teamwork programs improves personnel issues such as turnover and absenteeism.

The use of work teams is growing in the United States. In a study of *Fortune* 1000 companies in 1987, it was estimated that 70% of the companies use some type of work teams or problem-solving groups, whereas 27% of the companies use self-managing teams (Lawler, Mohrman, & Ledford, 1995). When the study was replicated in 1993, 91% of the companies reported using work teams, and 68% were using self-managing teams. Although the use of teams was widespread, most employees did not work in work teams. In most cases, less than 20% of a company's workers were members of teams.

Most of the emphasis on teamwork during the 1980s involved production or service employees (Safizadeh, 1991). Teamwork was seen as a new way in which to organize work, where decision-making control shifted to the employees actually performing the tasks. During the 1990s, the focus of teamwork activities changed. On the factory floor, companies that have been successful in developing teams are continuing their change efforts by increasing the use of self-managing teams (Manz, 1992). There also is increased emphasis on creating teams among professional and managerial employees (Katzenbach & Smith, 1993).

| BENEFITS OF TEAMWORK

Teamwork is increasing because teams are an effective way in which to improve performance and job satisfaction. Large-scale studies on the use of production work teams show that they are effective (Guzzo & Dickson, 1996). Teams improve both the efficiency and the quality of organizational performance. The use of teams also provides the flexibility needed to operate in today's rapidly changing business world. In addition, when the use of work teams is widespread in organizations, the organizations tend to show improvements in other performance areas such as employee relations. However, teams can develop performance problems that limit their effectiveness, and the initial transition to teamwork can be a difficult process for many organizations.

Besides increasing organizational effectiveness, the implementation of work teams often leads to improvements in job satisfaction and quality of worklife (Sundstrom et al., 1990). Teams have these beneficial characteristics because they provide social support to employees, encourage cooperation, and help make jobs more interesting and challenging. In addition, the transition to teamwork requires training that improves employees' technical and interpersonal skills. This increase in training often is viewed as a personal benefit by employees.

The benefits of teamwork are realized only when teams are working on jobs that are suited for teamwork and the organizations are willing to support them. Table 16.1 presents a set of task and organizational characteristics that are necessary conditions for the use of a team.

| PROBLEMS OF TEAMWORK

Although there are many benefits to both organizations and employees, there are some problems created by the use of teams and the transition to teamwork. Research on teamwork in work settings often provides contradictory results. Many of the studies on *quality circles* (i.e., temporary teams that provide suggestions about how to improve quality) show that these teams are not effective, whereas studies of factory work groups have widely variable results. One of the problems here is that teamwork programs are implemented with little consideration of their applicability, and new programs are introduced rather than trying to make existing programs work better.

Teamwork programs such as quality circles provide only limited power to teams. These programs often lead to small short-run improvements in performance, but they do not lead to long-term performance improvements (Guzzo & Dickson, 1996). The shift to self-managing work teams with a substantial shift of power to the teams is more likely to result in significant long-term performance improvements. However, the transition to self-managing teams can be difficult in organizations that have traditional management control systems.

TABLE 16.1
When Is a Team Appropriate?

1. The work contains at least some skilled activities.
2. The team can form a meaningful unit within the organization with clearly defined inputs and outputs and stable boundaries.
3. Turnover within the team is minimal.
4. Valid performance evaluation systems exist for both the team and its members.
5. Timely feedback is possible.
6. The team is capable of measuring and controlling the important variances in the workflow.
7. The tasks are highly interdependent so that members must work together.
8. Cross-training is supported by management.
9. Jobs can be designed to balance group and individual tasks.

SOURCE: "Job Design," L. Davis and G. Wacker, in G. Salvendy (Ed.), *Handbook of Human Factors.* Copyright © 1987. Reprinted by permission of John Wiley & Sons Inc.

Effective work teams have norms that support high-quality performance and a level of group cohesiveness that provides social support for the members. However, work teams can have problems with norms and cohesiveness. Teams with bad performance norms might not be effective and may be highly resistant to change. Low levels of group cohesiveness may limit team members' ability to work together, whereas high levels of group cohesiveness may lower employees' performance orientation and impair decision making and creativity (Nemeth & Staw, 1989).

Implementing work teams often creates problems. Conflicts exist between team development and the traditional hierarchical control systems in many organizations (Hackman, 1990a). Teams also suffer from implementation problems due to resistance to change. Teamwork requires a supportive organizational context to foster teams' growth and development.

DIFFERENCES AMONG WORK TEAMS

Teams exist at different levels of the organizational hierarchy, ranging from production to professional to managerial teams. At each level, the use of teams creates different risks and opportunities for organizations. These are outlined in Table 16.2. In the following subsections, production, professional, and managerial teams are examined in more detail.

TABLE 16.2
Risks and Opportunities for Work Teams

	Risks	*Opportunities*
Production teams	Controlled by technology Resistance from management	Continuity of work Ability to improve team and product
Professional teams	Team and work both are new Evaluation and rewards	Clear purpose and deadline Interdependence
Top management teams	Absence of organizational context Not bonded	Self-designing Substantial power

SOURCE: "Creating More Effective Work Groups in Organizations," R. Hackman, in R. Hackman (Ed.), *Groups That Work (and Those That Don't)*. Copyright © 1990. Reprinted by permission of Jossey-Bass Inc., a subsidiary of John Wiley & Sons Inc.

Production teams run the risk of being overwhelmed by their tasks and the technology used to perform them. The technology controls how these teams operate, leaving little leeway for the teams to make changes. Because of their focus on production, members may ignore the social development of their teams. Managers and supervisors may resist giving production teams the responsibility and authority they need to operate as teams. However, team members have the advantage of working together for long periods of time. This gives them the chance to refine both their teams and the tasks they perform.

The main problem for professional teams is that they must perform unique jobs that they cannot fully prepare for in advance. Not only are teams' tasks novel, but typically so are the teams themselves. The projects that they work on typically are time limited, so they must quickly develop structures and processes to operate as teams. The main advantage that teams have is that they often have clear and specific goals and deadlines. In addition, their tasks often are highly interdependent. These factors can help to orient and motivate team members to work together.

Top management teams suffer in the absence of supportive organizational contexts. They operate in competitive environments that are not supportive of teamwork. In addition, there often are loose boundaries between team membership and members' positions in their organizations, thereby making it difficult to determine what teams' tasks are. The special opportunity of top management teams comes from their power in their organizations. These teams' actions can have significant impact on the operations of their organizations. In addition, these teams have the ability to set their own purposes and goals, thereby allowing them to focus on the issues they view as most important for their organizations.

| PRODUCTION TEAMS

The increasing competitive pressure of the 1980s forced many U.S. companies to search for alternatives to the ways in which they operated. This was especially true for manufacturing companies that were challenged by competition from low-wage foreign-based companies. One of the main approaches that U.S. companies adopted to meet this challenge was the use of work teams. Three factors predicted whether manufacturing companies were willing to make the transition to work teams: competing internationally, having high-skill technology, and having a worker-oriented corporate culture (Appelbaum & Batt, 1994).

There are two major types of factory teams: teams that are integrated into jobs and teams that operate as parallel structures (Appelbaum & Batt, 1994). In the integrated approach, jobs are redesigned to be performed by teams. Workers then are given the power and authority to continue redesigning their jobs to promote continuous improvement in operations. Quality circles are an example of the parallel approach. The jobs remain the same, but workers are organized into teams so as to analyze work issues to improve quality or performance. Quality circle teams have specific functions that are distinct from members' work assignments. The main problem that these types of teams encounter is that the solutions they generate might not be implemented by their organizations.

Factory work teams vary in their levels of power and domains of control. From a leadership perspective, teams can be categorized as either supervised teams, semi-autonomous teams, or self-managing teams. Most companies use supervised teams, whereas few companies use self-managing factory teams. Work teams also vary widely depending on their domains of control. Some teams have control only over direct work activities, whereas other teams also control personnel issues such as hiring, training, and performance evaluation.

A new form of factory teamwork emerged as a major organizational form in the United States during the 1980s (Appelbaum & Batt, 1994). It combined aspects of the European sociotechnical systems approach and the Japanese lean production model with American human resources policies. This model, called *American team production,* leads to a redistribution of power in factories so that work teams have the ability to control their own fates. Probably the most famous example of this new model is General Motors' Saturn facility. The main features of this new model relate to the organization of work, human resources policies, and quality.

Work is reorganized into self-managing teams. Continuous improvement is expected because the workers have decision-making authority over their jobs and work is viewed as a system that can be modified. Workers are more likely to come up with improvements if they can look across the work system, and the use of teams gives them this broader perspective. It is up to the workers to establish their work processes and modify them as needed. These teams vary in what areas they control and how independent they are from management. However, at a minimum, they control their own work processes and work areas.

The team structure creates the potential to improve performance, but it is changes in human resources policies that provide the incentive to do so. Teams often are given control over hiring and training new employees. They are given authority to evaluate each other and develop other personnel policies. In addition, they typically work under team incentive programs that reward improvements in team operations.

In nearly all cases of this shift to teamwork, quality has been one of the central concerns. There are several reasons for this. If only cost and productivity are important, then the time lost in team meetings might not be worth the expense. The benefits of teamwork are not in short-run cost savings but rather in quality improvements and long-run improvements in operations. Without a concern about quality and the potential loss in markets, managers rarely are willing to support the investment in the development of teams.

The shift to work teams in factories faces a number of barriers (Appelbaum & Batt, 1994). These barriers relate to the existing technical infrastructure, unions, and the managerial power structure. Often, production technology is designed for individuals to operate separate machines (Hackman, 1990a). This is an impediment to the use of teams. This is why some of the best examples of factory teams occur in new factories that have been designed for teams. Although unions initially were hesitant to support changes, the positive attitudes of workers toward the use of teams often have made unions supportive of change. The largest impediments lie in management. Managers are not accustomed to sharing power with work teams. The fact that shifts to teamwork often lead to reductions in organizational levels (and, therefore, reductions in the numbers of managers) also discourages managerial support of teams.

| PROFESSIONAL TEAMS

Professionals often are organized into task forces or project teams. These are temporary teams brought together to perform single tasks and then disbanded. These types of professional teams have several unique characteristics. Their tasks, group processes, products, and team members are unique and nonrepeatable. These teams' projects usually are given limited time frames, so the teams must go through all of the stages of group development fairly quickly.

Project teams typically are composed of people from multiple functional areas in organizations, with little overlap of skills and knowledge (Gersick & Davis-Sacks, 1990). Consequently, the ability of the teams to discuss, negotiate, and make group decisions is very important because there are no authorities with the knowledge to make better decisions.

The nonroutine nature of the tasks and the lack of long-term relationships among the people forming these types of teams make developing and using teamwork norms and procedures more important than for other types of teams. These teams do not have the luxury of allowing group norms to evolve slowly while the teams develop. Team development is made more difficult because the teams do not know what their projects will require at the onset. The importance of various team members and procedures may change as the projects develop.

These teams' members face unique conflicts. They are both autonomous and dependent. The teams can act with relative independence because the project boundaries are distinct from the normal actions of their organizations. However, all team members are responsible to both their teams and the parts of the organizations they represent. When projects are over, team members will return to their functional areas. This creates an internal conflict within each team member.

One important type of professional project team is a research and development (R&D) team. R&D teams can be organized in several ways (Edosomwan, 1989). They can be highly interdependent in their design work, or the leaders can serve as integrators for work groups of independent technical professionals. Whereas most R&D teams are project teams that have limited durations, some teams have relatively long lives because they stay with particular products throughout their life cycles.

R&D teams have a number of characteristics that may make them operate differently from other types of teams. The personnel working on R&D projects are mostly technical professionals with highly specialized knowledge backgrounds. Most organizations separate their R&D teams from their production and operations personnel and also manage these technical professionals differently. The types of tasks performed in R&D are by definition nonroutine, so traditional management approaches that focus on control and regularity are inappropriate. These unique characteristics of R&D work and employees have both advantages and disadvantages for the development of teamwork.

One of the main advantages of R&D teams is due to the nature of their tasks (Hackman, 1990a). In most cases, R&D projects require the integrated efforts of professionals with a variety of technical skills. The complexity of the tasks requires multiple skills and mutual interdependence. Although this sometimes can be accomplished without teamwork, a team approach is an obvious benefit. In addition, R&D work is challenging, important, and viewed as high status compared to other types of professional work. This also helps to promote a sense of teamwork.

The R&D function is considered important for many organizations, and R&D professionals and managers typically are highly valued by organizations. Technical professionals are highly skilled, in relatively short supply, and expensive to recruit and retain. Because of the value of these professionals' skills, organizations are more willing to provide training to maintain their skills and are more willing to provide other job benefits to encourage retention (Carnevale, Gainer, & Schulz, 1990). Because they are expensive employees to retain, organizations are more willing to provide them with adequate resources and tools to perform their jobs.

R&D teams also have some important disadvantages with regard to developing and supporting teamwork. R&D professionals are selected for their professional skills, and these skills do not necessarily include social and communication skills. Rewards, another problem that exists in R&D teams, may limit the development of teamwork (Ellis & Honig-Haftel, 1992). R&D professionals often are individualists who would prefer to be rewarded for their personal efforts. This may discourage their commitment to teamwork where their individual efforts are incorporated into their teams and are not easy to identify and reward.

Performance evaluations also may be a problem for R&D teams. Because R&D projects can be complex and ill defined, it often is difficult to determine whether success or failure is due to the employees' efforts and abilities or to the nature of the tasks (Sundstrom et al., 1990). In many R&D organizations, the performance evaluation process is further complicated by matrix management structures in which technical professionals have both project and functional managers who may be involved in the evaluation process. These dual loyalties may make any performance evaluation seem unfair (O'Dell, 1989).

| TOP MANAGEMENT TEAMS

Forming top management teams is very difficult, and it is not clear whether such teams are needed to run organizations (Katzenbach & Smith, 1993). There is likely to be substantial resistance from top-level managers to working in teams. However, when top management teams are used to set strategic directions for organizations, their decisions have important impacts on people in the organizations. Compared to other types of teams, these teams have considerable power, authority, and independence.

Most organizations are run by *working groups* rather than by top management teams. In these loose groups, there are strong leaders, individual work products and accountability, and indirect performance measures. The goals of these groups are the same as their organizations' goals. Although these groups discuss issues and make decisions that affect their organizations, the managers who are members operate independently. The groups provide advice to the leaders and coordination to implement decisions, but they do not perform integrated tasks for which members are mutually accountable.

The effectiveness of top management teams is related to heterogeneity of functional expertise (Guzzo & Dickson, 1996). In other words, diversity of skill and knowledge improves performance of these teams. The different backgrounds of the members of top management teams can encourage creativity. Added to this is the power that the team members have to implement their decisions. This offers the potential to implement creative solutions to organizational problems. The value of top management teams depends on the situation. When organizations face turbulent environments in which changes are necessary for success, the value of top management teams increases.

There are several reasons why an organization would shift from a single leader to a top management team approach (Eisenstat & Cohen, 1990). A team's decision is more likely to represent the wide variety of interests in the organization. A team with members of varied backgrounds is better able to develop creative solutions to problems. Participation in the decision-making process is likely to encourage more support for implementation of decisions. Communication and coordination among the major parts of the organization should improve with teamwork at the top. The job of leading a large organization is simply too much for a single individual to perform well. Finally, participation in a top management team develops the skills of its members and makes the organization less vulnerable to disruptions due to turnover at the top.

The ultimate responsibility for the success of an organization typically rests with the leader (Eisenstat & Cohen, 1990). In U.S. culture, it is difficult to develop the notion of mutual accountability and responsibility at the top of an organization. Even for organizations with top management teams, the notion of single organizational leaders is difficult to avoid. This is one of the barriers to developing successful teams at the top. Consequently, top management teams typically have only as much power and authority as their leaders are willing to give them.

One of the most difficult problems for top management teams is managing the level of competition among the team members (Eisenstat & Cohen, 1990). This competition can lead to fragmentation, where team members become involved in conflicts that are left unresolved. If teams do not resolve these internal conflicts, then executives are likely to remove power from the teams by making more decisions unilaterally. This creates a cycle of team fragmentation and then leader avoidance, from which top management teams find it difficult to recover.

Being members of a top management team is a significant benefit to the individual participants (Eisenstat & Cohen, 1990). Not only does it help to improve their careers, but it also is valuable training in running an organization. However, other managers not on the team can resent not being included. The use of top management teams can create power struggles among upper-level managers. Consequently, some team members play it safe and try to agree with the leader. This type of conformity can reduce the value of the team.

SUPPORTING WORK TEAMS

Sundstrom (1999b) identifies the types of organizational supports that need to be provided for work teams. These organizational supports relate to establishing an appropriate foundation for teams, supporting the team process (leading, training, measuring and providing feedback, and rewarding teams), and establishing a proper infrastructure.

The foundations of teamwork relate to establishing a team structure and staffing the team. The organization needs to establish an appropriate structure for the work team by defining the team's responsibilities and authority, establishing the team's scope or boundaries, providing sufficient resources, and developing a system of accountability. Selection and staffing issues are important to ensure that the team has the right mix of knowledge, skills, and abilities to complete the task.

The main team processes are leading, training, measuring and providing feedback, and rewarding the team. It is important for the team leader to align and coordinate the team's actions with the rest of the organization, provide direction to the team, and support team members through coaching. Training is needed to develop teamwork and team liaison skills. Measurement and feedback systems help the team to improve the way in which it functions. Reward systems are needed to provide incentives for individual and team performance and to encourage cooperation among teams within the organization.

A team's infrastructure relates to the availability of information resources, communication technology, and the design of the physical work environment. Information systems should provide the team with convenient and responsive data access to support the task. Communication technology is needed to link team members and to provide internal and external linkages to distant team members, customers, and suppliers. The physical environment can support teamwork by providing space for individual work, teamwork, and informal social interaction.

The importance of these various support systems depends on the type of team. Measurement and feedback systems are very important for production and service teams because these teams need to track their performance in order to improve the ways in which they operate. Communication and information technologies are very important for project teams because of the analytic nature of their work and the need to coordinate members who may reside in different locations.

THE PROBLEMS WITH USING WORK TEAMS

Although different types of teams have different characteristics and issues, there also are some important commonalties among teams at work. Hackman (1990a), in an analysis of a variety of types of work teams, identified several "trip wires" or common problems in the design and management of work teams. Reviewing these trip wires illustrates the challenges that need to be surmounted so as to use teams successfully.

CALLING PEOPLE A TEAM BUT MANAGING THEM AS INDIVIDUALS

Employees can be organized to work in one of two ways. Job assignments can be given to individuals, with a supervisor controlling and coordinating the activities of the whole. Or, the task can be handed over to a team whose members have joint responsibility for performing and managing the task. Either way can be successful. What cannot be successful is treating people as individual performers and telling them that they are working as a team. This not only confuses people but also creates cynicism about teamwork.

There are several ways in which this problem can occur. The notion of teams is trendy, so sometimes managers want to refer to workers as teams for this reason. In other cases, organizations try to set up teams, but managers do not give the teams sufficient power and control. The organizational cultures may be so individualist that teams cannot fit into the environments. When the reward and career development systems are individually oriented, it is difficult to get employees to commit to teams.

Teams must be specifically designed so as to be beneficial to organizations. This includes establishing boundaries for the teams, defining group tasks with collective responsibility, and giving the teams authority to manage these tasks. In some organizations, this might be impossible because the organizational cultures or external environments might not allow it.

FALLING OFF THE AUTHORITY BALANCE BEAM

Managers and teams have to balance the issues of authority and responsibility in organizations. Teams can be given too much authority, especially if they have not matured enough to know how to operate. Managers may be concerned about handing over authority to teams when their organizations still hold them responsible for the teams' performance. However, if managers try to retain too much control over teams, then most of the benefits of teamwork will be lost.

Achieving a good balance between a team and management is difficult. Not only is there the issue of how much authority should be given to the team, but there also is the issue of what areas of responsibility should be covered. A team is able to handle more authority and responsibility as it matures. The difficulty for a manager is to not give away too much authority at the beginning of the team's life and to learn when to turn over more authority as the team gains experience.

Providing a clear goal for a team is one way in which to empower the team. A clear direction helps the team to form its own objectives and to motivate performance. Without clear direction, a team often will become mired in unproductive activities. Once the goals are established, the organization should turn over to the team most of the authority to control how the task is accomplished.

ASSEMBLING A GROUP OF PEOPLE, TELLING THEM IN GENERAL TERMS WHAT NEEDS TO BE ACCOMPLISHED, AND THEN LETTING THEM FIGURE IT OUT

In many cases, the jobs that individuals perform at work are overly defined. People are locked into ways of working that may not be optimal. When work teams are formed, they are viewed as a way in which to free people from past constraints. However, teams will not be effective if they simply are told to figure out what their jobs are. This gives teams less structure than they need to operate successfully.

Teams require structures that define their tasks and memberships. The limits of their authority should be explicitly stated. When they are given appropriate structures, teams are able to focus on developing their internal processes and procedures for performing their tasks. When they are not given appropriate structures, teams can become mired in unfocused attempts to create them.

An enabling structure for a team has three components. First, a well-designed team motivates its members through meaningful work, enough autonomy to perform the task, and feedback about results. Second, a well-structured team has clear boundaries and includes members with sufficient skills and knowledge to perform the task successfully. Finally, a team needs a clear understanding of the extent and limits of its authority and accountability.

SPECIFYING CHALLENGING TEAM OBJECTIVES BUT SKIMPING ON ORGANIZATIONAL SUPPORTS

A challenging objective can provide direction and motivation for a team, but without sufficient resources to perform the task, the team eventually will stop being motivated by the goal. For the full potential of the team to be realized, the organization must actively support teamwork. The types of support that the team needs include a reward system that recognizes team performance, an education system that provides training and technical support, an information system that helps the team to make decisions and monitor performance, and the material resources to complete the task.

It can be difficult for an organization to supply these supports, especially if the organizational culture has an individualist focus. It is difficult to change performance evaluation and reward systems. The organization might not have the trainers and facilitators to support team development. Information and control systems might be designed for managers and not easily changed to support a team. Finally, it might be difficult for the team to adapt the existing technology and space for its needs or to obtain resources in the existing organizational system.

A team-oriented organization is different from a traditional organization, and the transition is not an easy one to make. The work systems and policies designed to support and control individual work do not change easily. In addition, not all managers may want to support an organizational innovation that threatens their power in the organization.

ASSUMING THAT MEMBERS ALREADY HAVE THE SKILLS AND KNOWLEDGE THEY NEED TO WORK AS A TEAM

Once teams have started, organizations sometimes just leave them alone. There are good reasons not to interfere too much with the internal operations of teams. However, a hands-off approach can limit teams' effectiveness if its members do not have the skills and knowledge they need.

Managers have an important role as coaches to help develop members' skills in working as teams. There is no one best way in which to lead or facilitate work teams; the needs of different types of teams and different maturity levels of members are too variable. However, the value of coaching is not a substitute for other factors. Teams need structures, clear goals, and resources to succeed. When teams are failing because of a lack of these contextual factors, coaching will not help.

Finally, research suggests that what happens early on in a team's existence is likely to have continuing effects. Because of this, it is important for the organization and leader to help the team get a good start. Building the team at the beginning prepares it to handle problems and crises later. The leader should not wait until a crisis occurs before teaching the team how to manage its group processes.

SUMMARY

The use of teams in the workplace has been increasing rapidly during the past two decades. This trend started with factory teams and then moved up the organizational hierarchy. Teams are popular because they are effective at improving performance and job satisfaction. However, teams are not useful in all situations. Teams run into problems when they are not used appropriately, and they often encounter resistance in nonsupportive organizational environments.

The different types of work teams have their own sets of risks and opportunities. Production teams are ongoing, so they have time to develop as teams, but they often are controlled by outside forces. Professional teams have clear purposes and deadlines, but they must form anew for each project. Top management teams have the power to implement their decisions, but their members have difficulty in working together cooperatively.

Factory teams can be either integrated into their jobs or used in parallel to promote improvements in quality or other factors. Factory teams also vary in how much power and what areas of control they have. A new model of factory teamwork has developed that uses self-managing teams, supportive human resources policies, and an emphasis on quality. Although factory teams face a number of barriers to implementation, they have a track record of success.

Professional teams often are temporary teams that have been organized around projects. The unique nature of the tasks and the lack of existing relationships among the people make forming effective teams challenging. R&D teams are an example of professional teamwork. These teams have the benefits of motivating tasks that require teamwork, and they receive high levels of support from their organizations. However, they may lack people with teamwork skills and the right organizational incentives for working together.

Top management teams have the greatest potential to affect the success of organizations, but they may be the most challenging types of teams to develop. Single leaders run most organizations, and it often is unclear what the roles of top management teams should be. In addition, upper-level managers often are very competitive, so communication and coordination can be difficult. However, these often are highly competent people with a diversity of skills and knowledge. Their potential to develop and implement creative solutions to problems is great.

All types of teams require supports from their organizations to operate successfully and encounter challenges in their development. The organizational supports needed for teams include establishing effective team structures; supporting the team process with leadership, training, and rewards; and providing physical and technological infrastructures. The challenges that organizations encounter using teams relate to power and authority issues, development of appropriate jobs and goals, and provision of resources and leadership.

ACTIVITY: UNDERSTANDING THE DIFFERENCES AMONG WORK TEAMS

Objective. Work teams exist at different organizational levels. Production and service teams typically are used to produce products or provide services, professional teams are used to plan and coordinate projects or design new products, and management teams are used to run organizations and plan organizational change programs. These teams perform different functions and must face different issues to succeed.

Activity. For each type of work team (see Activity Worksheet 16.1 on the following page), analyze and discuss the biggest obstacles the team faces, the biggest benefits to the organization of using this type of team, and the types of supports the team needs from its organization.

Analysis. Compare the three types of teams, noting their commonalties and differences.

Discussion. Given the information derived from this analysis, what should organizations do to help encourage the successful use of teams in the workplace?

ACTIVITY WORKSHEET 16.1
Analysis of Work Teams

Production and service teams	Obstacle:	
	Benefit:	
	Support:	
Professional teams	Obstacle:	
	Benefit:	
	Support:	
Management teams	Obstacle:	
	Benefit:	
	Support:	

Chapter 17

TEAM BUILDING

T*eam building* is the term used to describe the variety of approaches to improving the operation of teams in organizations. Team-building programs typically focus on improving teamwork skills, developing social relations, and solving problems that disrupt teams' performance. One of the central concepts of team building involves evaluating teams' performance and using this information to improve the teams' operations. Organizations have an important role in team building of developing performance evaluation and reward systems that encourage teams to improve their operations.

➤➤ *LEARNING OBJECTIVES*

1. What are some of the different definitions of team building?
2. What are some of the reasons why organizations do not use team building?
3. What are some of the criteria for determining whether teams are effective?
4. What are the symptoms of ineffective teams?
5. What are the main types of team-building activities?
6. What are the characteristics of a good performance evaluation system?
7. Why is doing group process evaluations important for teams?
8. What are the benefits of and problems with individual, team, and organizational reward programs?

WHAT IS TEAM BUILDING?

Organizational development is a set of social science techniques designed to promote changes in organizations that enhance personal development and increase organizational effectiveness. Team building is a type of organizational development intervention that focuses on improving the operations of work teams. Team building means regularly taking time to evaluate the performance of teams so as to find ways in which to overcome obstacles and develop more productive patterns of work. To be effective, organizational development needs to be viewed as an ongoing activity for teams.

There are a variety of perspectives toward team building that emphasize different goals and approaches. Rather than trying to combine these perspectives to create a single view, the following is a sample of the different perspectives toward team building:

- Team building is a problem-solving process that focuses on the following three issues. What keeps the team from being effective? What changes could improve the team's effectiveness? What is the team doing now that is effective that it wants to continue? (Dyer, 1995)
- A team-building program uses three different tactics. First, the program can have a task focus that examines the team's problems and attempts to develop solutions to them. Second, it can take a group process or relationship focus, using exercises and activities to improve the way in which the group operates and the interpersonal relationships among team members. Third, it can take a structural approach and develop new norms, rules, and procedures to improve the operation of the team. (French & Bell, 1984)
- Team building means making sure that the team has common goals and that members can work together to achieve them. The main priority in team building is to develop a strong sense of belonging to the team. Unless the team members can identify with one another and see themselves as a team, it will be impossible to organize them toward accomplishing a common goal. (Hayes, 1997)
- What does it mean to develop a team? It means creating a team with the appropriate mix of skills including both technical and group process skills. It also means improving performance by changing the way in which the team operates. The team development process includes organizing work and roles, acquiring the necessary skills and resources, establishing the necessary relationships inside and outside of the

team, and changing the situation to facilitate performance. (Mohrman, Cohen, & Mohrman, 1995)

- Team building assumes that a successful team can be developed through training and practice. A team must learn how to set goals, structure work assignments, coordinate efforts, and develop a sense of group identity. (Forsyth, 1999)

| ORGANIZATIONAL CONTEXT OF TEAM BUILDING

Team building requires examining the organizational context for the team (Hayes, 1997). Many organizations trying to implement teamwork fail to appreciate how their current practices and cultures limit the ability of teams to operate. Effective teamwork requires a supportive organizational environment. It might not be useful to focus on the internal problems that a team is having if the source of the problems lies in the surrounding organization. For example, it is difficult to promote cooperation among team members when the performance evaluation and reward system focuses on individual accomplishments and ignores team accomplishments.

The context under which the team operates has a greater impact on performance than do the internal competencies of the team members (Mohrman et al., 1995). Therefore, team development also must focus on building the relationship between the team and its organizational context. Too often, a team-building program will focus on internal development when the key to performance problems is external to the team.

One of the central organizational context issues for a team is the performance evaluation and reward system of the organization. Performance evaluation systems have the potential to provide a team with feedback that can be used to analyze the team's operations and develop improvements. Reward systems provide motivation for the team members to work together and strive to be more effective. Although a performance evaluation and reward system typically is not considered a team-building program, it is an effective way for an organization to encourage and motivate a team to improve how it operates.

| EVALUATING TEAM-BUILDING PROGRAMS

Although many organizational leaders say that teams are important and that team building is an important activity, their actions do not necessarily support their words (Dyer, 1995). Most companies that use teams do little in the way of team development. They fail to include teamwork in their organizations' philosophies or reward systems. Top managements focus on financial issues, often ignoring the value of teamwork as a means of improving performance. The result is mixed signals about teamwork and the value of team building.

There are several reasons why organizations overlook the importance of team-building activities. They are limited by a lack of knowledge about how to do team building and the availability of competent professionals who can run team-building programs. Managers often do not understand the benefits of team building, so they do not reward teams that spend time doing it. Team members also are skeptical about the value of team building, so they are reluctant to spend the time doing it.

Part of the problem that team-building programs have with gaining organizational support is their reputation. Managers often are subject to fads, and team-building programs have suffered from this problem. During the 1960s, encounter groups encouraged people to share their true feelings with each other. Establishing good social relations among team members requires open communications, but this approach can be carried too far. An overemphasis on self-disclosure can create problems for group members in work settings. For example, perhaps one's boss should not know the employee's inner feelings about the boss. Team building through wilderness experiences are enjoyable activities, but it can be difficult to translate these experiences into solving work problems with current teams. In many organizations, rumors about poorly run team-building programs of the past limit support for team building.

Sundstrom, DeMeuse, and Futrell (1990) performed an extensive analysis of the effectiveness of team-building programs. They found that most evaluation studies examine the internal operations of the teams, measuring factors such as communication, cohesion, and satisfaction. Although these factors improved due to team building, the studies did not actually measure whether the teams' performance improved. The relatively few studies that have measured performance often found that team building did not improve performance. Team-building interventions that focused on teams' control over work were more effective than morale-boosting activities at improving performance (Cotton, 1993).

The success of team-building programs depends on several factors (Dyer, 1995). Top managements must provide support for teamwork and team-building programs. Organizational reward systems should support the use of team building so as to encourage team members to take the programs

---

TABLE 17.1
Criteria for Effective Teams

- Clear goals and values
- People understand their roles and assignments
- Climate of trust and support
- Open communication
- Full participation in decisions
- Commitment to implement decisions
- Supportive leaders
- Constructive handling of differences
- Structure consistent with goals, task, and people

SOURCE: W. Dyer, *Team Building: Current Issues and New Alternatives* (pp. 15-16). Copyright © 1995 by Addison-Wesley Publishing Company Inc. Reprinted by permission of Addison-Wesley Longman.

---

seriously. Time must be made available for teams to engage in team-building activities. Finally, team-building programs are improved when the interventions are linked with actions to improve the external relations of the teams.

DOES YOUR TEAM NEED TEAM BUILDING?

To determine whether team building is needed, teams need to have criteria for effective teams and an understanding of the types of problems that can interfere with team performance. Table 17.1 presents a set of criteria that can be used to evaluate the effectiveness of teams.

Effective teams have clear goals and values that are understood and accepted by all of the team members. Goal setting can help to provide the objectives and task assignments for teams. The team members must understand their assignments and how their roles fit into their teams' activities. The team climates provide trust and support among the team members so that they are willing to share their ideas and feelings with each other. All the team members participate in teams' communication processes, and teams strive to make most decisions through consensus. Once decisions have been made, team members accept them and commit to implementing the decisions. Leaders are supportive of team members and help facilitate team processes. Differences of opinion are recognized and handled rather than ig-

TABLE 17.2
Symptoms of Ineffective Teams

- Loss of production
- Increase in grievances or complaints
- Evidence of hostility or conflicts among members
- Confusion about assignments and relationships
- Decisions misunderstood or not enacted
- Apathy and general lack of interest
- Lack of initiative, innovation, or good problem solving
- Ineffective meetings
- High dependency on the leader

SOURCE: W. Dyer, *Team Building: Current Issues and New Alternatives* (pp. 79-80). Copyright © 1995 by Addison-Wesley Publishing Company Inc. Reprinted by permission of Addison-Wesley Longman.

nored. Finally, team structures and procedures are consistent with how the team operates and what they want to accomplish.

Table 17.2 presents a set of symptoms of team problems that indicate when team building is needed. Many of these symptoms identify the effects rather than the causes of problems (Dyer, 1995). In many cases, the two causal factors are conflicts between team members and leaders and difficulties among team members. Conflicts with team leaders often lead to overconformity, resistance to leaders, an authoritarian leadership style, and a lack of trust. Problems among team members often lead to fighting, lack of trust, personality conflicts, disagreements (with limited attempts to resolve them), building cliques or subgroups, and missed deadlines.

Team members often blame individuals for team problems rather than recognizing that it is teams' processes that are responsible. Team conflicts and confusion are good examples of problems that often are blamed on individuals but that really are the responsibility of teams. These problems can be dealt with through team building.

For example, how does one deal with two team members who are constantly arguing with each other? If one believes that the conflict is due to a "personality clash," then there is no solution except to get rid of one or both of the team members. One cannot simply rearrange an individual's personality to prevent future clashes. A more useful approach is to view conflict as a violation of expectations about what is to be done, how it is to be done, and when it should be done. Expectations focus on behavior, and behavior is open to change. The team can discuss its expectations about performance and goals and can negotiate an agreement that will allow the conflicting team members to work together.

In a similar manner, when there is confusion among team members, this confusion typically arises from unclear assignments and relationships. Solving this problem focuses not on the individual team members but on the team processes. Teams need to better clarify the roles of all team member rather than blaming them for not performing unstated assignments.

TYPES OF TEAM-BUILDING PROGRAMS

Categorizing the many different types of programs that typically are used for team building is difficult because there is no agreed-on set of techniques. The following subsections describe five different types of team-building programs: goal setting, role definition, interpersonal process skills, cohesion building, and problem solving.

| GOAL SETTING

The goal-setting process is designed to clarify the purpose of the team. This approach involves clarifying the team's goals and developing more specific objectives. This typically is done through consensus building so as to create agreement about and commitment to the team's goals. Objectives are developed to further define the team's tasks, and action plans are established that include team member assignments. The final step in a goal-setting program is to develop an evaluation and feedback system given that the success of goals improves with the addition of feedback (Locke & Latham, 1990).

A goal-setting program can be narrowly focused on the team's immediate performance criteria or broadly focused on the values and mission of the team and organization. This broader view is designed to develop a common vision for the team by exploring the underlying values and purpose of the team. The broader approach is useful for teams that will exist for a long time and for teams whose members come from diverse backgrounds (Hayes, 1997).

| ROLE DEFINITION

The role definition approach focuses on clarifying individual roles, group norms, and the shared responsibilities of team members. Conflict between roles and ambiguity about one's roles in the team can create stress and disrupt performance. Team members need to know both their own roles and the roles that others perform. Role definition activities help clarify one's roles and define the relationships among team members' roles. By clarifying the duties and task relationships among team members, coordination is improved and the team is better prepared to perform its task.

There are several approaches that can be used to help the team define its roles (Hayes, 1997). The negotiation approach has team members analyze their work situations and identify the things that other people could do to improve their effectiveness. This includes behaviors that they would like to see increased or decreased. The team members then negotiate changes in each other's behaviors so as to get what they want from the other members of the team.

An alternative approach has the team members interact, and group process observers analyze the roles that members perform in the team. These observations then are used to evaluate the team's performance. The typical result of this analysis shows that the team is underusing certain types of behaviors and is relying on a limited range of behaviors. This information can be used to help improve the team's interactions.

The value of the role definition approach is that it allows team members to see themselves from the outside, through the eyes of an observer or other members. This allows members to develop different perspectives for understanding how they operate and teaches them how to adjust their styles of interacting in ways that improve the operation of the team.

| INTERPERSONAL PROCESS SKILLS

Team members need to learn how to coordinate their efforts with other members and work together as a team. There are a variety of team process skills that members can learn to perform, such as decision making, problem solving, and negotiating. Some of a team's task problems are related to a lack of these teamwork skills, so teaching team members interpersonal process skills is one approach to team building.

Teaching group process skills is more than just lecturing. In team building, a team typically is given simulated activities or exercises to perform so as to practice these skills (Scholtes, 1988). The use of simulations allows the team to practice various group process skills and analyze the results. For example, the team can practice decision-making techniques in a desert survival exercise rather than waiting until it has to make an important project decision.

Process consultants often are used to facilitate these group exercises, observe how the team operates, and then comment on the group process (Forsyth, 1999). Feedback from these outside observers is viewed as a key part of the learning experience. This approach to learning traditionally has been viewed as the best way in which to improve group work skills.

| COHESION BUILDING

The purpose of cohesion building is to foster a sense of team spirit and build the interpersonal connections among team members. When successful, it strengthens the team's morale, increases trust and cooperation, and helps the team to develop a group identity. Cohesion building is done through techniques that create a sense of unity and belonging, a climate of mutual understanding, and a sense of pride in the team (Hayes, 1997). The goal is to increase the sense of being a part of the team. Once team members have this relationship firmly established, they will become more committed to the team's goals and more supportive of the actions of the other members.

Creating a sense of unity helps to develop a sense of cooperation and belonging. One technique is to identify team boundaries so that team members have a greater sense of being part of something separate. Once they begin to see themselves as part of a unique group, they will see more similarities among their fellow team members and more differences with outside groups. These psychological distinctions will encourage commitment to the team.

Building a sense of pride in the team also helps to build relations among team members. Pride also is enhanced by professionalism, so skills training can help to improve one's image of the team. Various techniques, such as celebrations for team successes, can demonstrate the team's accomplishments and help to build pride in the team.

One popular type of cohesion-building activity is an outdoor experience program. In this type of program, the team leaves its work environment and meets in an outdoor setting. Team members are presented with a series of challenges that they must deal with as a team. For example, they might have to cross a river using ropes or climb a mountain wall. By working together to meet these challenges, the team develops a sense of cohesion and accomplishment.

PROBLEM SOLVING

Team building is designed to improve the operation of the team. Rather than starting with an approach to team building, the team could start with an analysis of its problems. The problem-solving approach to team building starts with problem identification and analysis. The problems can come from performance data, objective outside sources, or internal team communication. Information about team problems is gathered through surveys, interviews, and/or group discussions. This information then is organized and shared with the team. Early on, a diagnostic session is used to clarify the problems and identify the team's strengths and weaknesses.

The diagnosis stage ends with a discussion of how the team should proceed to take actions to solve its problems. A standard problem-solving approach is used to generate alternatives and develop solutions. An action plan is developed for implementing the proposed changes in how the team operates.

This sounds like a fairly straightforward approach to diagnosing a team's problems, but it can be difficult for a team to conduct. Often, by the time the team recognizes that it has a problem, the underlying conflict makes resolution difficult. Outside consultants often are needed to help the team to analyze itself, develop alternatives, and negotiate acceptable solutions.

IMPROVING TEAMS WITH EVALUATION AND FEEDBACK

Although not typically considered a team-building activity, developing a team-oriented performance evaluation system and using the information to provide feedback to a team is an important way in which to improve how teams operate. Performance evaluations can be used to measure the team's success and provide input to the organization's reward system. This helps to motivate the team to perform better. In addition, feedback from the performance evaluations can be used by the team to identify and correct problems in its operations.

| TEAM PERFORMANCE EVALUATIONS

Performance evaluations are a key process in improving the operation of a team (Mohrman et al., 1995). The information from evaluations can be used directly to affect performance by showing the team what adjustments need to be made in how it is performing. There also are indirect benefits. Evaluations can identify when goals and objectives no longer are valid so that the team can modify its direction. The information can identify problems in the situation that the organization needs to correct. The impact of evaluating a team's performance goes beyond providing feedback to the team. Good performance information helps the organization to evaluate its use of the team and helps to establish criteria for rewarding the team and its members.

The key to developing a good measurement system is making sure that it captures key aspects of both team goals and organization goals. The lack of clear team goals and accountability is one of the main reasons why work teams fail (Jones & Moffett, 1999). Team performance measurements should relate to contributions to the organization. It is important to make sure that the measurements relate to factors that the team can influence (Zigon, 1997). In addition, the measures should focus on the results of the team's performance, not on the internal activities of the team, because the team should be free to accomplish its goals in the way it wants.

The development of team performance measures should be a participative process that includes team members, management, and possibly customers. Participation is important to gain acceptance and to ensure that the measures are useful for the team. Typically, a team performance measurement system contains 5 to 10 different measures (Jones & Moffett, 1999). Sometimes, there is value in creating a performance composite that gives a single score for a team. This helps the team to track overall performance over time. The purpose of measurement and feedback is to improve performance by using the information. Therefore, it is better to have a simpler system that team members can relate to than to have a sophisticated system that team members might have difficulty in interpreting.

For some types of teams, such as sports and action teams, the team measurement systems may include both individual and team performance measures. Individual performance measures relate to most organizations' reward systems, they may help to reduce social loafing and other motivation problems, and the information is useful to identify the types of assistance or coaching that specific individuals need. For other types of teams, such as production and project teams, the evaluations might measure only the team's performance due to the difficulty in accurately measuring individual performance separate from team performance.

| USING FEEDBACK

Building a fully functioning team requires learning how to operate better. The essence of this learning is getting feedback on how well the team is performing. Feedback is information from performance evaluations that is provided to the team. The team cannot wait until the end of the project to find out whether it needs to improve. The team needs to get feedback on an ongoing basis so as to learn and improve.

Team performance feedback can have both positive and negative effects on team motivation and problem solving. It can help to motivate the team to reach its goals and is an important source of information that the team can use to identify and solve problems. However, the team must accept negative feedback as a source of useful information rather than as a criticism of its performance. If the team is performing poorly, then feedback that is too negative can discourage the team and reduce motivation. Also, constant negative feedback can damage group cohesion and lead to conflict and scapegoating.

One of the most difficult aspects of evaluating a team's performance is how to use the information. An individual or a team tends to become defensive when being evaluated. No one likes to hear negative information about one's performance even though the information is needed if one is to improve. There are several techniques that can help to make a team better able to accept feedback about its performance.

- When providing feedback, focus on the future. Focusing on the past makes people defensive. Focus the information on how to improve future performance.
- Feedback should focus on specific behaviors. Providing general information does not help the team to identify what changes are needed in its behavior.
- Feedback should focus on learning and problem solving. The information that is provided should help the team to improve, not just focus on its deficiencies.

One of the reasons why teams do not evaluate their group processes is that they prefer to ignore their problems. Team members try to avoid conflict and often are unwilling to tell other team members when they are dissatisfied with the others' performance. This desire to avoid trouble means that problems are hidden and go unresolved until they get so large that they are difficult to manage. The best way in which to prevent this self-destructive pattern of behavior is to conduct regular group process evaluations. A technique for conducting group process evaluations is presented at the end of this chapter.

TEAM REWARD SYSTEMS

An organization's reward system is an important way in which to encourage a team to improve how it operates. Rewarding teamwork is important because rewards have the potential to influence the motivation of individual team members, the amount of interdependence and coordination within the team, and the quality of the group process. All of these factors affect team effectiveness. Because of this, more organizations are beginning to use some type of team-based pay plan (DeMatteo, Eby, & Sundstrom, 1998).

There are three different approaches to rewarding performance: individual, team, and organizational. *Individual* reward systems are good at motivating high performers but may discourage cooperation and teamwork. *Team* and *organizational* approaches are better at encouraging teamwork. There also are in-between options. For example, production workers and professionals often are evaluated and rewarded for individual performance. However, their cooperativeness and participation in teams can be included in their individual evaluations.

The success of different types of team rewards depends on the type of group task (Cohen & Bailey, 1997). If the task is highly interdependent, then team rewards work best. If the team's task is fairly independent, then individual reward systems work best.

| INDIVIDUAL REWARDS

In most organizations, rewards are based on people's job descriptions. Pay is based on the perceived value of the job that is to be performed (Lawler, 1999). Specific jobs have salary ranges attached to them, and people are paid based on their jobs and periodic performance evaluations from their managers.

One approach to making individual reward systems more responsive to teamwork is to change the performance evaluation system. Including factors such as cooperation and team participation into the evaluation can do this. However, managers often are not aware of the internal operations of a team. They focus on the results of the team's efforts, not on how the results occur.

To deal with this evaluation problem, some organizations use a multiple-rater system for performance evaluations (sometimes called 360° feedback). The individual's performance evaluation includes input from team members, managers, subordinates, suppliers, and customers (Thompson, 2000). This helps to reduce bias from the manager and also deals with problems created by using only team members. Team members' ratings of each other can be biased by friendships and a reluctance to be negative when rewards are attached to the evaluations.

An alternative approach is to pay an employee for the skills or competencies that he or she possesses (Lawler, 1999). A skill-based pay system helps to create a culture that encourages personal growth and development. The primary benefit of this approach is to improve the flexibility of the team to perform its task. It is most commonly used when the team members' skills are not too widely divergent and the team's actions are highly interdependent. For example, factory workers who are multiskilled can take over each other's jobs when bottlenecks occur or when some team members are absent. Professional teams that provide an integrated service to customers, such as insurance or banking, also use multiskilling to improve customer service.

| TEAM REWARDS

Team rewards provide rewards based on the successful performance of the team. There are a number of reasons why organizations are adopting team-based rewards (DeMatteo et al., 1998). Organizations are organizing work into teams, organizational hierarchies are flattening, and technology is creating new interdependencies among the parts of organizations. These changes make it more difficult to accurately evaluate individual performance separate from that of work groups. The increasing use of teams has created the need to encourage cooperation among team members and to motivate them as groups. Team rewards have the potential to encourage more cooperative behavior.

However, the potential of using team-based rewards is limited. Individual behavior is more sensitive to individual rewards than to group rewards. Team reward programs may reduce motivation if they are not perceived as fair. Fairness problems can arise from social loafing. This can reduce the motivating impact of team-based rewards, especially for high-performing team members. A survey of field research projects examining the impact of team-based rewards found mixed support for their effectiveness compared to individual-based reward systems (DeMatteo et al., 1998). The most important factor affecting the success of team rewards was task interdependence among team members. Interdependence is crucial for the success of team-based rewards because it tends to reduce the social loafing problem.

The effectiveness of team-based reward programs depends on the characteristics of the rewards, the organization, and the team. The team rewards should be large enough to be a noticeable difference in one's pay (often assumed to be about 10% of one's salary). To encourage cooperativeness, the reward should be distributed equally among all team members. The reward needs to be congruent with the organization's culture, strategy, and structure. Team rewards are more effective when the organization's culture supports teamwork and when work teams are integrated into the operation of the organization. Effective team rewards require clear team goals, measurable performance standards, and a task that requires integrated teamwork.

It can be difficult to develop appropriate team-based rewards for some types of teams. Project teams can be difficult to reward. An organization often will reward project team members when they successfully complete the project. This is a good team incentive. However, many team members come and go during the course of a project, so it is difficult to determine who should share in the rewards. An alternative is to rely on organization-wide rewards, such as profit sharing, to reward successful teamwork.

| ORGANIZATIONAL REWARDS

From an organizational perspective, there can be a problem with a team-based reward system. Organizations typically have multiple teams, and team-based incentives can encourage competition and conflict among teams. When an organization's work requires close connections among teams, the use of team-based rewards actually may reduce overall organizational performance. Team-based rewards sometimes may encourage competition with other teams in the organization. In addition, when work is highly interdependent throughout the organization, measuring the performance of individual teams may be difficult. This is why organization-wide incentive systems or profit sharing may be useful.

Profit-sharing programs can be calculated and distributed to people in a variety of ways (Thomas & Olson, 1988). The success of these programs depends more on the organizational context and participants' beliefs than on the specific formulas used to calculate the rewards. The biggest problem with organization-wide reward systems is the difficulty in establishing a connection between a team member's actions and the performance of the organization. This is especially true in larger organizations.

In U.S. culture, it is difficult to get away from individual-based reward systems. However, organizations can use multiple-performance reward systems. In most work environments, team-based rewards are added to existing compensation systems (DeMatteo et al., 1998). Most organizations use individual-based salary systems as their primary methods of compensation. In addition, compensation can be based on skills, individual merit, team-based incentives, and organizational incentives. It is not really an issue of choosing which system is best; instead, it is selecting the right combination of approaches. The right combination is likely to depend on the goals and operational characteristics of the organization.

SUMMARY

Team building is a type of organizational development that focuses on improving the operation of teams. To be effective, it should be an ongoing activity for teams. Team building examines both the internal processes and organizational contexts of teams. Although team-building programs have been shown to be effective, organizations and teams often are reluctant to conduct them.

Deciding whether a team needs team building requires criteria for effective and ineffective teams. Effective teams have clear goals and tasks, open communication climates, supportive leaders, and procedures for managing tasks and problems. Ineffective teams have unresolved conflicts and hostilities, confusion about goals and tasks, low levels of motivation, and high dependence on their leaders.

There are many different types of team-building activities. Goal setting is used to clarify a team's goals and objectives. Role definition clarifies individual roles and helps to establish group norms. Interpersonal process skills use training activities to teach members how to work together as a team. Cohesion building tries to create a team identity and improve the social relations among team members. Problem solving identifies the team's main problems and works with the team to develop and implement solutions.

Performance evaluations provide important information to help a team improve its operations. Evaluation measures should be developed through a participative process and linked to both team and organizational goals.

Feedback from performance evaluations allows the team to learn how to perform better. Regular assessment of the team's group process is helpful, although the team needs to learn how to handle negative information constructively.

Rewards can help to motivate individual performance and cooperation in the team. Individual reward systems are good at motivating individual performance but may reduce cooperation and commitment to the team. Team-based rewards encourage cooperation but might not encourage individual motivation. Organizational reward systems encourage cooperation among teams and commitment to the overall goals of the organization. Reward systems that combine the benefits of these three types can be created.

ACTIVITY: GROUP PROCESS EVALUATIONS

Objective. One of the central ways in which to promote the development of a team is through group process evaluations. This can be done in one of two ways. Either the team can do its own self-evaluation, or an outside observer can watch the team operate and conduct an evaluation. After the evaluation is completed, the team should discuss this feedback and decide how to use the information.

Activity. Distribute the group process evaluation form (Activity Worksheet 17.1) to a team and have the members complete it at the end of a team meeting. Then, have the team discuss the results of the evaluation and how it could use this information.

ACTIVITY WORKSHEET 17.1
Group Process Evaluation Form

What is the team doing well?

What areas of improvement are needed?

Analysis. How did the team members respond to the feedback they received? Was the team able to use this information to help improve the ways in which it operates?

Discussion. What is the value of doing group process evaluations? How regularly should teams do group process evaluations? Should group process evaluations be performed by the team members or by an outside observer? What are the benefits and costs of each approach?

REFERENCES

Adler, N. (1986). *International dimensions of organizational behavior.* Boston: Kent.

Adler, P. (1991). Workers and flexible manufacturing systems: Three installations compared. *Journal of Organizational Behavior, 12,* 447-460.

Alberti, R., & Emmons, M. (1978). *Your perfect right.* San Luis Obispo, CA: Impact Publishers.

Allen, V., & Levine, J. (1969). Consensus and conformity. *Journal of Experimental Social Psychology, 5,* 389-399.

Amabile, T. (1983). The social psychology of creativity. *Journal of Personality and Social Psychology, 45,* 357-376.

Amabile, T. (1996). *Creativity in context.* Boulder, CO: Westview.

Amason, A. (1996). Distinguishing the effects of functional and dysfunctional conflict on strategic decision making: Resolving a paradox for top management teams. *Academy of Management Journal, 39*(1), 123-148.

Ancona, D., & Caldwell, D. (1990). Information technology and work groups: The case of new product teams. In J. Galegher, R. Kraut, & C. Egido (Eds.), *Intellectual teamwork: Social and technological foundations of cooperative work* (pp. 173-190). Hillsdale, NJ: Lawrence Erlbaum.

Ancona, D., & Caldwell, D. (1992). Demography and design: Predictors of new product team performance. *Organizational Science, 3,* 321-331.

Appelbaum, E., & Batt, R. (1994). *The new American workplace.* Ithaca, NY: IRL Press.

Aranda, E., Aranda, L., & Conlon, K. (1998). *Teams: Structure, process, culture, and politics.* Upper Saddle River, NJ: Prentice Hall.

Armstrong, D., & Cole, P. (1995). Managing distances and differences in geographically distributed workgroups. In S. Jackson & M. Ruderman (Eds.), *Diversity in work teams: Research paradigms for a changing workplace* (pp. 187-215). Washington, DC: American Psychological Association.

Asch, S. (1955, Winter). Opinions and social pressure. *Scientific American,* pp. 31-35.

Axelrod, R. (1984). *The evolution of cooperation.* New York: Basic Books.

Axley, S. (1996). *Communication at work: Management and the communication-intensive organization.* Westport, CT: Quorum Books.

Bales, R. (1966). The equilibrium problem in small groups. In A. Hare, E. Borgatta, & R. Bales (Eds.), *Small groups: Studies in social interactions* (pp. 444-476). New York: Knopf.

Bass, B. (1985). *Leadership and performance beyond expectations.* New York: Free Press.

Battaglia, B. (1992). Skills for managing multicultural teams. *Cultural Diversity at Work, 4,* 4-12.

Baugh, S., & Graen, G. (1997). Effects of team gender and racial composition on perceptions of team performance in cross-functional teams. *Group and Organization Management, 22,* 366-384.

Beebe, S., & Masterson, J. (1994). *Communicating in small groups.* New York: HarperCollins.

Belbin, R. (1981). *Team roles at work.* Oxford, UK: Butterworth Heinemann.

Benne, K., & Sheats, P. (1948). Functional group members. *Journal of Social Issues, 4,* 41-49.

Bennis, W., & Biederman, P. (1997). *Organizing genius: The secrets of creative collaboration.* Reading, MA: Addison-Wesley.

Bikson, T., Cohen, S., & Mankin, D. (1999). Information technology and high-performance teams. In E. Sundstom (Ed.), *Supporting work team effectiveness* (pp. 215-245). San Francisco: Jossey-Bass.

Bikson, T., & Gutek, B. (1984). *Implementation of office automation.* Santa Monica, CA: RAND.

Blake, R., & Mouton, J. (1969). *Building a dynamic corporation through grid organizational development.* Reading, MA: Addison-Wesley.

Brewer, M. (1995). Managing diversity: The role of social identities. In S. Jackson & M. Ruderman (Eds.), *Diversity in work teams: Research paradigms for a changing workplace* (pp. 47-68). Washington, DC: American Psychological Association.

Brown, S. (1996). A meta-analysis and review of organizational research on job involvement. *Psychological Bulletin, 120,* 235-255.

Burgess, R. (1968). Communication networks: An experimental reevaluation. *Journal of Experimental Social Psychology, 4,* 324-327.

Burnstein, E., & Vinokur, A. (1977). Persuasive arguments and social comparison as determinants of attitude polarization. *Journal of Experimental Social Psychology, 13,* 315-332.

Burpitt, W., & Bigoness, W. (1997). Leadership and innovation among teams: The impact of empowerment. *Small Group Research, 28,* 414-423.

Bushe, G. (1988). Cultural contradictions of statistical process control in American manufacturing organizations. *Journal of Management, 14,* 19-31.

Byrne, R. (1984). Overcoming computer phobia. In S. Evans & P. Clarke (Eds.), *The computer culture* (pp. 76-101). Indianapolis, IN: White River Press.

Cacioppo, J., Petty, R., & Morris, K. (1983). Effects of need for cognition on message evaluation, recall, and persuasion. *Journal of Personality and Social Psychology, 45,* 805-818.

Caldwell, B., & Uang, S. (1994). Interactions of situation, social, and technological constraints in information technology use in organizations. In G. Bradley & H. Hendrick (Eds.), *Human factors in organizational design and management* (Vol. 4, pp. 531-536). Amsterdam: Elsevier Science.

Cannon-Bowers, J., & Salas, E. (1998). Team performance and training in complex environments: Recent findings from applied research. *Current Directions in Psychological Science, 7,* 83-87.

Carnevale, A., Gainer, L., & Meltzer, A. (1990). *Workplace basics: The essential skills employers want.* San Francisco: Jossey-Bass.

Carnevale, A., Gainer, L., & Schulz, E. (1990). *Training the technical work force.* San Francisco: Jossey-Bass.

Carnevale, A., & Stone, S. (1995). *The American mosaic: An in-depth report on the future of diversity at work.* New York: McGraw-Hill.

Carnevale, P. (1986). Strategic choice in mediation. *Negotiation Journal, 2,* 41-56.

Castore, C., & Murnighan, J. (1978). Determinants of support for group decisions. *Organizational Behavior and Human Performance, 22,* 75-92.

Chaiken, S. (1979). Communicator physical attractiveness and persuasion. *Journal of Personality and Social Psychology, 37,* 1387-1397.

Cheng, J. (1983). Interdependence and coordination in organizations: A role system analysis. *Academy of Management Journal, 26,* 156-162.

Cohen, S., & Bailey, D. (1997). What makes teams work: Group effectiveness research from the shop floor to the executive suite. *Journal of Management, 23,* 239-290.

Cohen, S., Ledford, G., & Spreitzer, G. (1996). A predictive model of self-managing work team effectiveness. *Human Relations, 49,* 643-676.

Cole, R. (1989). *Strategies for learning: Small-group activities in American, Japanese, and Swedish industry.* Berkeley: University of California Press.

Collins, J., & Porras, J. (1994). *Built to last: Successful habits of visionary companies.* New York: HarperCollins.

Cosier, R., & Dalton, D. (1990). Positive effects of conflict: A field assessment. *International Journal of Conflict Management, 1,* 81-92.

Cotton, J. (1993). *Employee involvement.* Newbury Park, CA: Sage.

Cox, T. (1995). The complexity of diversity: Challenges and directions for future research. In S. Jackson & M. Ruderman (Eds.), *Diversity in work teams: Research paradigms for a changing workplace* (pp. 235-245). Washington, DC: American Psychological Association.

Culnan, M., & Markus, M. (1987). Information technologies. In F. Jablin, L. Putnam, K. Roberts, & L. Porter (Eds.), *Handbook of organizational communication: An interdisciplinary perspective* (pp. 420-443). Newbury Park, CA: Sage.

Daft, R., & Lengel, R. (1986). Organizational information requirements, media richness, and structural design. *Management Science, 32,* 554-571.

Dalkey, N. (1969). *The Delphi method: An experimental study of group decisions.* Santa Monica, CA: RAND.

Davis, L., & Wacker, G. (1987). Job design. In G. Salvendy (Ed.), *Handbook of human factors* (pp. 431-452). New York: John Wiley.

Davis, S. (1984). *Managing corporate culture.* Cambridge, MA: Ballinger.

Dawes, R. (1988). *Rational choice in an uncertain world.* San Diego: Harcourt Brace Jovanovich.

Deal, T., & Kennedy, A. (1982). *Corporate cultures.* Reading, MA: Addison-Wesley.

Deci, E. (1975). *Intrinsic motivation.* New York: Plenum.

Delbecq, A., Van de Ven, A., & Gustafson, D. (1975). *Group techniques for program planning.* Glenview, IL: Scott Foresman.

de Leede, J., & Stoker, J. (1999). Self-managing teams in manufacturing companies: Implications for the engineering function. *Engineering Management Journal, 11*(3), 19-24.

DeMatteo, J., Eby, L., & Sundstrom, E. (1998). Team-based rewards: Current empirical evidence and directions for future research. *Research in Organizational Behavior, 20,* 141-183.

Dennis, A., & Valacich, J. (1993). Computer brainstorms: More heads are better than one. *Journal of Applied Psychology, 78,* 531-537.

Dertouzos, M. (1997). *What will be: How the new world of information will change our lives.* New York: Harper.

Deutsch, M., & Gerard, H. (1955). A study of normative and informational social influence upon individual judgment. *Journal of Abnormal and Social Psychology, 51,* 629-636.

Devine, D., Clayton, L., Philips, J., Dunford, B., & Melner, S. (1999). Teams in organizations: Prevalence, characteristics, and effectiveness. *Small Group Research, 30,* 678-711.

Dewey, J. (1910). *How we think.* New York: Heath.

Diehl, M., & Stroebe, W. (1987). Productivity loss in brainstorming groups: Toward a solution of a riddle. *Journal of Personality and Social Psychology, 53,* 497-509.

DiSalvo, V., Nikkel, E., & Monroe, C. (1989). Theory and practice: A field investigation and identification of group members' perception of problems facing natural work groups. *Small Group Behavior, 20,* 551-567.

Dyer, W. (1995). *Team building: Current issues and new alternatives.* Reading, MA: Addison-Wesley.

Eagly, A., Karau, S., & Makhijani, M. (1995). Gender and the effectiveness of leaders: A meta-analysis. *Journal of Personality and Social Psychology, 117,* 125-145.

Eagly, A., Wood, W., & Chaiken, S. (1978). Casual inferences about communicators and their effect on opinion change. *Journal of Personality and Social Psychology, 36,* 424-435.

Edosomwan, J. (1989). *Integrating innovation and technology management.* New York: John Wiley.

Eisenstat, R., & Cohen, S. (1990). Summary: Top management groups. In R. Hackman (Ed.), *Groups that work (and those that don't)* (p. 78). San Francisco: Jossey-Bass.

Ellis, L., & Honig-Haftel, S. (1992, March). Reward strategies for R&D. *Research Technology Management,* pp. 16-20.

Falbe, C., & Yukl, G. (1992). Consequences for managers using single influence tactics and combination of tactics. *Academy of Management Journal, 35,* 638-652.

Farmer, S., & Roth, J. (1998). Conflict-handling behavior in work groups: Effects of group structure, decision process, and time. *Small Group Research, 29,* 669-713.

Feldman, D. (1984). The development and enforcement of group norms. *Academy of Management Review, 9,* 47-53.

Finegan, J. (1993, July). People power. *Inc.,* pp. 62-63.

Fisher, R., Ury, W., & Patton, B. (1991). *Getting to yes: Negotiating agreement without giving in* (2nd ed.). Boston: Houghton Mifflin.

Fodor, E. (1976). Group stress, authoritarian style of control, and use of power. *Journal of Applied Psychology, 61,* 313-318.

Ford, R., & Fottler, M. (1995). Empowerment: A matter of degree. *Academy of Management Executive, 9*(3), 21-31.

Forsyth, D. (1999). *Group dynamics* (3rd ed.). Belmont, CA: Wadsworth.

Forsyth, D., & Kelley, K. (1996). Heuristic-based biases in estimates of personal contributions to collective endeavors. In J. Nye & A. Brower (Eds.), *What's social about social cognition? Research on socially shared cognitions in small groups* (pp. 106-123). Thousand Oaks, CA: Sage.

Franz, C., & Jin, K. (1995). The structure of group conflict in a collaborative work group during information systems development. *Journal of Applied Communication Research, 23,* 108-127.

Franz, R. (1998). Task interdependence and personal power in teams. *Small Group Research, 29,* 226-253.

French, J., & Raven, B. (1959). The bases of power. In D. Cartwright (Ed.), *Studies in social power* (pp. 150-167). Ann Arbor: University of Michigan Press.

French, W., & Bell, C. (1984). *Organizational development: Behavioral science interventions for organization improvement* (3rd ed.). Englewood Cliffs, NJ: Prentice Hall.

Gallaway, G. (1996). Facilitating the utilization of information resources in an organization through a sociotechnical systems approach. In O. Brown & H. Hendrick (Eds.), *Human factors in organizational design and management* (5th ed., pp. 95-100). Amsterdam: Elsevier Science.

Gandz, J., & Murray, V. (1980). The experience of workplace politics. *Academy of Management Journal, 23,* 237-251.

Gardenswartz, L., & Rowe, A. (1994). *The managing diversity survival guide.* Burr Ridge, IL: Irwin.

Gersick, C. (1988). Time and transition in work teams: Toward a new model of group development. *Academy of Management Journal, 31,* 9-41.

Gersick, C., & Davis-Sacks, M. (1990). Summary: Task forces. In R. Hackman (Ed.), *Groups that work (and those that don't)* (pp. 146-153). San Francisco: Jossey-Bass.

Gibb, J. (1961). Defensive communication. *Journal of Communication, 11,* 141-148.

Gigone, D., & Hastie, R. (1997). The impact of information on small group choice. *Journal of Personality and Social Psychology, 72,* 132-140.

Gilovich, T., Savitsky, K., & Medvec, V. (1998). The illusion of transparency: Biased assessments of others' ability to read one's emotional states. *Journal of Personality and Social Psychology, 75,* 332-346.

Goethals, G., & Nelson, E. (1973). Similarity in the influence process: The belief-value distinction. *Journal of Personality and Social Psychology, 25,* 117-122.

Graen, G., & Uhl-Bien, M. (1995). Relationship-based approach to leadership: Development of leader-member exchange (LMX) theory of leadership over 25 years. *Leadership Quarterly, 6,* 219-247.

Greenberg, J., & Baron, R. (1997). *Behavior in organizations: Understanding the human side of work* (6th ed.). Upper Saddle River, NJ: Prentice Hall.

Guzzo, R., & Dickson, M. (1996). Teams in organizations: Recent research on performance and effectiveness. *Annual Review of Psychology, 47,* 307-338.

Gwynne, S. (1990, October 29). The right stuff. *Time,* pp. 74-84.

Hackett, D., & Martin, C. (1993). *Facilitation skills for team leaders.* Menlo Park, CA: CRISP Publications.

Hackman, R. (1986). The psychology of self-management in organizations. In M. Pallak & R. Perloff (Eds.), *Psychology and work* (pp. 89-136). Washington, DC: American Psychological Association.

Hackman, R. (1987). The design of work teams. In J. Lorsch (Ed.), *Handbook of organizational behavior* (pp. 315-342). Englewood Cliffs, NJ: Prentice Hall.

Hackman, R. (1990a). Creating more effective work groups in organizations. In R. Hackman (Ed.), *Groups that work (and those that don't)* (pp. 479-504). San Francisco: Jossey-Bass.

Hackman, R. (1990b). Work teams in organizations: An orienting framework. In R. Hackman (Ed.), *Groups that work (and those that don't)* (pp. 1-14). San Francisco: Jossey-Bass.

Hackman, R. (1992). Group influences on individuals in organizations. In M. Dunnette & L. Hough (Eds.), *Handbook of industrial and organizational psychology* (pp. 199-267). Palo Alto, CA: Consulting Psychologists Press.

Hackman, R., & Morris, C. (1975). Group tasks, group interaction process, and group performance effectiveness: A review and proposed integration. *Advances in Experimental Social Psychology, 8,* 47-99.

Hackman, J., & Oldham, G. (1980). *Work redesign.* Reading, MA: Addison-Wesley.

Hackman, R., & Walton, R. (1986). Leading groups in organizations. In P. Goodman (Ed.), *Designing effective work groups* (pp. 72-119). San Francisco: Jossey-Bass.

Hare, A. (1982). *Creativity in small groups.* Beverly Hills, CA: Sage.

Harkins, S., & Jackson, J. (1985). The role of evaluation in eliminating social loafing. *Personality and Social Psychology Bulletin, 11,* 457-465.

Harris, T. (1993). *Applied organizational communication: Perspectives, principles, and pragmatics.* Hillsdale, NJ: Lawrence Erlbaum.

Harvey, J. (1988). *The Abilene paradox and other meditations on management.* Lexington, MA: Lexington Books.

Hayes, N. (1997). *Successful team management.* London: International Thomson Business Press.

Hemphill, J. (1961). Why people attempt to lead. In L. Petrullo & B. Bass (Eds.), *Leadership and interpersonal behavior* (pp. 201-215). New York: Holt, Rinehart & Winston.

Herrenkohl, R., Judson, G., & Heffner, J. (1999). Defining and measuring employee empowerment. *Journal of Applied Behavioral Science, 35,* 373-389.

Hersey, P., & Blanchard, K. (1993). *Management of organizational behavior: Utilizing human resources.* Englewood Cliffs, NJ: Prentice Hall.

Higgins, E. (1999). Saying is believing effects: When sharing reality about something biases knowledge and evaluations. In L. Thompson, J. Levine, & D. Messick (Eds.), *Shared cognition in organizations: The management of knowledge.* Mahwah, NJ: Lawrence Erlbaum.

Hill, G. (1982). Group versus individual performance: Are $N + 1$ heads better than 1? *Psychological Bulletin, 91,* 517-539.

Hitrop, J. (1989). Factors associated with successful labor mediation. In K. Kressel & D. Pruitt (Eds.), *Mediation research* (pp. 241-262). San Francisco: Jossey-Bass.

Hofstede, G. (1980). *Culture's consequences: International differences in work related value.* Beverly Hills, CA: Sage.

Hogg, M. (1992). *The social psychology of group cohesiveness: From attraction to social identity.* New York: New York University Press.

Hollander, E., & Offerman, L. (1990). Power and leadership in organizations. *American Psychologist, 45,* 179-189.

Hurwitz, A., Zander, A., & Hymovitch, B. (1953). Some effects of power on the relations among group members. In D. Cartwright & A. Zander (Eds.), *Group dynamics: Research and theory* (pp. 483-492). New York: Harper & Row.

Insko, C., Schopler, J., Graetz, K., Drigotas, S., Currey, K., Smith, S., Brazil, D., & Bornstein, G. (1994). Interindividual-intergroup discontinuity in the prisoner's dilemma game. *Journal of Conflict Resolution, 38,* 87-116.

Jackson, A., & Ruderman, M. (1995). Introduction: Perspective for understanding diverse work teams. In S. Jackson & M. Ruderman (Eds.), *Diversity in work teams: Research paradigms for a changing workplace* (pp. 1-13). Washington, DC: American Psychological Association.

Jackson, S. (1992). Team composition in organizational settings: Issues in managing an increasingly diverse workforce. In S. Worchel, W. Wood, & J. Simpson (Eds.), *Group process and productivity* (pp. 138-173). Newbury Park, CA: Sage.

Janis, I. (1972). *Victims of groupthink.* Boston: Houghton Mifflin.

Janis, I., & Mann, L. (1977). *Decision making.* New York: Free Press.

Janz, B., Colquitt, J., & Noe, R. (1997). Knowledge worker team effectiveness: The role of autonomy, interdependence, team development, and contextual support variables. *Personnel Psychology, 50,* 877-905.

Jehn, K. (1995). A multimethod examination of the benefits and detriments of intragroup conflict. *Administrative Science Quarterly, 40,* 256-282.

Jehn, K., & Shaw, P. (1997). Interpersonal relationships and task performance: An examination of mediating processes in friendship and acquaintance groups. *Journal of Personality and Social Psychology, 72,* 775-790.

Johnson, D., & Johnson, F. (1997). *Joining together: Group theory and group skills* (6th ed.). Boston: Allyn & Bacon.

Johnson, D., Maruyama, G., Johnson, R., Nelson, D., & Skon, L. (1981). Effects of cooperative, competitive, and individualistic goal structures on achievement: A meta-analysis. *Psychological Bulletin, 89,* 47-62.

Jones, G., & George, J. (1998). The experience and evolution of trust: Implications for cooperation and teamwork. *Academy of Management Review, 23,* 531-546.

Jones, R., & Brehm, J. (1970). Persuasiveness of one and two sided communications as a function of awareness when there are two sides. *Journal of Experimental Social Psychology, 6,* 47-56.

Jones, S., & Moffett, R. (1999). Measurement and feedback systems for teams. In E. Sundstom (Ed.), *Supporting work team effectiveness* (pp. 157-187). San Francisco: Jossey-Bass.

Kanter, R. (1977). *Men and women of the corporation.* New York: Basic Books.

Karau, S., & Williams, K. (1993). Social loafing: A meta-analytic review and theoretical integration. *Journal of Personality and Social Psychology, 65,* 681-706.

Karau, S., & Williams, K. (1997). The effects of group cohesion on social loafing and social compensation. *Group Dynamics: Theory, Research, and Practice, 1,* 156-168.

Katzenbach, J., & Smith, D. (1993). *The wisdom of teams.* Cambridge, MA: Harvard Business School Press.

Kayser, T. (1990). *Mining group gold.* El Segundo, CA: Sherif Publishing.

Kemery, E., Bedeian, A., Mossholder, K., & Touliatos, J. (1985). Outcomes of role stress: A multisample constructive replication. *Academy of Management Review, 28,* 363-375.

Kerr, N., & Bruun, S. (1983). Dispensability of member effort and group motivation losses: Free rider effects. *Journal of Personality and Social Psychology, 44,* 78-94.

Keysar, B. (1998). Language users as problem solvers: Just what ambiguity problem do they solve? In S. Fussell & R. Kreuz (Eds.), *Social and cognitive approaches to interpersonal communication* (pp. 175-200). Mahwah, NJ: Lawrence Erlbaum.

Kidder, T. (1981). *The soul of the new machine.* New York: Avon.

Kiesler, S. (1986, January). The hidden messages in computer networks. *Harvard Business Review,* pp. 46-60.

Kiesler, S., Siegel, J., & McGuire, T. (1984). Social aspects of computer mediated communication. *American Psychologist, 39,* 1123-1134.

Kilmann, R., & Saxton, M. (1983). *The Kilmann-Saxton Culture Gap Survey.* Pittsburgh, PA: Organizational Design Consultants.

Kipnis, D. (1976). *The powerholders.* Chicago: University of Chicago Press.

Kipnis, D., & Schmidt, S. (1982). *Profiles of organizational influence strategies: Influencing your subordinates.* San Diego: University Associates.

Kipnis, D., Schmidt, S., Swaffin-Smith, C., & Wilkinson, I. (1984). Patterns of managerial influence: Shotgun managers, tacticians, and bystanders. *Organizational Dynamics, 12*(3), 58-67.

Kirkpatrick, S., & Locke, E. (1991). Leadership: Do traits matter? *Academy of Management Executive, 5,* 48-60.

Kivlighan, D., & Jauquet, C. (1990). Quality of group member agendas and group session climate. *Small Group Research, 1,* 205-219.

Klein, J. (1984, September). Why supervisors resist employee involvement. *Harvard Business Review,* pp. 87-93.

Knight, G., & Dubro, A. (1984). Cooperative, competitive, and individualistic social values. *Journal of Personality and Social Psychology, 46,* 98-105.

Krauss, R., & Fussell, S. (1991). Perspective-taking in communication: Representations of other's knowledge in reference. *Social Cognition, 9,* 2-24.

Langfred, C. (2000). Work group design and autonomy: A field study of the interaction between task interdependence and group autonomy. *Small Group Research, 31,* 54-70.

Larson, C., & LaFasto, F. (1989). *Teamwork: What must go right/what can go wrong.* Newbury Park, CA: Sage.

Larson, J., Foster-Fishman, P., & Franz, T. (1998). Leadership style and discussion of shared and unshared information in decision making groups. *Personality and Social Psychology Bulletin, 24,* 482-495.

Latane, B., Williams, K., & Harkins, S. (1979). Many hands make light the work: The causes and consequences of social loafing. *Journal of Personality and Social Psychology, 37,* 822-832.

Laughlin, P., & Hollingshead, A. (1995). A theory of collective induction. *Organizational Behavior and Human Decision Processes, 61,* 94-107.

Lawler, E. (1986). *High involvement management.* San Francisco: Jossey-Bass.

Lawler, E. (1999). Creating effective pay systems for teams. In E. Sundstom (Ed.), *Supporting work team effectiveness* (pp. 188-214). San Francisco: Jossey-Bass.

Lawler, E., & Mohrman, S. (1985, January). Quality circles after the fad. *Harvard Business Review,* pp. 85-71.

Lawler, E., Mohrman, S., & Ledford, G. (1995). *Creating high performance organizations: Practices and results of employee involvement and quality management in Fortune 1000 companies.* San Francisco: Jossey-Bass.

Lea, D., & Brostrom, L. (1988). Managing the high-tech professional. *Personnel, 65*(6), 12-22.

Levi, D. (1988). *The role of corporate culture in selecting human resources policies.* Unpublished manuscript, Northern Telecom.

Levi, D., & Cadiz, D. (1998). *Evaluating teamwork on student projects: The use of behaviorally anchored scales to evaluate student performance.* ERIC Document No. TM029122.

Levi, D., & Lawn, M. (1993). The driving and restraining forces which affect technological innovation. *Journal of High Technology Management Research, 4,* 225-240.

Levi, D., & Rinzel, L. (1998). Employee attitudes toward various communications technologies when used for communicating about organizational change. In P. Vink, E. Koningsveld, & S. Dhondt (Eds.), *Human factors in organizational design and management* (Vol. 6, pp. 483-488). Amsterdam: Elsevier Science.

Levi, D., & Slem, C. (1990). *The human, social, and organizational impact of electronic mail.* Unpublished manuscript, Institute for Information Studies.

Levi, D., & Slem, C. (1995). Team work in research and development organizations: The characteristics of successful teams. *International Journal of Industrial Ergonomics, 16,* 29-42.

Levi, D., & Slem, C. (1996). The relationship of concurrent engineering practices to different views of project success. In O. Brown & H. Hendrick (Eds.), *Human factors in organizational design and management* (Vol. 5, pp. 25-30). Amsterdam: Elsevier Science.

Levine, J. (1989). Reaction to opinion deviance in small groups. In P. Paulus (Ed.), *Psychology of group influence: New perspectives* (pp. 187-232). Hillsdale, NJ: Lawrence Erlbaum.

Lewin, K. (1951). *Field theory in social science.* New York: Harper.

Likert, R. (1961). *New patterns in management.* New York: McGraw-Hill.

Locke, E., & Latham, G. (1990). *A theory of goal setting and task performance.* Englewood Cliffs, NJ: Prentice Hall.

Lord, R. (1985). An information processing approach to social perceptions, leadership, and behavioral measurement. *Research in Organizational Behavior, 7,* 87-128.

Lott, A., & Lott, B. (1965). Group cohesiveness as interpersonal attraction: A review of the relationships with antecedent and consequence variables. *Psychological Bulletin, 64,* 259-309.

Lumsden, G., & Lumsden, D. (1997). *Communicating in groups and teams.* Belmont, CA: Wadsworth.

Manufacturing Studies Board. (1986). *Human resources practices for implementing advanced manufacturing technology.* Washington, DC: National Academy Press.

Manz, C. (1992). Self-leading work teams: Moving beyond self-management myths. *Human Relations, 45,* 1119-1140.

Mayo, E. (1933). *The human problems of an industrial civilization.* Cambridge, MA: Harvard University Press.

McAllister, D. (1995). Affect and cognition based trust as foundations for interpersonal cooperation in organizations. *Academy of Management Journal, 38,* 24-59.

McClelland, D., & Boyatzis, R. (1982). Leadership motive pattern and long-term success in management. *Journal of Applied Psychology, 67,* 737-743.

McComb, S., Green, S., & Compton, W. (1999). Project goals, team performance, and shared understanding. *Engineering Management Journal, 11*(3), 7-12.

McGrath, J. (1984). *Groups: Interaction and performance.* Englewood Cliffs, NJ: Prentice Hall.

McGrath, J. (1990). Time matters in groups. In J. Galegher, R. Kraut, & C. Egido (Eds.), *Intellectual teamwork: Social and technological foundations of cooperative work* (pp. 23-62). Hillsdale, NJ: Lawrence Erlbaum.

McGrath, J., Berdahl, J., & Arrow, H. (1995). Traits, expectations, culture, and clout: The dynamics of diversity in work groups. In S. Jackson & M. Ruderman (Eds.), *Diversity in work teams: Research paradigms for a changing workplace* (pp. 17-45). Washington, DC: American Psychological Association.

McGrath, J., & Hollingshead, A. (1994). *Groups interacting with technology.* Thousand Oaks, CA: Sage.

McGregor, D. (1960). *The human side of enterprise.* New York: McGraw-Hill.

McGrew, J., Bilotta, J., & Deeney, J. (1999). Software team formation and decay. *Small Group Research, 30,* 209-234.

McIntyre, R., & Salas, E. (1995). Measuring and managing for team performance: Lessons from complex environments. In R. Guzzo & E. Salas (Eds.), *Team effectiveness and decision making in organizations* (pp. 9-45). San Francisco: Jossey-Bass.

McKenna, E. (1994). *Business psychology and organizational behavior.* Hillsdale, NJ: Lawrence Erlbaum.

Meindl, J., & Ehrlich, S. (1987). The romance of leadership and the evaluation of organizational performance. *Academy of Management Journal, 30,* 91-109.

Milgram, S. (1974). *Obedience to authority.* New York: Harper & Row.

Mittleman, D., & Briggs, R. (1999). Communication technologies for traditional and virtual teams. In E. Sundstom (Ed.), *Supporting work team effectiveness* (pp. 246-270). San Francisco: Jossey-Bass.

Mohrman, S. (1993). Integrating roles and structure in the lateral organization. In J. Galbraith & E. Lawler (Eds.), *Organizing for the future* (pp. 109-141). San Francisco: Jossey-Bass.

Mohrman, S., Cohen, S., & Mohrman, A. (1995). *Designing team-based organizations*. San Francisco: Jossey-Bass.

Moreland, R., Argote, L., & Krishnan, R. (1996). Socially shared cognition at work. In J. Nye & A. Bower (Eds.), *What's social about social cognition?* Thousand Oaks, CA: Sage.

Moreland, R., & Levine, J. (1982). Socialization in small groups: Temporal changes in individual-group relations. *Advances in Experimental Social Psychology, 15,* 137-192.

Moreland, R., & Levine, J. (1989). Newcomers and old-timers in small groups. In P. Paulus (Ed.), *Psychology of group influence* (pp. 143-186). Hillsdale, NJ: Lawrence Erlbaum.

Moreland, R., & Levine, J. (1992). Problem identification by groups. In S. Worchel, W. Wood, & J. Simpson (Eds.), *Group process and productivity* (pp. 17-48). Newbury Park, CA: Sage.

Moscovici, S. (1985). Social influence and conformity. In G. Lindzey & E. Aronson (Eds.), *The handbook of social psychology* (pp. 347-412). Hillsdale, NJ: Lawrence Erlbaum.

Mullen, B., & Copper, C. (1994). The relation between group cohesiveness and performance: An integration. *Psychological Bulletin, 115,* 210-227.

Mullen, B., Johnson, C., & Salas, E. (1991). Productivity loss in brainstorming groups: A meta-analytic integration. *Basic and Applied Psychology, 12,* 3-24.

Mullen, B., Salas, E., & Driskell, J. (1989). Salience, motivation, and artifacts as contributors to the relationship between participation rate and leadership. *Journal of Experimental Social Psychology, 25,* 545-559.

Murnighan, J. (1981). Group decision making: What strategies should you use? *Management Review, 25,* 56-62.

Myers, D., & Lamm, H. (1976). The group polarization phenomenon. *Psychological Bulletin, 83,* 602-627.

Nadler, J., Thompson, L., & Morris, M. (1999, August). *Schmooze or lose: The efforts of rapport and gender in e-mail negotiations.* Paper presented at the annual meeting of the Academy of Management, Chicago.

Nemeth, C. (1979). The role of an active minority in intergroup relations. In W. Austin & S. Worchel (Eds.), *The social psychology of intergroup relations* (p. 348). Pacific Grove, CA: Brooks/Cole.

Nemeth, C. (1997). Managing innovation: When less is more. *California Management Review, 40*(1), 58-66.

Nemeth, C., & Staw, B. (1989). The trade-offs of social control and innovation in groups and organizations. In L. Berkowitz (Ed.), *Advances in experimental social psychology* (pp. 195-230). San Diego: Academic Press.

Nkomo, S. (1995). Identities and the complexity of diversity. In S. Jackson & M. Ruderman (Eds.), *Diversity in work teams: Research paradigms for a changing workplace* (pp. 247-253). Washington, DC: American Psychological Association.

Northcraft, G., Polzer, J., Neale, M., & Kramer, R. (1995). Diversity, social identity, and performance: Emergent social dynamics in cross-functional teams. In S. Jackson & M. Ruderman (Eds.), *Diversity in work teams: Research paradigms for a changing workplace* (pp. 69-95). Washington, DC: American Psychological Association.

Nye, J., & Forsyth, D. (1991). The effects of prototype-based biases on leadership appraisals: A test of leadership categorization theory. *Small Group Research, 22,* 360-379.

O'Dell, C. (1989, November 1). Team play, team pay: New ways of keeping score. *Across the Board,* pp. 38-45.

Offner, A., Kramer, T., & Winter, J. (1996). The effects of facilitation, recording, and pauses on group brainstorming. *Small Group Research, 27,* 283-298.

Orpen, C. (1979). The effects of job enrichment on employee satisfaction, motivation, involvement, and performance: A field experiment. *Human Relations, 32,* 189-217.

Orsburn, J., Moran, L., Musselwhite, E., Zenger, J., & Perrin, C. (1990). *Self-directed work teams: The new American challenge.* Homewood, IL: Business One Irwin.

Osborn, A. (1957). *Applied imagination.* New York: Scribner.

Osgood, C. (1962). *An alternative to war and surrender.* Urbana: University of Illinois Press.

Ouchi, W. (1981). *Theory Z: How American business can meet the Japanese challenge.* Reading, MA: Addison-Wesley.

Parks, C. (1994). The predictive ability of social values in resource dilemmas and public good games. *Personality and Social Psychology Bulletin, 20,* 431-438.

Parks, C., & Sanna, L. (1999). *Group performance and interaction.* Boulder, CO: Westview.

Pascale, R., & Athos, A. (1981). *The art of Japanese management.* New York: Simon & Schuster.

Paulus, P. (1998). Developing consensus about groupthink after all these years. *Organization Behavior and Human Decision Processes, 73,* 362-374.

Pavit, C. (1993). What (little) we know about formal group discussion procedures. *Small Group Research, 24,* 217-235.

Peters, T., & Waterman, R. (1982). *In search of excellence.* New York: Harper & Row.

Peterson, R., & Nemeth, C. (1996). Focus versus flexibility: Majority and minority influence can both improve performance. *Personality and Social Psychology Bulletin, 22,* 14-24.

Podsakoff, P., & Schriesheim, C. (1985). Field studies of French and Raven's bases of power. *Psychological Bulletin, 97,* 387-411.

Pokras, S. (1995). *Team problem solving.* Menlo Park, CA: CRISP Publications.

Poole, M. (1983). Decision development in small groups: A multiple sequence model of group decision development. *Communication Monographs, 50,* 321-330.

Prochaska, R. (1980). The management of innovation in Japan: Why it is successful. *Research Management, 23,* 35-38.

Pruitt, D. (1981). *Negotiation behavior.* New York: Academic Press.

Pruitt, D. (1986). Trends in the scientific study of negotiation. *Negotiation Journal, 2,* 237-244.

Pruitt, D., & Carnevale, P. (1993). *Negotiation in social conflict.* Pacific Grove, CA: Brooks/Cole.

Rahim, M. (1983). A measure of styles of handling interpersonal conflict. *Academy of Management Journal, 26,* 368-376.

Raven, B., Schwarzwald, J., & Koslowsky, M. (1998). Conceptualizing and measuring a power/interaction model of interpersonal influence. *Journal of Applied Social Psychology, 28,* 307-333.

Reichwald, R., & Goecke, R. (1994). New communication media and new forms of cooperation in the top management area. In G. Bradley & H. Hendrick (Eds.), *Human factors in organizational design and management* (Vol. 4, pp. 511-518). Amsterdam: Elsevier Science.

Rice, R., Instone, D., & Adams, J. (1984). Leader sex, leader success, and leadership process: Two field studies. *Journal of Applied Psychology, 69,* 12-31.

Robbins, S. (1974). *Managing organizational conflict.* Englewood Cliffs, NJ: Prentice Hall.

Rohlen, T. (1975). The company work group. In E. Vogel (Ed.), *Modern Japanese organization and decision making* (pp. 185-209). Tokyo: Tuttle.

Rosenberg, L. (1961). Group size, prior experience, and conformity. *Abnormal and Social Psychology, 63,* 436-437.

Ross, L., & Ward, A. (1995). Psychological barriers to dispute resolution. In M. Zanna (Ed.), *Advances in experimental social psychology* (Vol. 27, pp. 255-304). San Diego: Academic Press.

Safizadeh, M. (1991). The case of workgroups in manufacturing operations. *California Management Review, 33*(4), 61-82.

Sakuri, M. (1975). Small group cohesiveness and detrimental conformity. *Sociometry, 38,* 340-357.

Savage, C. (1990). *Fifth generation management: Integrating enterprises through human networking.* Bedford, MA: Digital Press.

Schein, E. (1988). *Process consultation: Its role in organizational development.* Reading, MA: Addison-Wesley.

Schein, E. (1992). *Organizational culture and leadership* (2nd ed.). San Francisco: Jossey-Bass.

Scholtes, P. (1988). *The team handbook: How to use teams to improve quality.* Madison, WI: Joiner Associates.

Scholtes, P. (1994). *The team handbook for educators.* Madison, WI: Joiner Associates.

Schwenk, C. (1990). Effects of devil's advocacy and dialectical inquiry on decision making: A meta-analysis. *Organizational Behavior and Human Decision Processes, 47,* 161-176.

Shaw, M. (1978). Communication networks fourteen years later. In L. Berkowitz (Ed.), *Group processes* (pp. 351-356). New York: Academic Press.

Shaw, M. (1981). *Group dynamics: The psychology of small group behavior.* New York: McGraw-Hill.

Sherif, M. (1966). *In common predicament: Social psychology of intergroup conflict and cooperation.* Boston: Houghton Mifflin.

Siegel, S., & Fouraker, L. (1960). *Bargaining and group decision making.* New York: McGraw-Hill.

Simon, H. (1979). *The science of the artificial* (2nd ed.). Cambridge: MIT Press.

Slavin, R. (1985). Cooperative learning: Applying contact theory in desegregated schools. *Journal of Social Issues, 41,* 45-62.

Slem, C., Levi, D., & Young, A. (1995). Attitudes about the impact of technological change: Comparison of U.S. and Japanese workers. *Journal of High Technology Management Research, 6,* 211-228.

Smith, K., Carrol, S., & Ashford, S. (1995). Intra- and interorganizational cooperation: Toward a research agenda. *Academy of Management Journal, 38,* 7-23.

Spreitzer, G., Cohen, S., & Ledford, G. (1999). Developing effective self-managing work teams in service organizations. *Group and Organization Management, 24,* 340-367.

Sproull, L., & Kiesler, S. (1991). *Connections: New ways of working in the networked organization.* Cambridge: MIT Press.

Srull, T., & Wyer, R. (1988). *Advances in social cognition.* Hillsdale, NJ: Lawrence Erlbaum.

Stasser, G. (1992). Pooling of unshared information during group discussions. In S. Worchel, W. Wood, & J. Simpson (Eds.), *Group process and productivity* (pp. 17-48). Newbury Park, CA: Sage.

Stasser, G., & Titus, W. (1985). Pooling of unshared information in group decision making: Biased information sampling during discussion. *Journal of Personality and Social Psychology, 48,* 1467-1478.

Stein, M. (1975). *Stimulating creativity.* New York: Academic Press.

Steiner, I. (1972). *Group process and productivity.* New York: Academic Press.

Stewart, G., & Manz, C. (1995). Leadership for self-managing work teams: A topology and integrative model. *Human Relations, 48,* 747-770.

Stogdill, R. (1974). *Handbook of leadership.* New York: Free Press.

Stoner, J. (1961). *A comparison of individual and group decision making involving risk.* Unpublished master's thesis, Massachusetts Institute of Technology.

Strassmann, P. (1985). *Information payoff.* New York: Free Press.

Sundstrom, E. (1999a). The challenges of supporting work team effectiveness. In E. Sundstom (Ed.), *Supporting work team effectiveness* (pp. 2-23). San Francisco: Jossey-Bass.

Sundstrom, E. (1999b). Supporting work team effectiveness: Best practices. In E. Sundstom (Ed.), *Supporting work team effectiveness* (pp. 301-342). San Francisco: Jossey-Bass.

Sundstrom, E., DeMeuse, K., & Futrell, D. (1990). Work teams. *American Psychologist, 45,* 120-133.

Sweeney, J. (1973). An experimental investigation of the free rider problem. *Social Science Research, 2,* 277-292.

Taha, L., & Caldwell, B. (1993). Social isolation and integration in electronic environments. *Behaviour and Information Technology, 12,* 276-283.

Tajfel, H. (1982). Social psychology of intergroup relations. *Annual Review of Psychology, 33,* 1-39.

Tajfel, H., & Turner, J. (1986). The social identity theory of intergroup behavior. In S. Worchel & W. Austin (Eds.), *Psychology of intergroup relations* (pp. 2-24). Chicago: Nelson-Hall.

Taylor, F. (1923). *The principles of scientific management.* New York: Harper.

Thomas, B., & Olson, M. (1988). Gain sharing: The design that guarantees success. *Personnel Journal, 67*(5), 73-79.

Thomas, K. (1976). Conflict and conflict management. In M. Dunnette (Ed.), *Handbook of industrial and organizational psychology* (pp. 889-935). Chicago: Rand McNally.

Thomas, K. (1992). Conflict and conflict management: Reflections and update. *Journal of Organizational Behavior, 13,* 265-274.

Thompson, L. (2000). *Making the team: A guide for managers.* Upper Saddle River, NJ: Prentice Hall.

Thompson, L., & Hastie, R. (1990). Judgment tasks and biases in negotiation. In B. Sheppard, M. Bazerman, & R. Lewicki (Eds.), *Research on negotiations in organizations* (Vol. 2, pp. 1077-1092). Greenwich, CT: JAI.

Thompson, L., & Hrebec, D. (1996). Loose-loose agreements in interdependent decision making. *Psychological Bulletin, 120,* 396-409.

Thomsett, R. (1980). *People and project management.* New York: Yourdon Press.

Tjosvold, D. (1995). Cooperation theory, constructive controversy, and effectiveness: Learning from crisis. In R. Guzzo & E. Salas (Eds.), *Team effectiveness and decision making in organizations* (pp. 79-112). San Francisco: Jossey-Bass.

Tolbert, P., Andrews, A., & Simons, T. (1995). The effects of group proportions on group dynamics. In S. Jackson & M. Ruderman (Eds.), *Diversity in work teams: Research paradigms for a changing workplace* (pp. 131-159). Washington, DC: American Psychological Association.

Triandis, H. (1994). *Culture and social behavior.* New York: McGraw-Hill.

Triplett, N. (1898). The dynamogenic factors in pace-making and competition. *American Journal of Psychology, 9,* 507-533.

Tushman, M., & Nadler, D. (1986). Organizing for innovation. *California Management Review, 28*(3), 74-92.

Tsui, A., Xin, K., & Egan, T. (1995). Relational demography: The missing link in vertical dyad linkage. In S. Jackson & M. Ruderman (Eds.), *Diversity in work teams: Research paradigms for a changing workplace* (pp. 97-129). Washington, DC: American Psychological Association.

Tuckman, B., & Jensen, M. (1977). Stages of small group development revisited. *Group and Organizational Studies, 2,* 419-427.

Uhl-Bien, M., & Graen, G. (1992). Self-management and team-making in cross-functional work teams: Discovering the keys to becoming an integrated team. *Journal of High Technology Management Research, 3,* 225-241.

Uzzi, B. (1997). Social structure and competition in interfirm networks: The paradox of embeddedness. *Administrative Science Quarterly, 42,* 35-67.

Van de Ven, A., & Delbecq, A. (1974). The effectiveness of nominal, Delphi, and interacting group decision making processes. *Academy of Management Journal, 17,* 605-621.

Van der Vegt, G., Emans, B., & Van de Vliert, E. (1998). Motivating effects of task and outcome interdependence in work teams. *Group and Organization Management, 23,* 124-144.

Van Gundy, A. (1981). *Techniques of structured problem solving.* New York: Van Nostrand Reinhold.

Van Gundy, A. (1987). *Creative problem solving: A guide for trainers and management.* New York: Quorum Books.

Van Maanen, J., & Barley, S. (1985). Cultural organization: Fragments of a theory. In P. Frost (Ed.), *Organizational culture* (pp. 31-54). London: Sage.

Vroom, V., & Jago, A. (1988). *The new leadership: Managing participation in organizations.* Englewood Cliffs, NJ: Prentice Hall.

Vroom, V., & Yetton, P. (1973). *Leadership and decision making.* Pittsburgh, PA: University of Pittsburgh Press.

Walker, H., Ilardi, B., McMahon, A., & Fennell, M. (1996). Gender, interaction, and leadership. *Social Psychology Quarterly, 59,* 255-272.

Wall, V., & Nolan, L. (1987). Small group conflict: A look at equity, satisfaction, and styles of conflict management. *Small Group Behavior, 18,* 188-211.

Walton, R., & Hackman, J. (1986). Groups under contrasting management strategies. In P. Goodman & Associates (Eds.), *Designing effective work groups* (pp. 168-201). San Francisco: Jossey-Bass.

Walton, R., & McKersie, R. (1965). *A behavioral theory of labor negotiations.* New York: McGraw-Hill.

Wanous, J. (1980). *Organizational entry: Recruitment, selection, and socialization of newcomers.* Reading, MA: Addison-Wesley.

Wanous, J., & Youtz, M. (1986). Solution diversity and the quality of group decisions. *Academy of Management Journal, 29,* 149-159.

Watson, R., DeSanctis, G., & Poole, M. (1988). Using a GDSS to facilitate group consensus: Some intended and unintended consequences. *MIS Quarterly, 12,* 463-476.

Wech, B., Mossholder, K., Steel, R., & Bennett, N. (1998). Does work group cohesiveness affect individuals' performance and organizational commitment? *Small Group Research, 29,* 472-494.

Wegner, D. (1986). Transactive memory: A contemporary analysis of the group mind. In B. Mullen & G. Goethals (Eds.), *Theories of group behavior* (pp. 185-208). New York: Springer-Verlag.

Weldon, E., Jehn, K., & Pradhan, P. (1991). Processes that mediate the relationship between a group goal and improved group performance. *Journal of Personality and Social Psychology, 61,* 555-569.

Wellins, R., Byham, W., & Wilson, J. (1991). *Empowered teams.* San Francisco: Jossey-Bass.

Wellins, R., & George, J. (1991). The key to self-directed teams. *Training and Development Journal, 45*(4), 26-31.

Wheelan, S. (1994). *Group process: A developmental perspective.* Boston: Allyn & Bacon.

Wilder, D. (1986). Social categorization: Implications for creation and reduction of intergroup bias. In L. Berkowitz (Ed.), *Advances in experimental social psychology* (Vol. 19, pp. 291-355). San Diego: Academic Press.

Wilder, D. (1990). Some determinants of the persuasive power of in-groups and out-groups. *Journal of Personality and Social Psychology, 59,* 1202-1213.

Williams, J., & Best, D. (1990). *Measuring sex differences: A multination study.* Newbury Park, CA: Sage.

Witeman, H. (1991). Group member satisfaction: A conflict-related account. *Small Group Research, 22,* 24-58.

Worchel, S., Andreoli, V., & Folger, R. (1977). Intergroup cooperation and intergroup attraction: The effect of previous interaction and outcome of combined effort. *Journal of Experimental Social Psychology, 13,* 131-140.

Youngs, G. (1986). Patterns of threat and punishment reciprocity in a conflict setting. *Journal of Personality and Social Psychology, 51,* 541-546.

Yukl, G. (1989). Managerial leadership: A review of theory and research. *Journal of Management, 15,* 251-289.

Yukl, G. (1994). *Leadership in organizations* (3rd ed.). Englewood Cliffs, NJ: Prentice Hall.

Yukl, G., & Guinan, P. (1995). Influence tactics used for different objectives with subordinates, peers, and supervisors. *Group and Organization Management, 20,* 272-297.

Zaccaro, S., & Marks, M. (1999). The roles of leaders in high-performance teams. In E. Sundstrom (Ed.), *Supporting work team effectiveness* (pp. 95-125). San Francisco: Jossey-Bass.

Zander, A. (1977). *Groups at work.* San Francisco: Jossey-Bass.

Zander, A. (1994). *Making groups effective.* San Francisco: Jossey-Bass.

Zanna, M. (1993). Message receptivity: A new look at the old problem of open versus closed mindedness. In A. Mitchell (Ed.), *Advertising: Exposure, memory, and choice.* Hillsdale, NJ: Lawrence Erlbaum.

Zigon, J. (1997, January-February). Team performance measurement: A process for creating performance standards. *Compensation and Benefits Review,* pp. 38-48.

Zuboff, S. (1988). *In the age of the smart machine.* New York: Basic Books.

AUTHOR INDEX

SUBJECT INDEX

ABOUT THE AUTHOR

Daniel Levi is a Professor in the Psychology and Human Development Department at Cal Poly, San Luis Obispo. He has an M.A. and a Ph.D. in environmental psychology from the University of Arizona. He teaches classes in group dynamics and in social, environmental, and organizational psychology. In addition, he teaches classes in teamwork and the psychology of technological change in courses primarily for engineering students at Cal Poly.

He has conducted research and worked as a consultant with factory and engineering teams for companies such as Nortel Networks, TRW, Hewlett-Packard, and Philips Electronics. In addition, he has researched international team projects related to concurrent engineering.

His research and consulting with factory teams primarily has focused on the use of teams to support technological change and the adoption of just-in-time and quality programs. This work examined a variety of team issues including job redesign, training, compensation, supervision, and change management approaches. His work with professional teams primarily has been done with engineering design teams. These projects examined the use of concurrent engineering, self-management, and the globalization of teams. The topics of this work included the impact of information technology on teams, facilitation and training needs for professional teams, and the impacts of organizational culture and leadership.

Early work on the present book was sponsored by an engineering education grant from NASA. This project focused on the development of teamwork skills in engineering students working on multidisciplinary projects.